THE MESSIANIC STAR

THE MESSIANIC STAR
New Light on the Star of Bethlehem

by
Martin Wells

SOPHIA CENTRE PRESS
MMXXII

The Messianic Star: New Light on the Star of Bethlehem
by Martin Wells

Sophia Centre Press
University of Wales Trinity Saint David
Ceredigion
SA48 7ED
United Kingdom
www.sophiacentrepress.com

Typeset by: Daniela Puia
Cover design: Jenn Zahrt
Cover image: Hieronymous Bosch, *Triptych of the Adoration of the Magi* (~1495)

ISBN: 978-1-907767-12-8

Names: Wells, Martin, 1972- author.

Title: The messianic star : new light on the Star of Bethlehem / by Martin Wells.

Description: Ceredigion, United Kingdom : Sophia Centre Press, [2022] | Series: Studies in cultural astronomy and astrology ; vol. 12 | Includes bibliographical references and index.

Identifiers: ISBN: 978-1-907767-12-8 (paperback) | 978-1-907767-62-3 (ebook)

Subjects: LCSH: Star of Bethlehem--Biblical teaching. | Stars--Religious aspects--Christianity. | Jesus Christ--Messiahship--Biblical teaching. | Jesus Christ--Nativity--Biblical teaching. | Astronomy in the Bible. | Bible and astrology. | BISAC: RELIGION / Biblical Commentary / General. | RELIGION / Biblical Criticism & Interpretation / General. | RELIGION / Biblical Studies / Prophecy. | BODY, MIND & SPIRIT / Astrology / General.

Classification: LCC: BS655 .W45 2022 | DDC: 220.8/5238--dc23

Printed worldwide by Lightning Source

CONTENTS

ACKNOWLEDGEMENTS

This book began its life in the early 2000s, first as a Masters degree and then as a PhD project. Though, in fact, it had *really* begun many years before in the dim and distant 1990s as an attempt to write a new biography of Jesus. Common sense and the sheer scale of the task led me to narrow the scope to the Infancy Narratives and then specifically the Star of Bethlehem. Yet even this became a major undertaking, one that would consume almost every free hour and weekend of my life for over a decade.

Therefore, my first debt of gratitude must be to my wife, Cheryl, who gave me the time to research, write and re-write this long work. Without her, this book would simply not exist. Secondly, I must thank my PhD supervisors at St David's University College (as it was then known), now University of Wales Trinity Saint David: the late Professor D.P. Davies, Dr James Robinson, and my examiners, Professor J. Keith Elliot and Associate Professor Nick Campion. Finally, I thank the Sophia Press for their guidance and skilful editing over the years, turning an academic text of great length and detail (and which had far too many footnotes) into the more readable book you see before you.

Herod:	Now then, lords, you may speak frankly from your hearts of the cause that moves you, even though we realize that your words might bring us to grief.
Jaspar:	Lord King, to briefly explain our purpose, it is true that not long ago, God manifested a star to us. It follows a course completely different from that of other stars. When we heeded its clear and obvious mystery, we remembered what the prophet Balaam promised us, who said that a beautiful star will appear when the high Christ in incarnated to reign over the Jews. The prophet has shown us the meaning of the sign: that the King is born.

Arnoul Greban, *The Mystery of the Passion*, c1450.

The fates rule our sphere, and all things stand fast by sure decree; the long seasons are marked out in fixed career. As we are born, we die, and our end depends on our beginning.

Manilius, *Astronomica* 4.14–16

INTRODUCTION

Much has been written on the origin and meaning of the Star of Bethlehem. The Star has been called a comet, nova, or meteor, the planet Venus, an astrological planetary conjunction, an occultation of the moon, an angel, and a miraculous object. What are we in the twenty-first century to make of Matthew's brief account of the Star?

It wouldn't be over-generalising to state that the majority of arguments for astrological or astronomical solutions have come from the pens (or rather, computers) of astronomers. An examination of Star literature published in the past fifty years shows that the majority have appeared in journals such as the *Journal of the Royal Astronomical Society of Canada*, *Quarterly Journal of the Royal Astronomical Society*, *Journal for the History of Astronomy* and *The Observatory*. These specialist studies and their leakage into mainstream public thought via media coverage have kept the popular astrological view predominant.

The fact the Star remains so elusive (the Gospel of Matthew provides only a few lines on the event) is a strong lure for those who wish to finally settle 'astronomy's greatest mystery'.[1] As Nicola Denzey says:

> Modern scholars—most often scientists—consider the star a sort of historical puzzle that can be solved by science; they scan records, documents, and data to find likely celestial events that then might have been (mis)interpreted as a portent of Christ's advent.[2]

The lure of this unsolved puzzle is evident from books such as *The Star of Bethlehem Mystery* and *Astronomical Enigmas: Life on Mars, the Star of Bethlehem and Other Milky Way Mysteries*.[3] And as journalist Jonathan Leake wrote in the *Times*:

> Despite the near-universal acceptance of [the] story by Christians, St Matthew's Gospel has long been a source of argument amongst astronomers who have found it impossible to agree upon an astronomical event which fits his description of 'a star in the east' that moved as the Magi travelled.[4]

What *was* the Star of Bethlehem?

CHAPTER 1:
MATTHEW'S GOSPEL

In his book *What are the Gospels?* Richard Burridge observed:

> The anonymous and traditional nature of the gospels gives us no clear idea of their social setting, geographical provenance or the occasion(s) which prompted their production.[1]

We need to use internal evidence to elicit the social background to the gospels.

The name 'Matthew' was associated (and widely accepted) quite early with the Gospel text. Scholarly debate centres on the external patristic testimony of Papias, the Bishop of Hierapolis (about 100 CE); a lost work preserved in a later text by Eusebius (about 260-340 CE) and the title (perhaps already known by about 125 CE) ΕΥΑΓΓΕΛΙΟΝ ΚΑΤΑ ΜΑΘΘΑΙΟΝ (*The Gospel According to Matthew*). Of significance is the language of the original autograph (Hebrew or Greek) driven by Papias—perhaps the first to call 'Matthew' (Ματθαῖος) specifically by name—who claimed that Matthew wrote in Hebrew/Aramaic.

Also under discussion is whether Matthew was 'the tax collector' featured in Matthew 9.9 and elsewhere (the popular opinion of the Church Fathers), a later Jewish Christian or even a Gentile Christian. We'll probably never know who the author was as an historical figure, but the Gospel was certainly authored by one man (within and for a specific community, not for a particular school of thought), possibly a Jewish-Christian scribe skilled in interpretation.

The consensus is that Matthew was written between 75 CE (after the Gospel of Mark and the destruction of the Temple in 70 CE) and the mid-90s CE. (Mark is traditionally dated to around 65–75 CE, but whether Mark was composed before or after the destruction of Temple is unresolved.) The first known reference to a Matthean passage is by Clement of Rome (about 95-96 CE), while the first mention of the 'Gospel' is by Ignatius (died 107–115? CE).

Polycarp of Smyrna (lived about 69-155 CE) appears to have known Matthew, and the *Didache* (the anonymous early Christian treatise from about 100–110 CE) likewise exhibits evidence of having drawn from Matthew.

Certainly, four Gospels existed as a known collection by 180 CE. Tatian had compiled the *Diatessaron* (through [the] four [gospels]) in about 170 CE, while a collection known as τὸ εὐαγγέλιον τετράμορφον (*tetramorph*) was cited by the second-century CE Greek bishop Irenaeus.

Another temporal marker is Matthew's apparent conflict with Judaism, indicating a period when the community had become separated from post-70 CE Formative Judaism (the reorganisation of Judaism and the emergence of Rabbinic Judaism) and was beginning to emerge as its own distinctive Jewish-Christian church. The traditional fixed-point is the introduction in about 85 CE of a Synagogue liturgy called the *Birkath ha-minin* (blessing of the heretics).

Basing Matthew on an uncertain date for Mark puts us on shaky ground and dating can only be speculative at best. Somewhere between c. 70–100 CE is the generally accepted period.

Where Matthew originated from is equally as speculative, though modern scholarship tends to place Matthew in Syria, specifically Ἀντιόχεια (Antioch) on the Orontes, now in Turkey. This is the city where (according to Luke; Acts 11.26), the disciples were first called Χριστιανούς (Christian). Other suggested locations include Jerusalem; Palestine or Galilee; the city port of Caesarea Maritima (Samaria); Phoenicia; Alexandria; Transjordan and Edessa.

The first known reference to the Gospel of Matthew appears in the letters of Ignatius, the second (or third) Bishop of Antioch. John P. Meier, who views Matthew as part of second-generation Christianity within the Antiochene Church (70-100 CE), states, 'It may be no accident that Ignatius of Antioch is the first Father of the Church to use passages from Matthew.'[2] Matthew himself (Matthew 4.24) refers to Συρίαν (Syria), though this might describe a narrow territory that included northern Palestine from Damascus to Antioch.

There's also the prominent role Matthew gives to Simon Peter, an influential figure in the Antiochene Church, especially in later Christian tradition where Origen cites him as the first Bishop of Antioch (c49-56 CE).

The Antioch consensus is only a guess. There's no evidence that limits Matthew's community to Antioch alone. The fact we know so much about Antioch and its Christian community is one reason for its dominant position.

Evidence of Gentile-Jewish tension in Matthew could also be due to an urban Jewish-Christian community being close to Jewish synagogues and Gentile-Christian congregations. Such mixed communities could have existed anywhere. However, 'We are forced to work with the material we have, and Antioch is the best hypothesis in view of the evidence at our disposal.'[3]

The assumption that there must be a centralised Matthean community adheres to the consensus that the Gospels were written for specific local communities. Early Gospel texts, written on papyrus scrolls, would have belonged to the whole community and were produced to be read aloud— early Christians wouldn't yet have possessed their own private codex copies. Matthew's implied audience might not have been his actual historical audience, making provenance impossible to detect. Wide audiences were a generic feature of this genre, but even if a wide audience was intended for the Gospels, they'd still have been composed and influenced by their community setting.

Matthew's Gospel puzzlingly exhibits both a positive and negative position with regard to Judaism and the Gentiles. How can this tension and conflict be explained? Arguments place Matthew in a position *intra muros* (inside the walls, still connected to parent Judaism); *extra muros* (outside the walls, following a recent 'painful' separation but still primarily Jewish) or as part of an independent non-Jewish community with no remaining links to Judaism. Passages in Matthew fit all three positions.

The period of Matthew's composition is one during which Judaism had to come to terms with the catastrophic destruction of the Jerusalem Temple (the centre of Jewish religion and life), the subsequent fall of the Temple's dominant priestly aristocracy as a power base, and the aftermath of the failed revolt against Rome. Though over-simplistic, it isn't *wrong* to say that after the fall of the Sadducees, the Pharisees emerged as the dominant social force. They survived the destruction of the Temple due to their focus on the home and the law of the Torah. During this period, the Torah and its application to society replaced the then extinct Temple cult.

This emerging Judaism was still in its infancy and not fully formed during the composition of Matthew, but it must have been coherent enough to provide a body with which Matthew and his community could come into conflict and dispute. Significant for this period is the *Birkat ha-Minim*, the twelfth of eighteen benedictions and a curse on the Christians [*ve-ha-Notzrim*] and 'heretics' [*minim*] in the 80s CE that came out of the Rabbinic Council of Jamnia:

> For the apostates let there be no hope and may the kingdom of the arrogant be quickly uprooted in our days; and may the *Nazarim* and *Minim* instantly perish; may they be blotted from the book of the living, and not be written with the righteous. Blessed are you Lord, humbler of the arrogant.[4]

Whether this benediction and the Jamnian period that produced it has any bearing on Matthew's stance in regard to contemporary Judaism is still debated. Recent studies have criticised the traditional view of the *Birkat ha-Minim* due

to problems with dating, influence, original form and purpose. The current
view is that there's little evidence for blatant anti-Christian activity during this
period. Perhaps the *minim* represented many groups and didn't lead explicitly to
a decree expelling them from synagogues. With regard to dating, to use Jamnia
'as a fixed point for establishing early Christian material is like a hiker taking
a compass bearing on a sheep'.[5] Even if the *Birkat* no longer functioned as a
boundary between *intra* and *extra muros*, some kind of post-70 CE redrawing
of boundaries was in process and was a factor in the Matthean community's
relationship with Judaism.

> In time the descendants of the Matthean community and the tradition
> to which they belonged came to be called 'Christians' and saw
> themselves as distinct and at best only vaguely related to Judaism. At
> the time of the writing of the Gospel of Matthew, of course, no such
> self-understanding existed. The people of Matthew's community did
> not understand themselves as 'Christians'. On the contrary they were
> Jews.[6]

The 'parting of the ways' means the Matthean community is *outside* Judaism
but still responding to synagogue debate and hoping to convert individual Jews.
Passages that invite this *extra muros* position include:

1. Hostility towards the scribes and Pharisees (contrary to Matthew
    23.3, which is positive towards the Pharisees) whom Matthew
    associates with the Synagogue.

2. The ἐκκλησία (assembly, legislative body) with its own distinctive
    form of worship amongst whom Jesus will be present.

3. The transference of the Kingdom of God to a new people that
    included Gentiles.

It may be that Matthew was writing as a Jewish Christian 'critiquing other
Jews', which was different to the anti-Judaism of his Gentile contemporaries.[7]
Such polemical 'criticism from within' wasn't new and appears in Jeremiah,
Deuteronomy, Amos, 5 Ezra and the Dead Sea Scrolls. Gerben Oegema,
observing the role the rejection of Jesus by Israel plays in Matthew's Gospel,
states that 'the purpose of portraying Jesus as Messiah is partly to be understood
as an anti-Jewish apologetic.'[8]

Unfortunately, these polemical/apologetic passages in Matthew have
resulted in the Gospel being interpreted as 'anti-Jewish'—or worse, anti-Semitic.

Such an interpretation grew more acute as the historical context was gradually lost over time and the Gospel evolved into a purely Christian text, removed from its Jewish origins. Parting from Judaism wouldn't have been easy and Matthew's community can be viewed as a 'deviant Jewish association' but one with a more positive attitude toward Gentiles.[9]

The third view is that Matthew's community was a Gentile-Christian Church, completely separated from the Synagogue, a view deduced from the Gospel's apparent 'Gentile bias' (Matthew's is the only Gospel that uses the word ἐθνικός [gentile, heathen]). The general argument focuses on the following areas of Gentile bias in the Gospel:

(a). The Gentile elements in Christ's nativity, for example, Tamar, Rahab, Ruth, Bathsheba ('the wife of Uriah') in the genealogy, and the magi.

(b). The strong negative view towards Israel and its rejection.

(c). Matthew's 'apparent' ignorance of first-century BCE Jewish culture such as the Sabbath law, geography, population, the Shema, tephillin and Rabbinic titles.

(d). References to συναγωγὴ αὐτῶν (their synagogues) and οἱ γραμματεῖς αὐτῶν (their scribes). There are also many seemingly pro-Gentile passages.

Those who argue for a Gentile community dismiss Matthew's Jewish passages as anachronistic remnants of earlier positions, adopted even if Matthew didn't agree with them himself. Such dismissal would reduce important Matthean themes to the level of irrelevant archaisms. Given the strong Jewish nature of Matthew, it's unlikely to have been the product of a purely Gentile-Christian community.

Matthew's Jewish background can perhaps be seen most clearly in his use of Old Testament citations, introduced by fulfilment formulae. (Matthew would have been using the Jewish scriptures as translated into Greek in the third century BCE, known as the *Septuagint* (LXX). These are unique to the New Testament and have few equivalents in Jewish literature. While the first-century BCE literature of Qumran reveals a forward looking hope, Matthew (whose messiah has already arrived) is looking back to the Old Testament to legitimise his arrival and messianic status.

Fourteen prophetic citations appear in Matthew, of which five appear in Matthew 1–2.

1.22–23	ἵνα πληρωθῇ τὸ ῥηθεν ὑπο κυρίου διὰ τοῦ προφήτου λέγοντος [All this took place] *to fulfil what had been spoken by the Lord through the prophet*	Virgin birth	Isaiah 7.14
2.5–6	οὕτως γὰρ γέγραπται διὰ τοῦ προφήτου *For so it has been written through the prophet*	Born in Bethlehem	Micah 5.2, 4
2.14–15	ἵνα πληρωθῇ τὸ ῥηθεν ὑπο κυρίου διὰ τοῦ προφήτου λέγοντος [This was] *to fulfil what had been spoken by the Lord through the prophet.*	Flight into Egypt	Hosea 11.1
2.17–18	τότε ἐπληρώθη τὸ ῥηθεν διὰ Ἰερεμίου τοῦ προφήτου λέγοντος *Then was fulfilled what had been spoken through the prophet Jeremiah.*	Massacre of the Innocents	Jeremiah 31.15
2.23	ὅπως πληρωθῇ τὸ ῥηθεν διὰ τῶν προφητῶν ὅτι *So that what had been spoken through the prophets might be fulfilled.*	Return to Nazareth	Isaiah 4.3; 11.1; Judges 16.17?

These are employed by Matthew to portray Christ as having fulfilled the prophesied role of the Messiah. To Matthew, Jesus was the Messiah from birth and not merely from his baptism. Matthew's use of Jeremiah 31.15 takes on the new secondary fulfilment role of referring to Herod's Massacre of the Innocents). His use of formula citations can be connected to *enthymemes*, a rhetorical device of 'statement immediately followed by supporting reason'. Matthew is employing the 'internal proof of logical argument' where it's not the author of the text who reasons about the truth but the characters *within* the text via *enthymemes*.

> In many cases, the minor premise of the *enthymeme* is a scriptural quotation. The external evidence, which functions cumulatively to show that prophecy has been fulfilled in the birth of Jesus, is thus utilised to construct an argument internal to the text.[10]

Conflict with Judaism and the local synagogues led Matthew to write an infancy account that used Old Testament scriptures to present Jesus as a foretold saviour Messiah. The stumbling block between emerging Christianity and Judaism was the significant problem of Christ's crucifixion by the Romans in addition to his rejection by the Jews. As Jesus had died an ignoble death, he couldn't have been the messiah expected by the Jews, who was to lead Israel to redemption and freedom through war against the Romans. The issue of Jesus' death was an early problem for Jewish-Christians, who looked to the Old Testament for evidence of a suffering saviour. Hence, the apologetic passages in Matthew, Mark, Luke, John and Paul that turn the issue around and proclaim Jesus to be the Messiah *because he died* (an event foretold by Scripture). Matthew continues the tradition of being part apology (in response to Jewish criticism) and part affirmation (to reassure his community) that Christ not only died for our sins but was born the Jewish Messiah.

There's a lack of consensus on the subject of Matthew's literary structure as it can't be reduced to a particular pattern. He employs many literary and rhetorical structuring devices and techniques, for example, *inclusio*, contrasting doublets, *chiasmus* (inverted parallelism), repetition, narrative turning points, triads (divisions into three), numerical patterns, hinge texts and five-fold division. It's evident from the text that Matthew exhibits a rolling shift between narrative and discourse material:

1–4	Narrative	
5–7		Discourse
8–9	Narrative	
10		Discourse
11–12	Narrative	
13		Discourse
14–17	Narrative	
18		Discourse
19–23	Narrative	
24–25		Discourse
26–28	Narrative	

This pattern suggests that the structure of Matthew has been deliberately designed as a counterpart to the Pentateuch (the first five books of the Hebrew Torah attributed by ancient tradition to Moses). In Matthew, each discourse segment belongs to a narrative as follows:

Prologue: 1–2 Infancy Narrative

Book 1:   3.1–4.25 Narrative
            5.1–7.27 Sermon on the Mount

Book 2:   8.1–9.35 Narrative
            9.36–10.42 Mission and martyrdom discourse

Book 3:   11.2–12.50 Narrative and debate
            13.1–52 Kingdom of Heaven teaching

Book 4:   13.54–17.21 Narrative and debate
            17.22–18.35 Church administration discourse

Book 5:   19.2–22.46 Narrative and debate
            23.1–25.46 Eschatology discourse, farewell

Epilogue: 26.3–28.20 Last Supper to resurrection.

Each book also ends with the same repeated formula: καὶ ἐγένετο ὅτε τέλεσεν ὁ Ἰησοῦς (Now, when Jesus had finished). These discourses were designed to present Jesus as a new Moses, giver of a new law. Alternatively, it can be argued that the five discourses correspond to 'themes of Jewish festival year celebrations, taken in order from after Passover.'[11] It's been suggested that these five blocks of teaching were intended as a teaching manual, to provide both propaganda for the Church's missionary work and an apologetic shield against hostile synagogues. (Critics note that the crucial Matthew 26–28 passages don't fit the five-book format, and discourses such as 11.7–30 and 23.1–39 aren't marked off by the formulae.)

There's also a structure for Matthew based on the five 'marker' blocks of discourse material. A chiastic structure, whereby the great discourses of Matthew 5–7 with its nine beatitudes and Matthew 23–25 with its seven woes parallel one another, and Deuteronomy with its sixteen curses and four blessings could have been in Matthew's mind as he structured his gospel. Indeed, Matthew portrays Jesus, like Moses, going to his death with warnings and promises and both go up a mountain. Matthew 2 appears to be closely modelled on the birth of Moses as in Exodus 1.15–2.10. Taking this approach, Matthew 2 becomes the beginning of this theme; the origin of Christ (the Davidic Messiah) as the new Moses (lawgiver) and new redeemer of Israel.

What if we took each narrative and discourse section as a 'thought unit' on its own terms? When applied to Matthew 1–4, this results in the following structure (note the use of triads):

Title (1.1)
Historical preface (1.2–17)
Three infancy stories (1.18–25; 2.1–12; 2.13–23)
Three John the Baptist *pericopae* (extracts; 3.1–6, 7–12, 13–17)
Three pericopae that lead into the ministry (4.1–11, 12–17, 18–22)

As an extended introduction to the Gospel story, Matthew 1–4 tells us *who* Jesus is, *where* he is from, *how* he arrived, *why* he arrived, *when* he arrived and *what* he proclaims.

Matthew, Luke and the Synoptic Problem

When placed in parallel columns, the Greek text of Matthew, Mark and Luke reveal pericopae that strongly agree in their order of events, wording (vocabulary) and even editorial comments. The stated percentages vary but approximately 97% of Mark can be found in Matthew while 88% of Mark can be found in Luke. These three Gospels have therefore been termed *Synoptic* (Greek 'seen together'). The material is known as the Triple Tradition (TT), where Mark is the 'middle term' between Matthew and Luke, and covers the approximately 360 pericopae (mostly narrative material with some sayings) common across all three Synoptic Gospels.

TT Pericope	Matthew	Mark	Luke
Pilate delivers Jesus to be crucified	27.24–26	15.15	23.24–25
The road to Golgotha	27.31b–32	15.20b–21	23.26–32
The crucifixion	27.33–37	15.22–26	23.33–34
Jesus derided on the cross	27.38–43	15.27–32a	23.35–38
The two thieves	27.44	15.32b	23.39–43
The death of Jesus	27.45–54	15.33–39	23.44–48
Witnesses of the crucifixion	27.55–56	15.40–41	23.49

There's also the 'Double Tradition', around 200-250 verses (primarily 'sayings' [*logia*] of Jesus), which appear in Matthew and Luke but not Mark.

DT Pericope	Matthew	Luke
Centurion's servant	8.5–13	7.1–10
The cities of Galilee	11.20–24	10.12–15
Jesus' thanksgiving	11.25–27	10.21–22

The evil spirit	12.43–45	11.24–26
Parable (the lost sheep)	18.10–14	15.3–7
Parable (the talents)	25.14–30	19.11–27
Lament over Jerusalem	23.37–39	13.34–35

These DT agreements are either attributed to the existence of a hypothetical lost document known as 'Q' (Ger. *Quelle*—source; a collection of 'sayings' akin to the Gnostic Gospel of Thomas) or Lukan knowledge of Matthew. Simply stated, the Synoptic Problem is the search for an explanation of the literary relationship between Mark, Matthew and Luke to establish who borrowed from whom.

The search for a solution has generated a vast amount of literature over the centuries, but the most popular accepted consensus is that of the 'Two Source Hypothesis' (2SH): Markan priority + 'Q' with no direct relationship between Matthew and Luke. There's also the expanded 'Four Source Hypothesis' (4SH): Mark + 'Q' + *Sondergut* (independent 'special material' unique to Matthew or Luke, designated M and L respectively). Matthean *Sondergut* amounts to 485 verses, for example:

M Sondergut	Matthew
Infancy narrative	2.1–21
Pearls before swine	7.6
Peter walks on water	14.28–32
Blessing of Peter	16.17–19
Peter pays temple tax	17.24–27
Peter asks about forgiveness	18.21–22
Earthquake #1	27.51
Resurrection of the saints	27.52–53
Earthquake #2; angel of the Lord opens tomb	28.2
The great commission	28.16–20

The 2SH can be summarised as follows:

(a) In the TT, Matthew and Luke depend on Mark (Markan priority)

(b) In the DT, Matthew and Luke depend on a second source (Q)

(c) Matthew and Luke are independent of one another (*Sondergut*, 'Q' and TT)

The problem is that 'Q' remains a hypothetical literary construct and therefore the 2SH requires Matthew and Luke to have independently used both Mark and 'Q' in exactly the same way and with an improbably high degree of verbatim agreement. This unease over the requirement for 'Q' has led to DT solutions that remove it completely. These include:

- The Augustinian Hypothesis: (AH; Matthean priority > Mark used Matthew > Luke used Matthew)
- The Farrer Hypothesis: (FH; Markan priority > Matthew used Mark > Luke used Matthew and Mark)
- The Two Gospel (or Griesbach) Hypothesis: (2GH/GH; Matthean priority > Luke used Matthew > Mark used Matthew and Luke)

All propose that the DT can be explained via Luke's use of Matthew, removing the need for 'Q'. An alternative explanation for the DT is the 'Matthew Conflator Hypothesis' (MCH), which accepts Markan priority but proposes instead the less common view that Matthew was the last of the Synoptics to appear, having made use of Luke.

Of the many arguments against 'Q' and the 2SH, one of the most damaging is the direct evidence of the Major and Minor Agreements (MA) *between* Matthew and Luke *against* Mark, where Mark stops being the middle term—the 'Mark-Q overlap' (DT material added to TT material). As this creates the impossible scenario of 'Q' finishing Mark's sentences, such agreements suggest instead that Matthew used Mark and then Luke used Matthew and Mark, copying across those changes Matthew had made to Mark. For example, Matthew 26.68 and Lk 22.64 against Mark 14.65 (where Matthew and Luke add the additional τίς ἐστιν ὁ παίσας σε; [*Who is it that struck you?*], which Mark lacks).

From this brief over-view of the Synoptic Problem, three basic scenarios can be presented:

(1) Matthew and Luke are completely independent (2SH)

(2) Luke made use of Matthew (AH/FH/2GH)

(3) Matthew made use of Luke (MCH)

The impact of these three scenarios on Matthew 1–2 and Luke 1–2 will be examined in the next chapter.

CHAPTER 2:
THE NATIVITY AND INFANCY NARRATIVES

One well known method of reconciling the agreements and differences between Matthew 1–2 and Luke 1–2 remains the traditional harmonised 'nativity' sequence of Luke 1; Matthew 1; Luke 2.1–38; Matthew 2. Such literary harmonisation (which assumes the validity of both accounts) exists as early as the second century CE in Tatian's Diatessaron (where the episode of the magi occurs after the Temple presentation but before the flight to Egypt) and has continued through medieval mystery plays up to today's school nativities The approach creates significant narrative and chronological problems: 'Even the most determined harmonizer should be foiled by the impossibility of reconciling a journey of the family from Bethlehem to Egypt with Luke's account.'[1]

The infancy narratives do contain several agreements, though the number of common points varies among scholars. Excepting the proper nouns, Jesus ('Ισοῦς), Mary (Μαρία) and Joseph ('Ιωσήφ), there are two (the virgin conception and birth in Bethlehem); four (Mary isn't married, miraculous conception, birth in Bethlehem, raised in Nazareth) or more—the name of Jesus' father, the Spirit, the angel, the name, the time, the journey, geography, visitors and genealogy. For example, the *Jesus Seminar* lists five:

1. Parents of Jesus are engaged but don't yet live together

2. Conception of Jesus isn't through Mary's intercourse with Joseph

3. Birth takes place after Mary and Joseph begin living together

4. Birth is in Bethlehem

5. Birth takes place during reign of Herod

A longer list of eleven similarities comprises:

1. Parents, Mary and Joseph, are engaged but haven't yet had sexual relations

13

2. Joseph is of Davidic descent

3. Angelic announcement

4. Conception of Mary not via Joseph

5. Conception through the Holy Spirit

6. Angel asks for child to be named Jesus

7. Angel states Jesus is to be Saviour

8. Birth takes place after parents live together

9. Birth in Bethlehem

10. Birth during reign of Herod the Great

11. Child raised in Nazareth

There are numerous similar lists and eighteen parallels appear in *Beyond the Q Impasse*:[2]

1. Mary and Joseph will serve as parents for Jesus

2. Joseph is betrothed to Mary

3. Virginity of Mary

4. Conception by Holy Spirit

5. Jesus' family is from the line of David

6. Angelic annunciation

7. Child's name is given

8. Jesus as saviour

9. Child visited

10. Visitors worship

11. Jesus is born in Bethlehem

12. Herod is king

13. There is χαρὰν μεγάλην (great joy)

14. Use of δίκαιος, *righteous*

15. φόβος, *fear*

16. Abraham

17. Family's hometown is Nazareth

18. Genealogy

How many of these eighteen represent an actual similarity (not, for example, a verbal coincidence) is debatable.

Another interesting parallel is the witness of the heavens to Jesus' birth. In Matthew, this is the Star of Bethlehem, while in Luke it's the message of the angel and the singing of the heavenly host, reminiscent of Job 37.7.

Assuming literary independence, how can we account for the similarities between Matthew and Luke? We can begin by hypothesising a combination of known historical data (that Jesus was born during the reign of Herod and raised in Nazareth or at least in Galilee) and early core christological traditions that Jesus was:

- the Son of God
- from the line of David
- born in Bethlehem to a virgin(?) called Mary

Such traditions are scattered throughout the New Testament, though a 'virgin birth' only explicitly occurs in Matthew and Luke (if Παρθένος (*parthenos*) is understood correctly). Mark doesn't include a birth narrative, John only says that Jesus was born out of wedlock, and Paul (our earliest source) merely states that Jesus was born of a woman. (The virgin birth occurs in the only two New Testament documents that *do not* suggest Christ was pre-existent.) It's possible that the christological concept of the virgin birth *originated* with Matthew from his translation and/or use of the Greek Old Testament or Septuagint Isaiah 7.14 where the Hebrew צַלְמָה (*almah,* young woman; girl of marriageable age) was translated into the Greek Septuagint as Παρθένος (*parthenos,* virgin; the Latin *virgo* can also mean 'young woman'). Neither of these words explicitly refer to virginity.

The parallels provide us with an early independent attestation of a small body of pre-Gospel tradition regarding Christ's origins, and if the Evangelists followed the literary conventions of Josephus, they were 'unlikely to invent events without reference to some form of source.'[3]

Jesus' geographical location at the time of his birth is a critical element of the astrological/astronomical hypothesis in terms of celestial observations and calculations. However, Jesus' birth in Bethlehem can't be historical and has its origins in pre-existing messianic/christological tradition. That David the Shepherd was regarded to have been from Bethlehem wasn't invented by Matthew and Luke, therefore, a Bethlehem birth was a core condition required for Jesus to be the Davidic Messiah. Hence, Matthew's specific use of Micah 5.1 and 2 Samuel 5.2 (Matthew 2.5b–6) as formula citations and Luke's use of the historical census and shepherds.

The contradictory ways in which Matthew and Luke place Jesus in Bethlehem and explain his consequent return/migration to Nazareth point more logically to Galilee as his historical birthplace, especially as Nazareth is the assumption in the New Testament. The citation of Isaiah 9.1–2 at Matthew 4.12–16 to explain Jesus' move from Nazareth to Galilee is identical to Matthew's use of τῶν προφητῶν (the prophets; Matthew 2.23) to validate his move from Bethlehem to Nazareth, which suggests a messianic (narrative) purpose rather than an historical one. The census is employed by Luke for the same reason. Under Roman administration, Joseph had no reason to travel *from* his hometown *to* his place of birth. A Roman census required people only to return to their place of work and residence.

A move to Nazareth to escape the reach of the tetrarch Archelaus (4 BCE–6 CE) would be odd, as northern Galilee was ruled by another of Herod's sons, the tetrarch Antipas (4 BCE–39 CE), the executor of John the Baptist who (according to Luke) later wished to kill Jesus. The logic of this move makes little sense except as an explanation for Jesus' Nazarean origins.

Matthew's explanation for the move to Galilee is part of the need to provide an answer to the problem of why the Messiah came from the north. There was a clear political distinction between Galilee and Jerusalem and a feature of the New Testament is the need to justify Jesus' activity there. A shift in religious geography to the north (which had begun in the first century BCE) allowed for small, marginal northern towns and villages, especially in the heavily populated area of Galilee, to be home to the Messiah. Archaeological evidence also points to a Galilean origin. Given the lack of early Roman or Herodian-period finds in Judean Bethlehem, it's been argued that the northern *Bethlehem of Galilee* is Jesus' birthplace. Bethlehem of Galilee, unlike the town in Judea (which only has primarily Iron Age and Byzantine archaeology), contains much from the Herodian-period. The evidence for a Bethlehem birth is weak:

> Even if we leave aside the implausible publicity that Matt 2:3-5 attaches
> to Jesus' birth at Bethlehem, how can there have been such general

ignorance of Jesus' birthplace in Bethlehem when the parents would have had to come from there as strangers with their child to a small village in Galilee?[4]

And:

> The shift of his birthplace [from Nazareth] to Bethlehem is a result of religious fantasy and imagination: because according to scripture the messiah had to be born in Bethlehem, Jesus' birth is transferred there.[5]

The Bethlehem birth acts as a theological affirmation or truth (that Jesus was the royal Davidic Messiah) in the form of a historical narrative.

It's historically more probable that Jesus was born in the northern region of Galilee. If so, this weakens any Star hypothesis that relies on magi observing astronomical events centred on the southern Judean region of Bethlehem.

How do Matthew's and Luke's narratives compare? First, there's the overall tone. Luke's longer, more developed, narrative of 132 verses (147 if 3.23–38 is included) is one of welcoming celebration: peaceful and joyful with no threats of death. It even includes four hymns of praise. According to Luke, Jesus is taken to Bethlehem for the census and presented at the Temple (in the heart of Herodian Jerusalem), before returning safely to Nazareth without incident. Luke adds that Jesus and his family continued to return to Jerusalem each year for Passover.

There's also a structural difference. Luke (for christological purposes) presents the births of Jesus and John the Baptist in step parallel:

Introduction of parents	1.5–7 (John)	1.26–27 (Jesus)
Birth announcement	1.8–23 (John)	1.28–38 (Jesus)
Conception	1.23–25 (John)	2.6–7 (Jesus)
Birth and naming	1.59–66 (John)	2.21 (Jesus)
Response to birth	1.67–79 (John)	2.22–38 (Jesus)
Growth of child	1.80 (John)	2.39–40, 52 (Jesus)
Genealogy	–	3.23–38 (Jesus)

Matthew's narrative is significantly simpler and shorter (a mere 42 verses) and presents a faster moving series of linear events, which don't mention John. As the order of events is linear, the continuity of time principle is in effect—the narrator doesn't retrace his steps. The events provide a cause and effect situation, with each event triggering the next. Here we see an alternative (contradictory) genealogy followed by five short episodes, each ending with a Formula Citation:

1. Mary is found to be pregnant by the Holy Spirit; the Angel of the Lord speaks to Joseph; birth of Jesus (*not mentioned in the text*).

2. The Magi, following a Star (*origin not mentioned in the text*), arrive in Jerusalem looking for the King of the Jews; Herod and all Jerusalem are worried; Herod calls upon Council for advice; it's learnt that Bethlehem will be the birthplace of the Messiah; Herod secretly asks the magi to report to him; the magi follow Star to Bethlehem and pay homage; Magi warned in dream not to return to Herod.

3. Joseph, Mary and Jesus flee to Egypt.

4. Herod kills newborn children in Bethlehem.

5. Joseph, Mary and Jesus return from Egypt after Herod's death and settle in Nazareth.

Matthew's narrative is more male-centred with its emphasis on Joseph. Mary is left in the shadows in Matthew 1–2 in contrast to her dominant position in Luke.

Considering the many irreconcilable differences of narrative and chronology between Matthew and Luke, the probability they're describing the same set of events is almost nil. However, the number of agreements between Matthew 1–2 and Luke 1–2 (themes, locations, characters, order of events, Greek verbal agreements) suggest a level of literary dependence.

The absence of the magi, Massacre of the Innocents and journey to Egypt from Luke (plus the peripheral nature of Joseph) may result from Luke's desire to create a Christian Deuteronomy. Luke's shifting and omitting of Gentile characters such as the Syro-Phoenician woman and magi may be due to his need to show the Gentile mission as unfulfilled and in the future. The massacre is omitted as Luke treats bad characters as ambiguous (and with a touch of goodness), so an evil Herod is unacceptable. The journey to Egypt is gone as Luke's strict historical scheme requires Jesus' exodus to end in Jerusalem. Finally, Joseph is overshadowed by Mary due to the role of women in Luke's *kerygmatic* (proclaiming) theme of *Heilsgeschichte* (salvation history).

Luke kept his birth narrative in the same order as Matthew but it was supplemented by themes of wealth, poverty reversal and salvation-history. Thus, Luke redacted and reordered Matthew 1–2 to suit his own literary and theological purpose. Luke's substitution of 'shepherds following the word of the angel' (Luke's version of the Star) can be seen as due to the need for humble poverty to replace riches. There's also no interaction between Jesus and Gentiles until Acts.

Alternatively, there could be in Luke a desire to present a hidden Jesus, a Jesus out of sight of Herod and his court, with no shining heavenly Star pinpointing his location like a cosmic spotlight. Maybe Luke's removal of the magi was due to his negative view of magicians. This can be evidenced in Luke's depiction of Simon Magus, who was found 'practising magic' (μαγεύων) in Samaria, along with other magicians in Salamis and Ephesus.

One view is that Matthew was inspired by Luke's narrative with the differences being the result of the same creative freedom (though to a much greater extent) apparent in Matthew's reshaping, rearranging and reducing of much of his source material prior to Matthew 14. (For example, Matthew's rejection of Luke's emphasis on poverty.) It's been suggested that Matthew's 'accommodating attitude' towards the rich, and therefore the 'righteous poor ones', that appear in Luke 1-2 (for example, Zechariah, Elizabeth, Anna, the shepherds, Simeon; the lowly inn/stable) lies behind their absence from his own infancy narrative.

Matthew frequently abbreviates and shortens Mark and his much shorter infancy narrative doesn't necessarily infer an earlier, less mature text. For example, as Matthew's focus is on Jesus, Luke's passages on John become targets for omission. Luke's hymns were likewise omitted and replaced by Old Testament Formula Citations, as Matthew's 'extra muros' need to present Jesus as the Davidic Messiah required an male-centred, Joseph-oriented narrative, an alternative genealogy and a change from Nazareth to Bethlehem as the starting point of the story. And there may have been traditions *unknown* to Luke:

> If he [Matthew] knew a tradition about the visit of the magi he might have preferred it to Luke's account of the shepherds, since the magi were Gentiles (and thus could foreshadow the Great Commission and were of higher status than the shepherds.[6]

Likewise, of Matthew 2.13-23 (the Slaughter of the Innocents and escape to Egypt):

> These would have rung true to him as foreshadowing the hostility of Jewish leaders that led to Jesus' death (and perhaps of the Matthean community's own conflicts with non-Christian Jews).[7]

Such considerations would naturally lead to the omission of Luke's story of Jesus' presentation at Temple and his later friendly visits with the Jewish teachers.

The subject of Matthew and Luke's relationship is critical to an understanding of the historicity of the two birth narratives. If they were independent, why weren't Luke or Matthew aware of each other's traditions? If Luke used Matthew, why did he remove Matthew 2? If Matthew used Luke, why wasn't Luke aware of the magi-star traditions?

Luke begins his Gospel with a prologue or preface where he states that, since 'many' others (Greek plural πολλοὶ) have compiled narratives, he too has decided to write an account after παρηκολουθηκότι ἄνωθεν πᾶσιν ἀκριβῶς καθεξῆς (*investigating [in an orderly way] everything carefully from the first*). This is so a certain 'Theophilus' may know the truth. If, in his intention of writing a truthful, historical report or 'narrative' (be it in the form of Hellenistic historiography or Greek technical prose), Luke doesn't mention the magi, the star, the Massacre of the Innocents or flight into Egypt, how does this impact the historicity of Matthew 2? Did Luke undertake such research into his historical sources?

Luke is using a common rhetorical practice—stressing historical accuracy to his audience. By referring to the πολλοὶ (many) attempts before him and his own thorough examination, Luke affirms the age and reliability of the traditions he's relating, regardless of whether he conducted such research. This convention is also employed by Josephus, who cited the use of historical (Roman) documents. When Luke writes he covered πᾶσιν (*everything*) it's to convey 'the impression that nothing significant for his purpose was omitted'.[8] Luke's preface doesn't mean he was a true historian in the modern sense.

> Ancient authors passed on legends, invented edifying speeches, and engaged in wishful thinking to an even greater degree than do modern 'popular' biographies and historians . . . on the other hand, they also made use of good material, accurately remembered and transmitted.[9]

Like Josephus, Luke intented to write 'about actual events that have taken place in the actual past'.[10] Whether Luke had access to verifiable historical data unknown to the other Evangelists can't be known for sure, but he certainly aimed to place the mission of Jesus in a historical framework, continuing his narrative theme of salvation-history. Hence, Luke presents a prophetic form of historical narrative, a form closely linked to Roman historical events.

All historians are capable of error. Luke made dating errors such as the date of Quirinius' census. However, this isn't reason enough to completely dismiss him as factually unreliable. In fact, his accuracy in such points as the use of πολιτάρχης (*Politarch*) as a title could mean that Luke might also be accurate in matters for which we don't have independent attestation outside the New

Testament. Granting that Luke wasn't a thorough historical researcher (he relies on Mark for the majority of his material), he is still writing (even if only to a limited degree) within the conventions of Hellenistic historiography.

Why did Luke, after 'careful investigation', write such a fundamentally different account? Does this imply that Luke, if using Matthew 1–2 as a source or being aware of such infancy traditions, deliberately wrote out of his narrative the unique and powerful significance of the Star of Bethlehem to remove an early reference to Gentiles and to portray Christ as poor? Were the magi written out because Luke held a negative view of astrologers and magicians or because Matthew 2 was full of undesirable political undertones?

If Luke was placing Jesus within Roman history, a celestial phenomenon of significant messianic portent is conspicuous by its absence. Did a Star tradition exist independently of Matthew in the late first century CE? Can it be ascertained when it became attached to Jesus' birth and is there an earlier pre-Matthean source?

Luke's ignorance about the Star remains unusual if we consider the vast network of communication that existed throughout the Roman Empire. Information could travel swiftly and a letter could travel from Rome to Londinium in a week. However, oral teaching would have travelled much further and more effectively than written texts, especially given Christian use of the paraenetic Greek institution of hospitality: people and not texts spread the good news.

In oral cultures, a formal fixing of stories takes place so they become imprinted. When Luke writes that he used ὑπηρέται τοῦ λόγου (*servants of the word*) as a source, rather than an official in charge of the scrolls, he may mean (in early Christian terms) a witness to vital fixed traditions. Oral traditions would have shaped the stories about Jesus.

> The Gospels were written within the living memory of the events they recount. Mark's Gospel was written well within the lifetime of many of the eyewitnesses, while the other three canonical Gospels were written in the period when living eyewitnesses were becoming scarce, exactly at the point in time when their testimony would perish with them were it not put into writing.[11]

However, Luke's account ἀπ᾽ ἀρχῆς ἄνωθεν (*from the beginning*) only properly begins with John's ministry (when eyewitness testimony began) and *not* Luke 1–2. The infancy narrative was just 'a preliminary account' in order to provide 'an appropriate background'.[12]

This wide network of eyewitness testimony poses a significant problem for the historical veracity of Matthew 2. Why did no oral tradition of a Star and magician visit come from Jesus' family and disciples? Or spread out from the frightened population of the entire Judean capital? We'd expect such a unique and unusual episode (far more than a routine census) to have had produced vivid recall in the memory of thousands of potential eyewitnesses in Judea, the wider surrounding regions of Idumea, Samaria, Galilee and Decapolis or further afield in Syria, Nabatea, Egypt, Parthia or Rome.

Luke's ignorance of the infancy tradition as found in Matthew is critical for our understanding of Matthew as history. If these (imprinted) traditions didn't travel, did one exist prior to Matthew's composition? Given Luke's traditional composition date of c. 80–95 CE, this overlap of time with the composition of Matthew suggests there was no 'Star' and 'visiting magi' tradition outside Matthew's community in Antioch. (The dating of Luke is no less difficult than the dating of Mark and Matthew. The general consensus is some time between 80–85 CE.) The evidence suggests Matthew was the originator of the events presented in Matthew 2.

It's possible that Luke chose to ignore the events behind Matthew 2, presenting instead a narrative to suit his own audience. If this were the case (and it can never be proven), then his account of the birth of Jesus provides zero support to any historical understanding of Matthew 2. Of the possibility that a unique kernel of historical fact, known only to Matthew, lies behind the visit of the magi and the Star of Bethlehem, 'those who wish to maintain the historicity of the Matthean Magi story are faced with nigh insuperable obstacles'.[13]

> Close analysis of the infancy narratives makes it unlikely that either account is completely historical. Matthew's account contains a number of extraordinary or miraculous public events that, were they factual, should have left some traces in Jewish records or elsewhere in the NT.[14]

Many scholars, particularly those studying the historical Jesus, are of the same opinion.

> The birth and infancy stories demonstrate the storyteller's art in applying ancient lore and motifs to Jesus. For that reason they are imaginative constructs rather than reports of historical events... [Matthew 2.1–12 is] long on Pagan pageantry but short on history.[15]

Also:

The fact that Luke as well as Matthew has a birth narrative does not contribute anything to the historical credibility of Matthew's narrative. On the contrary, because the two accounts are incompatible their historical value is even less.[16]

One incompatible point of disagreement with Luke is the Massacre of the Innocents. Though some scholars argue for a real event, Josephus records no such massacre. Given his use of records belonging to Herod's friend and advisor Nicholaus of Damascus, it's improbable such an event occurred.

Some commentators have appealed to the *Testament of Moses* as evidence for such a massacre. This incomplete and partly illegible early first-century CE text was possibly adapted from an earlier original composed during the unpopular rule of Antiochus IV Epiphanes (175-164 BCE) and the Maccabean Revolt. Despite being of mixed dates, *The Testament of Moses* 6.2–7 reflects the later reign of Herod the Great with 6.4 stating that 'He will kill both old and young, showing mercy to none'. Josephus records acts of Herodian violence and murder against family and subjects alike, especially if they threatened his power. From such passages, it's possible to see Herod acting how Matthew 2 describes. Nevertheless, the *Testament of Moses* can't of itself support the historicity of Matthew 2.16-18 (my italics):

> It is not enough to say that Herod's general pattern of behaviour was such that the judicious removal of a small number of young children passed without comment—*it was precisely this kind of thing which the garrulous Josephus was anxious to record.*[17]

Recent debate describes the lack of evidence for such a massacre 'inconceivable' and views the event in Matthew as a theological apology justifying later views of Jesus' exalted status. However, it's also been argued:

> The archaeological and historical records support the likelihood of this event. Firstly, it is completely in character for Herod the Great to do such a thing as he was paranoid about the succession even executing some of his own offspring and wives! Secondly, Bethlehem was a very tiny town in Jesus' day. If all children under two were killed we still would not be talking about even 10 children in all likelihood. Such a small event in a small town, well off Josephus' radar screen when he wrote his history of the 'Jewish Wars' and even later his 'Antiquities' could easily have been missed by him . . . and it is an argument from silence to say it didn't happen because Josephus doesn't mention it.[18]

Not all of history is recorded. However, it's unlikely that Matthew alone would have been aware of an event in Herodian history unknown to Luke, Josephus or Nicolaus (or indeed the rest of the Greco-Roman world).

There is a case made that Matthew 2 may have in fact 'fuelled' the growing popular image of Herod as a tyrant and certainly all the references to Herod within Matthew 2.16 match those within Josephus: threats to Herod's rule from rivals leading to anger and executions. And that only in the later *Antiquities* (c. 93 CE) was Herod was portrayed (for unknown reasons) in a more tyrannical light. This tradition most famously appears in about 400 CE in Marcobius' apocryphal quote from Augustus that 'it is better to be Herod's pig (ὖς) than his son (ὗιυς) (word play on the Greek for 'pig' and 'son').

Matthew's tension and conflict in relation to his local urban Jewish neighbours and his use of Formula Citations strongly suggests that his infancy narrative existed as apologetic christological propaganda: a defence (using Old Testament citations) in the face of Jewish objection and criticism to explain/justify exactly why Jesus (the new Moses), despite his crucifixion and humble Galilean origins, truly was the expected Davidic Messiah. Matthew 1–2 can be seen as the result of a need to maintain continuity with the past. By taking the genealogy of Jesus back to Abraham, Matthew establishes Jesus' legitimacy and has provided a beginning and end that goes beyond the narrative in the earlier Mark.

CHAPTER 3:
WORDS AND THEIR MEANINGS

Matthew's description of the Star totals only forty-two words in four passages:

2:2   εἴδομεν γὰρ αὐτοῦ τὸν ἀστέρα ἐν τῇ ἀνατολῇ

      For we observed his star at its rising

2:7   Τότε Ἡρῴδης λάθρα καλέσας τοὺς μάγους ἠκρίβωσεν παρ᾽ αὐτῶν τὸν χρόνον τοῦ φαινομένου ἀστέρος

      The Herod secretly called for the wise men and learned from them the exact time when the star had appeared

2:9   ἰδοὺ ὁ ἀστήρ, ὃν εἶδον ἐν τῇ ἀνατολῇ προῆγεν αὐτούς, ἕως ἐλθὼν ἐστάθη ἐπάνω οὗ ἦν τὸ παιδίον

      and there, ahead of them, went the star that they had seen at its rising, until it stopped over the place where the child was.

2:10   τὸν ἀστέρα

      the star

From these scant references, we could view the following as *facts* about the Star:

1. It was seen by the wise men when they were in the east

2. It was observed at its *acronychal (evening) rising* up to 1-2 years previously

3. At this time, it had a distinct (*possible*) astrological meaning

4. It disappeared as they journeyed to Jerusalem

5. It was so insignificant that Herod and all Jerusalem had overlooked it

6. The same star appeared again when they left Jerusalem

7. It went before them again

8. It 'stood over' Bethlehem

As the original autograph of Matthew is unrecoverable, and we possess no New Testament fragments earlier than c. 125 CE and no Matthean fragments earlier than c. 200 CE, we must make do with the surviving Greek MSS, versions and Patristic citations that have survived. The earliest known text of Matthew 2 is the third-century MS 𝔭⁷⁰, which gives us only 2.13–16, 22–23. The first complete texts to include 2.1–12 come from the uncials, which are dated from the fourth-century. Manuscript evidence for Matthew 2 is relatively late.

I have isolated eight words and passages that characterise and shape our understanding of the Star.

1. ἀστέρα , ἀστήρ (*star*) (Matthew 2.2, 9, 10)

2. ἐν τῇ ἀνατολῇ (*in the east/at its rising*) (Matthew 2.2)

3. ἠκρίβωσεν (*ascertained, learned*) (Matthew 2.7)

4. τὸν χρόνον τοῦ φαινομένου ἀστέρος (*the exact time when the star had appeared*) (Matthew 2.7)

5. ἰδοὺ ὁ ἀστήρ, ὃν εἶδον ἐν τῇ ἀνατολῇ (*Behold, the star, which they had seen at its rising/the east*) (Matthew 2.1, 9)

6. προῆγεν (*went before*) (Matthew 2.9)

7. ἕως ἐλθὼν ἐστάθη ἐπάνω (*until [having come] it stood over the place*) (Matthew 2.9)

8. παιδίον (*child*) (Matthew 2.9, 11)

Such an analysis is essential, as astrological and astronomical arguments depend heavily on astrological interpretations of the Greek, in particular the specific technical interpretations of ἐν τῇ ἀνατολῇ (*in the east*), ἠκρίβωσεν (*ascertained*), προῆγεν (*went before*) and ἐστάθη ἐπάνω (*it stood over*). By determining the meaning of the words in their specific context in Matthew 2, we can determine whether the astrological/astronomical theory is a valid solution for the Star.

It is a great thing to know what the New Testament says. The next point to be considered is what the New Testament means. A book is made up of words; words have histories; they are flexible, living things; only rarely, if ever, is it possible to tie a word down to one unchangeable meaning that it will retain through all the changes and chances of language. This is true of even apparently simple words.[1]

The history of translating the Bible into English (whether by individuals or, as more common today, committees) can't be covered here, but the general issues revolve around *free* (phrase for phrase) translation (such as functional/dynamic equivalence, meaning-based translation and closest natural equivalence) against the more common *literal* (word for word) translation ('formal/verbal equivalence'). I'll use a literal, verbal equivalence approach.

Studies have highlighted the problems that can arise in translating the Greek New Testament and there several *word-study fallacies* which could result in an erroneous theological or technical interpretation. The four most relevant here are:

1. Appeal to unknown or unlikely meanings

2. Careless appeal to background material

3. False assumptions about technical meaning (*terminus technicus*)

4. Selective and prejudiced use of evidence

Ambiguity is a problem in translating from receptor to target language, caused when a word with two or more possible meanings results in the same sentence being interpreted in more than one way. Usually, the ambiguity can be solved by identifying the main semantic focus or by examining the context in which the word appears—by determining the *sense* of the word and those surrounding it. If meaning can't be determined by context, other sources of knowledge are required.

It's possible such ambiguity is unintentional. There's a distinction between *authorial* meaning and *audience*. From a literary perspective, this can be the distinction between the implied narrator and the response of the reader/audience. As astronomers who advocate the astrological/astronomical theory is one such 'audience' (providing their own context to the text and translating accordingly), we need to identify Matthew's original context and meaning with regard to the Star as neutrally as possible.

Whether or not Matthew used a specific Greek Old Testament text, he was grounded in Jewish themes and expectations. The key Matthean themes include those of eschatology, judgement, ecclesiology, Old Testament revelation, Davidic Christology and kingship.

1. ἀστέρα , ἀστήρ (*star*)

Many meanings (and solutions) have been attached by astronomers to the word 'star' in Matthew 2.2 (for example, nova, comet, planet, conjunction of many planets and occulation). Generally, ἀστήρ is used for a single star and ἄστρον for plural 'stars' but the usage is extremely varied. Of particular interest is Josephus' reference (*War* 6.289) to a *single* star (ἄστρον) that *stood over* Jerusalem.

The noun ἀστήρ can refer to a star, the fixed stars, a planet, or planets (οἱ ἑπτὰ ἀστέρες or πλανής ἀστήρ), but it can also describe a meteor/shooting star, comet, the sun, the moon, the zodiac itself or even a constellation. The second-century mathematician and astronomer Ptolemy (c. 100–165 CE), when referring to one of the then five known planets in his *Almagest*, always used the typical Hellenistic periphrasis '*star of...*' (i.e. ὁ ἀστήρ τοῦ Κρόνου – *the star of Saturn*).[2] In his *Tertrabiblos*, however, Ptolemy omits the 'star of...' and uses plain Διος (*Jupiter - Zeus*) or Κρόνου, etc.

In the New Testament, ἀστήρ is used 24 times but ἄστρον only four (never in Matthew). Outside Revelation (where ἀστήρ is used 14 times) Matthew has the highest usage of five, with all but one being in Matthew 2. The fifth appears in Matthew 24.29 and is used in the plural (οἱ ἀστέρες").

The LXX uses both ἀστήρ and ἄστρον as the chief translation for כּוֹכָב (ωιτη ἄστρον also used for בָּרָק, שַׁחַק and שָׁמַיִם) and can mean both 'star' singular and 'stars' plural.

The Hebrew כּוֹכָב (and the Syrian *Kaukbhâ*), are similar to the Akkadian *kakkabu* and it's been suggested that it was the colloquial name for Jupiter. However, Jupiter was referred to by the Babylonian name of Marduk, with *kakkabu* having the wider meaning of stars, constellations, planets and heavenly phenomena in general. The Ugaritic word *kkb* or *kbkb* also means 'star'. In a few cases כּוֹכָב is used metaphorically. Significantly, in Numbers 24.17, it was later interpreted as referring to a Davidic or messianic ruler.

In the works of Philo (20 BCE–40 CE), of his 120 uses of ἀστήρ or ἄστρον it's always in reference to 'a star', 'the stars', never to a planet, for which he uses the specific word πλανήτης or πλανής (*wanderer, roamer*).

Philo provides a prime example of how translators have chosen to represent the Greek in English. The translators of the 1929 LCL edition took οὐρανὸν ἀστέρων (*De Opificio Mundi* 45) to mean 'heavenly body/bodies' (as they do for the single usage of ἀστέρων in other instances), which could suggest a wider meaning including 'planets'. However, C.D. Yonge, in his 1854 English edition, uses 'stars in heaven.' Furthermore, the Loeb edition translates Philo's use of ἀστήρ in *Opif.* 31 as 'constellation', though Yonge just calls it a 'star above the heavens'.

> In selecting a term for 'star', it is important to avoid an expression which may relate to only one set of stars, that is to say, a particular constellation, since there may be connotations associated with such a constellation which can radically alter the intent of a particular passage. Some constellations, for example, may be regarded as kindly disposed toward mankind, while others may be regarded as hostile.[3]

Matthew's lack of specific expression has resulted in so much speculation about what the Star exactly was. The context of the passage varies depending on whether ἀστήρ is translated as a metaphor or symbol (for Christ), miraculous sign or angel, astrological event, or ordinary comet, nova or planet. This is a clear example of lexical ambiguity in action.

In the Greco-Roman world, stars and planets were routinely interpreted as divine beings with souls and intellect, or deified heroes placed among them. Stars as divine beings are in the prologue to Plautus' *Rudens* where the constellation Arcturus appears in human form 'agleam with shining star.' Was Matthew referring to a heavenly *body* or a heavenly *being*?

Plato wrote (*Timeus*, c. 360 BCE) that the universe is a living being 'in very truth possessing soul and reason by the providence of God.' As intelligence (νοῦς) and soul (ψυχή) were coexistent, the regular movements of the heavens were credited by Plato with both. Stars are also referred to as divine or gods in *Laws* and in the Pseudo-Platonic dialogue *Epinomis*, where the stars are gods and overseers of humanity.

Later, Aristotle wrote (*De Caelo* 285a, 29–30), 'the heaven is alive and contains a principle of motion'. The celestial sphere of fixed stars and the planetary spheres had pure souls and responded to the influence of the first unmoved mover—God. Yet *individual* stars weren't alive, though on this point Aristotle couldn't seem to make up his mind.

Plato was a strong influence on Philo who wrote that:

> The stars [ἀστέρες] found their place in heaven. Those who have made philosophy their study tell us that these too are living creatures [ζῷα], but of a kind composed entirely of Mind. Of these some, the planets [πλάνητες] appear to change their position by a power inherent in themselves, others do so as they are swept along in the rush of our universe, and these we call fixed stars.[4]

Philo also refers to both angels and stars as divine beings. However, the cosmos as a ζῷον wasn't a universal belief in Hellenistic philosophy. The notion was rejected by Boethus of Sidon, the Peripatetic Straton and the Epicureans.

This belief in the divinity of the stars was taken by (for example) the Pythagoreans and used to formulate their doctrine of the soul's immortality and its descent from and ascent to the stars at birth and death. Great men were often referred to as brilliant stars and to call someone a 'star' is still popular usage. Placing mythical figures and deified men among the stars to achieve astral immortality was known as καταστερισμός (*placing among the stars*). The Stoics accepted this doctrine, and their cosmological view of a close interconnection (συμπάθεια) between micro and macrocosm prevailed in Rome.

We can't ignore the plural *stars* found in a variant of the *Infancy Gospel of James* or *Protevangelium Jacobi*, an apocryphal infancy story (c. 160–200 CE). Though a later text, it's been picked up by at least one astronomer with regard to the astrological hypothesis.

2. ἐν τῇ ἀνατολῇ (Matthew 2.2)

Perhaps because the μάγοι were ἀπὸ ἀνατολῶν (Genesis, plural, feminine), having seen the Star ἐν τῇ ἀνατολῇ (dative, singular, feminine), older English Bible versions translated the singular ἀνατολή as 'in the east.' The difference between singular and plural and articular and anarthous (with or without an article) is significant for its translation.

Though it was noted as a 'possible technical expression' as far back as 1915 by A.H. McNeile, Walter Bauer was the most instrumental in highlighting the translation of 'rising' as opposed to 'east'. In his 1952 fourth edition of *Grieschisch-deutsches Wörterbuch* he translated ἀνατολή as *Aufgehen* based on the view that ἐν τῇ ἀνατολῇ has an article and is singular. Not long after, the 1956 *La Bible de Jérusalem* gave the earliest translation of the Greek as 'at its rising'.

The *Greek-English Lexicon of the New Testament* (BDAG) entry for ἀνατολῇ provides three interpretations:

(1) Upward movement of celestial bodies

(2) Position of the rising sun

(3) Change of darkness to light in the early morning

The *Greek-English Lexicon* (LSJ) entry provides the same interpretation (frequently in the plural) but notes the distinction between ἀνατολῇ—the rising above the horizon *of any heavenly body*, and ἐπιτολή—the rising of a *star at sunrise or sunset*

In modern translations, the phrase in Matthew 2 is now considered to refer to the astronomical *rising* of the Star (acronychally [evening] or heliacally [morning]) over the eastern horizon.

Examples from Greek horoscope texts demonstrate its usage in reference to the rising of planets. In *P. Oxy.* 1380 (a hymn to Isis) there are references to the 'rising sun' (ἥλιον ἀπ᾿ ἀνατολῆς) and the 'rising stars' (ἄστρ[ω]ν ἀνατολαῖς). Philo uses the word in this sense when he writes of the 'risings [of the stars]' (ἀνατολαῖς αὐτῶν) and the rising of the sun (ἀνατολάς). Diodorus Siculus (3.23) describes τὴν ἀνατολὴν τοῦ κυνός (*the rising of the dog-star* [Sirius]) while Ptolemy writes of the planets τῆς ἀνατολῆς μέχρι τοῦ πρώτου στηριγμοῦ, that is, 'rising to their first station'. This refers to *heliacal* risings.

In *1 Enoch* 18.15 the word is also used to refer to the rising of stars. Later, in *1 Enoch* 72–82 there's a passage that describes east and west as the directions of the *rising* and *setting* stars (*1 Enoch* 77.1–2):

The First quarter is called east because it is the chief (quarter)... (2) And the quarter in the west is called *netug* [diminished]because all celestial luminaries decrease there and go down.[5]

Enoch was also found at Qumran where 4Q209 reads:

And the great quarter (they call) the West quarter, because there go the stars of heaven; there they set and there all stars enter... [And the east (they call)] East because from there arise the bodies of the heavens; and also (they call it) *mizrah* because thence they arise.[6]

There appears to be confusion over the Greek technical terms for evening-morning risings and statements about 'risings' and 'settings' in modern editions of classics are 'notoriously untrustworthy.'[7] The Oxford English Dictionary defines *heliacal* rising as, 'said of the rising of a star when it first emerges from the sun's rays and becomes visible before sunrise' and *acronychal* rising as 'happening in the evening or at night-fall, vespertine, as the acronychal rising or setting of a star.' The star or planet rises in the east as the sun sets in the west, so Ptolemy uses ἡ ἀκρονύκτους φάσεις to describe the 'evening rise' of planets.

The waters are muddied by the word ἐπιτολή, which was also used as a technical term for the rising of stars. The LSJ entry cites:

(1) the rising of a star

(2) the season of a star's appearance in the heavens

(3) the rising of a star *as the sun rises or sets or just before sunrise or
     after sunset*

Usually, ἐπιτολή refers to heliacal risings and ἀνατολή to daily risings. The
intransitive is ἐπιτέλλω and this verb is the more usual usage for the rising of
stars.

The LSJ cites Geminus (70 BCE to 40 CE) as their source for (3) but Gustav
Teres, in his linguistic analysis of Matthew 2's astronomical expressions, also
made use of Geminus' work, ΕΙΣΑΓΩΓΗ ΕΙΣ ΤΑ ΦΑΙΝΟΜΕΝΑ to argue that
Matthew was writing of an *evening* rising at 2.2, 9 and a *morning* rising at 2.7.
Geminus makes a clear distinction between the technical uses of ἐπιτολή and
ἀνατολή.

However, ἀνατολή was also an acceptable alternative.

Another example is from the second-century BCE grammarian, Ptolemy of
Ascalon. He defined ἀνατολή as a term *only* applied to the sun and the moon,
with ἐπιτολή being the proper term for the rising of stars.

Tim Hegedus made a special study on early Christian responses to astrology
and noted the ambiguous usage of ἀνατολή, but he interprets Matthew's usage as
heliacal, arguing that the magi would have regarded this solar astrological omen
(birth of a cosmic power) as more significant than horoscopic astrology.

A horoscope by second-century CE astrologer Vettius Valens uses ἐπιτολή
to describe the *rising* of Sirius (he doesn't state whether this is an evening or
morning event). Ethelbert Bullinger, in his *Critical Lexicon*, doesn't cite ἀνατολή
in his section on 'rising' and it only appears in his entry for 'East' where he cites
it as 'a rising, esp. of the sun.'[8] That is, the *eastern* dawn.

Despite the astronomical interpretation of 'rising' it's apparent that *without
the article*, ἀνατολή was interchangeable with the senses of 'dawn' and 'east'.
The majority of its use in Hellenistic literature refers to 'dawn' where it became
shorthand for ἀνατολή ἥλίου (place where the sun rises). These senses were closely
linked and not distinct as they are in modern English.

The *Greek-English Lexicon of the New Testament Based on Semantic
Domains* (LN) defines ἀνατολή in terms of domain 15 ('linear movement')
sub-domain J ('come/go up, ascend'), 'to move up, especially of the upward
movement of the sun, stars, or clouds.' Thus ἀνατολή is also defined as domain
82 ('spatial orientations') sub-domain A ('north, south, east, west'). Where they
differ in their translation of 2.2 is that they take a backward step in noting the
possibility of it meaning geographical 'east' instead of the accepted 'rising'.

The word's usage for the direction of the rising sun gives us a double sense
of 'dawn' and 'east'. *Papyri Graecae Magicae, (PGM)* VI.4 refers to Helios

(the sun-god) as the 'rising sun', ἀνατολῇ τῇ τοῦ ἡλίου. Geminus (*Gem.* 13.3) also includes the usage of ἥλιος (*sun*) to refer to the cardinal point 'east'. This combining of ἥλιος with ἀνατολῇ can be seen in LXX where it occurs twenty-nine times. LXX Isaiah 14.12 speaks of a fallen star, who was titled 'Son of Dawn'— Πῶς ἐξέπεσεν ἐκ τοῦ οὐρανοῦ ὁ ἑωσφόρος ὁ πρωὶ ἀνατέλλων.

There are 176 instances of ἀνατολή in the LXX where it's used to translate מִזְרָח, יָצָא and קֶדֶם: The majority refer to an eastern direction/location, for example, Genesis 2.8 κατὰ ἀνατολάς (*eastward*); Genesis 10.30 ὄρος ἀνατολῶν (*mountain of the east*) and Genesis 11.2 ἀπὸ ἀνατολῶν (*from the east*). However, there always being an exception to the rule, 1 Esdras 5.46 (πρὸς τῇ ἀνατολῇ) provides evidence of articular use in connection with geographical east.

Philo is perhaps using the LXX when he has Balaam speak of being called ἀπ ἀνατολῶν. All of Josephus' 48 usages have the meaning of 'east' (from the Roman point of view) In the *Pseudepigrapha*, it occurs 41 times and 37 instances refer to 'east'.

In modern Greek the plural of ἀνατολῇ is a proper noun meaning 'various parts of Anatolia.' If the magi came from Anatolia, they would be *wise men from the west*.

Use of the arthrous singular noun in Matthew 2.2 has been translated as '*rising in the east*' (astronomical). Grammarians argue that if Matthew had meant *geographical* east he would have used the anarthrous *plural* (as he does in 2.1, 8.11 and 24.17).

However, examples of the singular to denote geographical east also exist. Philo uses a mixture of plural and singular phrases for the geographical east: ἀνατολὰς ('east'), προς ἀνατολὰς ('towards the east'), ἀνατολή ('by east'), απ᾽ ἀνατολῶν ('from the east').

In the LXX, only 15 of the 171 instances are in the singular (ten of them anarthous). The five that have the article cover a wide range of meanings: rising of the sun (Judges 5.31), dawn (2 Maccabees. 10.28), east (1 Esdras 5.46 and 2 Esdras 13.29), and growth (Ezekiel 16.7).

In later papyri, the singular appears in the second/third-century CE P. *Tebt.* 2.276 in relation to the *heliacal* rising of Venus and as points of time in P.*Oxy.* 4.725 (183 CE) and P.*Ryl* 1.27 (third century CE).

Given Matthew's use of the singular and plural, ἀνατολῇ is probably an example of *astronomical* terminology, though it's unclear whether it has any implicit or explicit *astrological* meaning, or refers to a morning or evening rising. Non-astronomical interpretations are also possible and may be intertwined with the astronomical sense.

Robert Gundry has suggested that Matthew's quotation and redaction of LXX Isaiah 9:1-2 provides evidence for the connection between Numbers 24.17, Christ's *rising* and the messianic Star. He says that Matthew has replaced Isaiah's φῶς λάμψει with φῶς ἀνέτειλεν (*a light has dawned*) so the *dawn* of Christ's ministry can link with the rising messianic Star, and notes that the Greek ἀνατέλλω has a double meaning of 'rise-shine brightly' providing a link to the allusion to Numbers 24.17 at Matthew 2.2, 9. Matthew may be using ἀνατέλλω to mean 'rise' rather than 'shine' in reference back to Matthew 2.2, 9 and Balaam's rising star.

W. D. Davies also notes that the messianic use of ἀνατολή in LXX Zech. 3.8; 6.12 was 'prepared for' in the LXX's use of ἀνατέλλειν in connection with the messianic age. In fact, Davies suggests that the Star and the use of the term ἐν τῇ ἀνατολῇ has connections to light and messianic usage.

Similarly, ἀνατολή can be given a Davidic interpretation. The term is used in the Benedictus (Luke 1.67–79) where Zechariah (1.78), filled with the Holy Spirit, calls Jesus ἀνατολὴ ἐξ ὕψους (*the rising sun from heaven*). In 1.78–79, Luke has clearly used the words of Zechariah (c. 519–517 BCE) the minor prophet who used the word צמח ('branch' or 'sprout') as a *title*. The LXX translation is given as Ἀνατολή.

The expression ἀνατολὴ ἐξ ὕψους has been given many interpretations, though it's generally accepted as an idiom meaning 'the rising sun from Heaven' ('[the] rising/dawning from [the] height').

Again, we see the association of ἀνατολή with the dawn and the *Patristic Greek Lexicon* cites its use for the rising sun ('hence *dawn* of future life') and also as a metaphor of Christ.

It's possible that ἀνατολὴ ἐξ ὕψους *might* mean 'Messiah *of God*.' However, in the LXX, where the phrase ἐξ ὕψους occurs six times, it means more 'from heaven' than 'from God'. Hence, it may refer to a *pre-existent* divine figure who will come out of heaven, bringing salvation (evoking the ἄγγελος of Isaiah 9.6) and associated with the light of dawn (ἀνατολή). In this interpretation Luke has transformed the 'messiah from below' (ὑποκάτωθεν αὐτοῦ ἀνατελεῖ) of LXX Zechariah 6.12 into the 'messiah from above.'

Apart from the notion of Luke 1.78 being a reference to a 'heavenly messiah', there exists the 'descendant of David' interpretation. In the LXX the ἀνατολῇ of Jeremiah 23.5 is a translation of צמח ('sprout', 'shoot', 'scion', a word that designates the future Davidic king).

Its presence in Zechariah was based on its established use as a metaphor for the future prosperity of the Davidic line, the restored royal ruler. In Zechariah's time this was Zerubbabel, the Davidic heir who is exhorted in an oracle to rebuild the temple.

A messianic interpretation of ἀνατολήν is possible and in the late first-century BCE 4QFlor 1:11 (=4Q174), it's written of the royal messiah, 'He is the Scion [צמח] of David who will arise with the Interpreter of the Law.' צמח has been translated as both as 'shoot' and 'branch'. The messianic epithet צמח דוד (branch/shoot of David) is also evident in the Dead Sea Scroll where Genesis 49.10, Numbers 24.17 and Isaiah 11.1–6 all appear.

These messianic oracles were also significant in early Christian writings. For example, LXX Isaiah 11.1 is quoted by Paul in Romans 15.12, a letter written c. 53–55 CE:

καὶ πάλιν Ἡσαΐας λέγει, Ἔσται ἡ ῥίζα τοῦ Ἰεσσαί, καὶ ὁ ἀνιστάμενος ἄρχειν ἐθνῶν, ἐπ' αὐτῷ ἔθνη ἐλπιοῦσιν

And again Isaiah says, 'The root of Jesse shall come, the one who rises to rule the Gentiles, in him the Gentiles shall hope.'

The translation of 'shoot' or 'growth' is more accurate than 'branch' as the latter doesn't fully translate the meaning of צמח, which is what comes *out of the ground*, not what branches out *from an existing trunk*. This better explains the LXX translation of ἀνατολή ('rising') in Zechariah 3.8 and 6.12.

If LXX ῥίζα refers to 'shoot' rather than 'root', Paul is referring to Jesus as the fulfilment of a promised appearance of the messianic son of David. He springs from the root as the shoot of a plant's old stump. The epistle to the Romans tells us that that the association between Christ and the messianic root/shoot was made early in Christian theology. There are other LXX passages where 'branch' and 'root' are used in connection with messianic prophecy and redemption.

What's noticeable in Matthew's Gospel is the number of redactional references to Jesus as υἱοῦ Δαυίδ. In the New Testament, this phrase appears only in the Synoptics where Matthew uses it ten times, and Mark and Luke five times between them (even then, Luke is using Mark). Matthew's concern with kingship and the messiah can also be seen in his use of the phrase βασιλεία τῶν οὐρανῶν (*king of Heaven*), which appears 32 times in Matthew and in no other Gospel.

What can we make of the argument that Matthew is presenting us with a messianic usage of ἀνατολῇ (with its light-dawn and/or root-branch-scion imagery)? The LXX translation of צמח as ἀνατολῇ has overtones of rising, growth, and light.

It's possible Matthew was playing with his use of ἀνατολῇ and gave the Star a double or even triple sense of a guiding light from the east (the direction of salvation/righteousness), rising at dawn and representing the arrival of the branch of David. The large number of Royal Davidic references in the Infancy Narrative alone highlights Matthew's purpose of pressing his readers to see Jesus as the legitimate heir of the Davidic throne and the expected royal Davidic Messiah. Christ's Davidic descent was accepted in early creedal-type formulations.

The nativity is therefore an important part of Matthew's Davidic Christology containing allusions to all three messianic passages—Genesis 49.10, Numbers 24.17 and Isaiah 11.1. Assuming that Matthew is the product of a primarily Jewish-Christian community, the Star of Bethlehem, is better seen in the light of messianism rather than that of Hellenistic astrology.

3. ἠκρίβωσεν (*ascertain*) (**Matthew 2.7**) and 4. ἠκρίβωσεν... τὸν χρόνον τοῦ φαινομένου ἀστέρος (*the exact time when the star had appeared*) (**Matthew 2.7**)

> Matthew generally shows little concern for chronological specification. Most of his pericopae are strung together with no account of the interval between them; we are simply left with the impression of great lapses of time.[9]

This is typical of Matthew's method (made more obvious by the artificial divisions of chapter and verse) and unknown periods of time occur frequently in the Infancy Narrative. One unknown length of time is how long the Star had been visible, a question linked to Jesus' age when the magi visit Bethlehem.

Matthew has Herod ἠκρίβωσεν (*ascertain*) the time of the appearance of the star, the answer to which he uses later when he orders the death of all the children under two. The Greek ἠκρίβωσεν is the third person aorist active indicative singular of the rare verb ἀκριβόω (Matthew uses the adverb ἀκριβῶς at 2.8 when Herod asks the magi to ἐξετάσατε ἀκριβῶς (*inquire 'carefully/diligently'*) into Jesus' whereabouts in Bethlehem) and also appears in 2.16. These are the only two uses of this aorist verb in the New Testament and it doesn't appear at all in the LXX. The adverbial usage, however, does occur in the LXX with the meaning 'to make diligent enquiry' (Deuteronomy 19.18 for יטב ; Daniel 7.19 for יצב).

As an aorist indicative verb, ἠκρίβωσεν indicates an absolute *past* time with reference to the time of speaking. Likewise, the prior participle καλέσας (literally, *having called*) is also aorist, supporting Herod's action as being a past action.

The BDAG and LSJ define ἀκριβόω as 'to understand, investigate or ascertain something *precisely, accurately and exactly*' and the 'to learn exactly or accurately' meaning was used by the Church Fathers.

According to some, the aorist ἠκρίβωσεν is a *terminus technicus* used in astrological interpretations, yet neither the BDAG nor LSJ provide any astrological reference.

Geminus writes of the rising and setting of stars over the horizon κατὰ τὸν λόγον ἀκρίβειαν. Here it refers to exactitude, and although an example of the verbs' use in an astronomical context, it isn't definitive.

Of the verb φαίνω (*shine, light, appear, be seen,* etc), the LN puts it into the semantic range of domain 24 ('sensory events and states'), sub-domain A ('See').[10] In Patristic usage its perfect active and passive meaning was 'appear, come into being, be made to manifest', that is, of Christ. It's a favourite Matthean word for he uses it the greatest number of times in the New Testament (14 compared to two in Mark and Luke.) Here we are dealing with its participle form, and the syntax of participles is a difficulty being (usually) heavily reliant on context and their relation to the main verb.

In Matthew 2.7b, the adjectival participle φαινομένου is used in the *passive* sense of an *appearing* star that is shining or producing light. If used in its given present tense, τὸν χρόνον τοῦ φαινομένου ἀστέρος could be translated as 'the time of the shining Star' or 'the time of the Star's shining'.

Of the passive usage φαίνω, the LSJ entry cites this voice as one of 'come to light, appear,' quoting one usage (Homer, *Il.* 8.556) as being 'frequently of the *rising* of heavenly bodies.' Homer does write, ἄστρα φαεινὴν ἀμφὶ σελήνην φαί νετέ ἀριπρεπέα but this refers more to an image of shining stars surrounding the moon above the Trojan camp.

A difficulty is that Koine Greek has the same endings for both middle *and* passive in the present tense and it isn't easy to determine which voice is in force. Although it's generally agreed that this participle is in the *passive* voice ('to come to light, appear, be manifest') perhaps it should be read as being in the middle.

As there's no clear explicit or even implicit indicator of an agent or any other instrument bringing about the appearance of the Star (it isn't implied that God is the agent), how can the participle be passive? Grammatically the participle is in the middle voice with the sentence being not 'of the Star *being made* to shine/appear' but 'of the Star shining/appearing.'

In New Testament Greek studies, the old time-based view of Greek verbs, which developed into the *Aktionsart* theory (where verbs are used in relation to *how,* and not strictly *when,* actions occurred), has led to *verbal aspect* theory whereby tense forms are selected based on the author's perspective (often sub- or unconsciously). In other words, it's *how the user wishes to conceive of and conceptualise an action* and therefore not strictly based on the action itself.

Though *present* in tense, this participle phrase can be regarded as having an *imperfective aspect* (progressive *continuous* past action) and 2.7b can be translated as 'the time the star had begun to be visible.'

In this case, the tense-form of the participle (which doesn't exist in imperfect form and would usually convey its imperfect past time from the context and tense of the main verb) has nothing to do with the main verb ἀκριβῶς (in *aorist indicative* form). Thus, an imperfect indicative could also be appropriate in a clause equivalent to this participial phrase, so Matthew might also have written: χρόνον ἐφ' ᾧ ἐφαίνετο ἀστήρ or χρόνον ὅτε ἐφαίνετο ἀστήρ.

Teres, presenting an astronomical meaning for φαινομένου, has used Geminus to interpret its use as referring specifically to a heliacal *morning* rising of Jupiter. Geminus refers to a planet's early visible appearance before the sun—ἑῴαν φαινομένην ἐπιτολὴν. Hesiod also uses φαινομένου when discussing the morning rising of Orion.

However, the *Protevangelium Jacobi* 21.7–8 uses μὴ φαίνεσθαι to refer to the *disappearance* of the stars (due to the exceptional brilliance [παμμεγέθη λάμψαντα] of the Star) and supports Matthew's use to mean 'appearance'. As a final point, Teres uses the present tense participle as corresponding to the *imperfect* to conclude, 'that the star was still visible on a nightly basis when Herod spoke to the Magi.'

Translating the participial phrase as 'shining' or 'appearance' doesn't alter its construction, as the phrase is *temporal* in sense, with the focus on the accusative χρόνον, that is: *when?* The BDAG, with regard to 2.7, interprets χρόνον as referring to '*a point in time* consisting of an occasion for some event.'

However, the LSJ entry cites the accusative form as meaning '*for a while, for a long* or *short time*', that is, *a duration of time*. The Greek 'could also, however, be read as pertaining to the star's duration ('time' = 'span of time') or, more precisely, to the length of time it was seen by the Magi.'[11]

If this is the case (we can never know for sure), Matthew is writing of the *duration* of the Star's shining as opposed to the date of the Star's appearance. Such a view doesn't affect Herod's action at 2.16 where the children are killed κατὰ τὸν χρόνον ὃν ἠκρίβωσεν παρὰ τῶν μάγων (*according to the time he that he had learned from the wise men.*)

Matthew 2.7 and 2.16 *could* demonstrate the presence of astrology in the text. Herod probes the magi for chronological information regarding a rising star, but all we have in the text is Herod asking the magi a simple question: *how long/from what time has the Star been shining?* The implication that this refers explicitly to astrology isn't clear.

An interesting variation appears in the *Protevangelium Jacobi*. Here, Herod doesn't want to know *what time* the sign appeared but *what the sign was*. The magi's reply was to describe the Star in more detail and offer a vague explanation on how it was interpreted:

Καὶ ἀνέκρινεν τοὺς μάγους λέγων αὐτοῖς· Τί εἴδετε σημεῖον ἐπὶ τὸν γεννηθέντα βασιλέα; Καὶ εἶπον οἱ μάγοι· Εἴδομεν ἀστέρα παμμεγέθη λάμψαντα ἐν τοῖς ἄστροις τούτοις καὶ ἀμβλύναντα αὐτούς, ὥστε τοὺς ἀστέρας μὴ φαίνεσθαι· καὶ οὕτως ἔγνωμεν ὅτι βασιλεὺς ἐγεννήθη τῷ Ἰσραήλ, καὶ ἤλθομεν προσκυνῆσαι αὐτῷ.

Then he questioned the astrologers: 'What sign have you seen regarding the one who has been born king?' And the astrologers said, 'We saw a star of exceptional brilliance in the sky, and it so dimmed the other stars that they disappeared. Consequently, we know that a king was born for Israel. And we have come to pay him homage.[12]

Perhaps the author of this later apocryphal narrative was trying to clarify Herod's brief exchange with the magi.

5. ἰδοὺ ὁ ἀστήρ, ὃν εἶδον ἐν τῇ ἀνατολῇ (Behold, the star, which they had seen at its rising/the east) (Matthew 2.1, 9)

The actions of the Star, magi and Herod could be seen to be consistent with the view that Matthew is referring to an astronomical event—a star rose above the horizon at some unspecified point in the past—and the magi interpreted this star as referring to Jesus. Yet from Matthew 2.9 onwards, the Star acts in a manner that moves far beyond its initial historical attributes.

Matthew writes that after departing from Jerusalem (in the southwestern direction of Bethlehem), the Star is again visible (2.9)—καὶ ἰδοὺ ὁ ἀστήρ, ὃν εἶδον ἐν τῇ ἀνατολῇ. The BDAG defines the use of ἰδοὺ in Matthew 2.9 as a demonstrative particle that has introduced something *new* or *unusual*.

It's used this way for the sudden appearance of the magi in Jerusalem (Matthew 2.1). In the LXX this is used chiefly for הִנֵּה (lo! Behold!). It's a favourite word of both Matthew (62 occurrences) and Luke (57) against Mark's mere seven. Matthew often uses καὶ ἰδοὺ to begin a narrative or introduce a new part of the story.

If the Star hadn't been visible up to this point, Matthew's use of ἰδοὺ suggests a sudden reappearance. Opinion is divided over whether the Star was always visible or had vanished before the magi reached Jerusalem.

Because Herod (and others) only *hear* (ἀκούσας) about the Star and don't see it, there's an object (perhaps last seen up to two years previously) which has 'suddenly' reappeared to the magi on their leaving Jerusalem. This explains Matthew's unnecessary reminder (ὃν εἶδον ἐν τῇ ἀνατολῇ) of a fact pointed out seven verses earlier—it was the return of same Star they'd seen before.

It's also been suggested that the magi were travelling at night, for a typical star—even a miraculous one—can't be seen during daylight. Travel by night would provide the opportunity for Matthew to 'speak anew of the star.'[13] Despite this, there's an early tradition of the journey having taken place during the day.

In the first four centuries of Christian reception history, the Star was always interpreted as a bright new object. But if the Star was so exceptional that it could be seen by day, and if it was a real historical event, how was it missed?

6. προάγω (Matthew 2.9)

Matthew next states (2.9) that the Star *'went before'* the magi [προῆγεν αὐτούς] after they depart from Herod. In 2.9, the verb προῆγεν derives from προάγω (LSJ *lead forward, escort on their way*; being made up of προ 'before, forth' and ἄγω 'to move or lead') and is used here in its intransitive form to mean 'to move ahead or in front of, *go before, lead the way, precede*.' The PLG also cites 'to lead forward.' Was there a reason why Matthew used this word instead of ἔμπροσθέν?

The LN classifies προάγω in domain 15 ('linear movement') and the three sub-domains, 15.142 (O. 'come/go prior to'), 15.143 (P. 'come/go in front of') and 15.171 (W. 'lead, bring, take'). Its usage in 2.9 might fit into sub-domain P with its range of 'to move in front of or ahead of, with the implication that both parties are moving in the same direction' or W, with its range of 'to bring forward or forth'.

Of all nineteen uses of προάγω in the works of Philo it's only used to mean 'advance', 'led on', 'bring forth', 'return' (of a garment). In the New Testament this verb is used twenty times, and its use is usually a clear one of 'being ahead, leading.' For example, Mark 11.9 refers to οἱ προάγοντες (*the ones leading the way*). Matthew uses the verb six times, the highest single usage in the New Testament. Four of these usages derive from Mark, but 2.9 and 21.31 are unique to Matthew. In the LXX 1 Kings 17.16, it refers to the forward advancement of Goliath, a translation of וגשׁ.

Retrograde motion

Gustav Teres interprets retrograde motion as the meaning behind προῆγεν and Michael Molnar (who sees the Star as being an *occultation* of Jupiter by the moon) refers to Ivor Bulmer-Thomas' 'clarification' that both προῆγεν and ἐστάθη ἐπάνω (*stood above*) are astrological terms. Bulmer-Thomas (who sees Jupiter as the star described by Matthew) in turn relies on G.J. Toomer's translation of Ptolemy's *Almagest*.

The OED defines 'retrograde' (from Latin *retrogradior*, *retrogradus*) as '*intr. Astr.* Of the Planets, etc: To go backward (in apparent motion) in the zodiac; to seem to travel from east to west.' This apparent movement is an illusion caused by the Earth's motion relative to the slower and more distant planets; the planet in question will appear to stop and then move in the opposite direction.

The event was well-known and Plato was also aware of planetary retrogradation. Plato uses the verb ἐπανακυκλέω (ἐπανακύκλησις)—D.R. Dicks translates this as 'additional circlings, backwards, retrograde' and the LSJ as '*return* of a circle *into itself*'. For Plato, retrograde movement was the result of a voluntary force (ἐθελούσιος). This was later taken up by Philo. In Enoch we find this reversal of planetary motion being punished for 'erring in their courses'.

Ptolemy discusses the mathematics of retrograde action in book twelve of his *Almagest*. He explains that the heavens rotate from east to west and G.J. Toomer provides the following translation of the Greek technical terms with regard to this rotation: εἰς τὰ προηγούμενα = '*towards the leading [parts]*' and εἰς τὰ ἑπόμενα = '*towards the following [parts]*'. The adjectives προηγούμενος (advance, in advance, leading) and ἑπόμενος (following) are used in the *Almagest* as well as his earlier *Star Catalogue*. The phrase εἰς τὰ προηγούμενα (ἑπόμενα) τῶν ζῳδίων ('*towards the leading (following) [parts] of the zodiacal signs*') is also frequently used in describing this motion.

Toomer states that he's settled for using 'in advance' for εἰς τὰ προηγούμενα, that is, for when Ptolemy refers to the daily motion of east to west. It's here that Toomer refers to 'retrogradation'. Geminus likewise writes εἰς τὰ προηγούμενα, which refers to *proceeding before* (going ahead of) the fixed stars. However, Geminus uses ὑπόλειψις for retrograde motion and προάγω for advancing forward. The LSJ entry for ὑπόλειψις gives its astronomical meaning as '*direct motion*, that is, eastwards along the ecliptic.' (Interestingly, they cite its use by Iamblichus (c. 250 CE–c330 CE) in his *de vita Pythagorica* 6:31 to mean 'occultation'.)

But *advancing* isn't the same as *retrograde* motion and Toomer notes that his translation of προήγησις (or προηγήσεις) as 'retrogradation/s' appears inconsistent with the translation elsewhere as 'motion in advance', but he explains that this would be 'too confusing' when applied to planets when they 'reverse their normal direction of motion.' Ptolemy also uses the word προηγούμενοι in his later astrological work, *Tetrabiblos* (1.24, 3.11), which F.E. Robbins translates as 'follow' or 'moving forward.'

Ptolemy's προηγούμενοι:

> Is essentially the same word that Matthew uses...[and that this]...
> corroborates the idea that the biblical account was applying technical
> astrological language that has since lost its meaning. Thus, the correct
> interpretation of the Magi's report is that the star was moving forward
> against the background stars, not in front of the Magi as they travelled
> from the east.[14]

The only element the two words have in common is the preposition προ with the
differences in aspiration and inflection between the two words creating an *apparent*
similarity. Hence, 'They cannot be used to link this item of Matthean vocabulary
with astrology.'[15]

There were also (unsurprisingly!) many Greek words that could be used to
mean 'retrograde movement of the planets.' I've already mentioned ὑπόλειψις and
ἐπανακυκλέω.

> Strangely enough, according to the ancient terminology, when the planets
> are 'moving forward' (in the direction of the diurnal movement, 'in the
> direction of the leading signs,' or east to west) they are 'retreating' (ἀναποδί
> ζοντες) with respect to their (west to east) motion in their own orbits...[16]

Of the word ἀναποδίζω, LSJ gives the basic meaning, 'make to step back, call back
and question' but also 'of the retrograde motion of the planets, reversal of planet's
motion'. Neugebauer and van Hoesen translate ἀναποδίζω as 'retrogradation'
in their translation of *P.Oxy 307*, a Greek Horoscope for 3 January 46 CE. This
word also appears in (LXX) Wis. 2.5 (καὶ οὐκ ἔστιν ἀναποδισμὸς) (*and none returns*).
Neugebauer and van Hoesen also translate as 'retrograde' the word ἀφαιρετικός (as
does the LSJ—'*of planetary motion*') that appears in *P. Oxy. 1476*, line 6. Two
further terms for retrograde are παλίνορσος and ὑποποδισμός. Hence, there appears to
be *seven* Greek words that can be used for 'retrograde'.

It's significant that the LSJ entry for the verb προάγω *doesn't give a single
astronomical citation*. Given its usage in classical astronomical texts, this is an
oversight or a further indication that its use in Matthew didn't mean retrograde in
an astronomical sense but *proceeding forward*.

Though the heavens appear to move east to west (diurnal motion), Bethlehem
lies six miles south-west of Jerusalem. Only an object outside the laws of physics
would be able to move in such a manner (unless it were a comet or meteor, but
those too have their fair share of problems as a source for the Star).

Molnar refers to this *technical term* as having 'lost its meaning'. He means 'lost its meaning today', but as Ptolemy's *Almagest* and *Tetrabiblos* were then standard texts (and for over a thousand years thereafter), it's hard to imagine the learned Fathers of the early Christian Church were unaware of the astronomical meaning of these words.

The reception history of the Star during the first four centuries doesn't reveal any astrological/astronomical meaning. With the existence of seven Greek words to describe retrograde motion, it's perhaps more accurate to translate Matthew's προῆγεν in its simplest sense—as an object that led (moved ahead of) the magi.

Guiding star as literary motif

There may also be a literary source behind the guiding star that backs this simpler translation for two out of the three of the Greek sources cited below use προάγω to refer to the *guiding action* of a light or star.

Ancient Ugaritic Literature (14th to 12th centuries BCE)

Within the Ugaritic and Canaanite myth of Baal, Asherah is placed upon a donkey, and led (along with the virgin Anat) by the gods Qodesh and Amrur to the home of El. The transliterated Ugaritic text of lines 16–17 are:

16. qdš yủḫdm. šbᶜr

17. åmrr. kkbkb. lpnm

The four English versions below give the same basic translation:

16. 'Qodesh took a torch'; 'Kadesh was lighted up'; 'Qidshu took the lead'; 'the Holy One began to lead.'

17. 'Amrur was like a star in front'; 'Amurr was kindled like a star in front'; 'Amuru trailed like a star'; 'the Most Blessed One like a guiding star.'

bᶜr has 'to lead' as one of its meanings and the double meaning of 'leading (a caravan)' and 'shining (like a star)'. Therefore, we have in these two lines both a guiding torch and a reference to the guiding qualities of stars.

Apollonius of Rhodes (c. 270–245 BCE)
In *The Argonautica* (a telling of the quest for the Golden Fleece), Jason, fleeing with the recently stolen fleece, remembers that the blind seer Phineus had told him they

would return home via an unknown route. After the Argo has revealed this secret route (to the river Danube), the goddess Hera sends a heavenly portent to guide the Argonauts on their way (*Argon.* 4.294–302):

Ὣς ἄρ᾽ ἔφη. τοῖσιν δὲ θεὰ τέρας ἐγγυάλιξεν
αἴσιον, ᾧ καὶ πάντες ἐπευφήμησαν ἰδόντες
στέλλεσθαι τήνδ᾽ οἶμον· ἐπιπρὸ γὰρ ὁλκὸς ἐτύχθη
οὐρανίης ἀκτῖνος, ὅπη καὶ ἀμεύσιμον ἦεν.
γηθόσυνοι δέ, Λύκοιο κατ αὐτόθι παῖδα λιπόντες,
λαίφεσι πεπταμένοισιν ὑπεὶρ ἅλα ναυτίλλοντο
οὔρεα Παφλαγόνων θηεύμενοι· οὐδὲ Κάραμβιν
γνάμψαν, ἐπεὶ πνοιαί τε καὶ οὐρανίου πυρὸς αἴγλη
μίμνεν ἕως Ἴστροιο μέγαν ῥόον εἰσαφίκοντο.

Thus he spake, and to them the goddess granted a happy portent, and all at the sight shouted apporoval, that this was their appointed path. For before them appeared a trail of heavenly light, a sign where they might pass. And gladly they left behind the son of Lycus and with canvas outspread sailed over the sea, with their eyes on the Paphlagonian mountains. But they did not round the Carambis, for the winds and the glean of the heavenly fire stayed with them till they reached Ister's mighty stream.[17]

Although this has been translated as a 'trail of heavenly fire' and a 'radiant light in the heavens' or 'a shooting star blazed its sky trail far beyond them,' 'shooting star' perhaps over-stretches the text.

Though this text doesn't use προάγω, we have an auspicious (αἴσιος) sign, in this instance a trailing (ὁλκὸς) heavenly beam of fire (οὐρανίης ἀκτῖνος), that brings great cheer (ἐπευφημέω) when it guides the Argonauts on their voyage until (ἕως) stopping at the river mouth, justifying the words of the seer Phineus. This echoes the magi's joy (χαρὰν μεγάλην) in being guided by the Star towards Bethlehem until (ἕως) it stopped over Jesus, justifying the prophecy they'd heard in Jerusalem.

Virgil (70–19 BCE)

In Virgil's *Aeneid* 2.694, Aeneas is guided by a star from Troy to the spot where Rome is to be founded (2.692–700):

Vix ea fatus erat senior, subitoque fragore
intonuit laevum, et de caelo lapsa per umbras

stella facem ducens multa cun luce cucurrit.
Illam, summa super labentem culmina tecti,
cernimus Idaea claram se condere silva,
signantemque vias; tum longo limite sulcus
dat lucem, et late circum loca sulfure fumant.
Hic vero victus genitor se tollit ad auras
adfaturque deos, **et sanctum sidus adorat.**

*Scarcely had the aged man thus spoken, when
with a sudden crash it thundered on the left and a
star shot from heaven, gliding through the shadows,
and drawing a fiery trail amid a flood of light. We
watch it glide over the palace roof and bury in
Ida's forest the splendour that marked its path; then
The long-drawn furrow shines, and far and wide all
abour reeks with sulphur. Ont his, indeed, my
father was vanquished and, rising erect, salutes the
gods,* **and worships the holy star.**

This 'shooting star' clearly equates to the star that guided the return of the Argonauts.

On the words 'et sanctum sidus adorat', Austin comments, 'It is hard not to suppose that these words may have brought to the mind of many a medieval Christian reader the thought of another star.'[18]

The *Aeneid*, as a great Roman classic, was widely known and available in the late first century CE, and a small papyrus fragment of 4.9 was even found at Masada. It was also written to glorify the Julian line as both Caesar and Augustus identified themselves with Aeneas. Indeed, the comet that appeared at Caesar's death in 44 BCE (the *sidus Iulium*, interpreted as both his soul joining the gods and the herald of Augustus' Golden Age) is represented in the *Aeneid* through numerous allusions to comets, flames or stars (especially the star of Venus).

Diodorus Siculus and Plutarch
In his *Library of History* 16.66.3, Diodorus Siculus (d. c. 21 BCE) describes the voyage of Timoleon (c. 411–337 BCE) to Sicily in a fleet of ten ships:

Ἴδιον δέ τι καὶ παράδοξον συνέβη γενέσθαι τῷ Τιμολέοντι κατὰ τὸν πλοῦν, τοῦ δαιμονίου συνεπιλαβομένου τῆς ἐπιβολῆς καὶ προσημαίνοντος τὴν ἐσομένην περὶ αὐτὸν εὐδοξίαν καὶ λαμπρότητα τῶν πράξεων. δι' ὅλης γὰρ τῆς νυκτὸς προηγεῖτο λαμπὰς καιομένη κατὰ τὸν οὐρανὸν μέχρι οὗ συνέβη τὸν στόλον εἰς την Ἰταλίαν καταπλεῦσαι.

During this voyage, a peculiar and strange event happened to Timoleon. Heaven came to the support of his venture and foretold his coming fame and the glory of his achievements, for all through the night he was preceded by a torch blazing in the sky up to the moment when the squadron made harbour in Italy

This story of the fleet being preceded by a burning torch (προηγεῖτο λαμπὰς) from heaven is also told by Plutarch. In the New Testament, John has Jesus refer to himself as ὁ ἀστὴρ ὁ λαμπὸς ὁ πρωϊνός (the bright morning star).

Both Diodorus and Plutarch report that priestesses of Persephone had previously dreamed the goddess would accompany Timoleon. The light from heaven was the presence of the goddess or her favour. Dreams and a guiding light are what we find in Matthew 2.

The motif of a star leading someone to a *precise house* is unusual, but the literary motif of guiding torches and stars wouldn't have sounded strange to Matthew's audience. However, there's another source that would have been recalled as easily in the mind of Matthew and his community, if not more so: the light or influence of guides (angels) sent by God.

Angelic guides

Angels were a significant feature of Jewish literature from the second century BCE right through into the Talmud, Midrash and later Hekhalot texts. Jewish interest in angels revolved around the heavenly sanctuary, the throne of God, the ascent to heaven, and the origin of fallen angels and demons (especially in apocalyptic literature) and their part in the war against evil (a focus of the literature of the Dead Sea Scrolls).

The idea of a star needn't necessarily denote an inanimate, celestial body. Indeed, several references in art and literature draw a connection between stars and angels. LXX Judg. 5.20 states that, Ἐξ οὐρανοῦ παρετάξαντο οἱ ἀστέρες, ἐκ τρίβων αὐτῶν παρετάξαντο μετὰ Σισαρα (*The stars fought from heaven, from their courses they fought against Sisera*) and LXX Job 38.7, Ὅτε ἐγενήθησαν ἄστρα, ᾔνεσάν με φωνῇ μεγάλῃ πάντες ἄγγελοί [Hb. *sons of God*] μου (*when the morning stars sang together and all the heavenly beings…*).

Alexander Toepel when pointing to planetary spirits/angels in Jewish literature notes the reference to angels and four trees in 4Q552–553 and argues that the trees (each ruling over a specific area) represent planets due to the planet-tree symbolism in Mithraic art. He further notes Daniel 10.13, 20 and 21 and the reference there to the angelic princes of Persia and Greece.

A a second-century fresco at Dura-Europos shows two stars depicted above the tomb of Christ that have been interpretated as representing the two angels who announced the resurrection (Luke 24.1–12; Matthew 28.1–10 and Mark 16.1–8 only have one angel). In the New Testament, Revelation 1.20 states that, οἱ ἑπτὰ ἀστέρες ἄγγελοι τῶν ἑπτὰ ἐκκλησιῶν εἰσιν (*the seven stars are the angels of the seven churches*) and there are interesting passages in the works of Philo where he interprets angels as the disembodied attendants of the stars. Philo uses the word χορός (*chorus*) to describe these invisible movers, a Hellenistic term for stars in general. Origen likewise speaks of the heavenly bodies being guided by angels.

Angels also descended from heaven to Earth, and in the first-century CE Jewish-Egyptian *Joseph and Aseneth* 14, an angel (ἄγγελος) *in the form of a star* descends from heaven.

Angels as guides and clouds are a part of the exodus out of Egypt. In LXX Exodus 14.19, as Moses led the children of Israel out of Egypt:

ἐξῆρεν δὲ ὁ ἄγγελός τοῦ θεοῦ ὁ προπορευόμενος τῆς παρεμβολῆς τῶν υἱῶν ʼΙσραήλ, καὶ ἐπορεύθη ἐκ τῶν ὄπισθεν· ἐξῆρεν δὲ καὶ ὁ στῦλος τῆς νεφέλης ἀπὸ προσώπου αὐτῶν καὶ ἔστη ἐκ τῶν ὀπίσω αὐτῶν

The angel of God who was going before the Israelite army moved and went behind them; and the pillar of cloud moved from in front of them and took its place behind them.

In Exodus 23.20 God explains, Καὶ ἰδοὺ ἐγὼ ἀποστέλλω τὸν ἄγγελόν μου πρὸ προσώπου σου (*I am going to send an angel in front of you*) and the guiding nature of this angel is repeated in three further passages.

Craig Keener, noting that the Star could only have given a general or symbolic indication of direction, suggests that, if it alludes to the guiding pillar of cloud in the wilderness, Matthew's use of the Star could be reminiscent of Israel's salvation history. Soares Prabhu has also drawn attention to this possible connection and its link to Balaam. Indeed, Benedict Vivano has argued for Numbers 9.15–23 being the source behind the movement of the Star in Matthew 2. He argues that the movement of the Star at Matthew 2.9 has as its source the moving cloud and fire that led the Israelites out of the desert.

The movement of the cloud at Numbers 9.15–23 was the unspoken divine command of God and its movements controlled the movements of the Israelites, just as the movement of the Star guided the magi to their destination. John Sturdy refers to this cloud as a 'theological representation of the accompanying presence of God in the form of a visible sign'[19] and Keener comments how the Star alludes to these pillar motifs, suggesting that it was used by God 'in a manner reminiscent of Israel's salvation history.'[20]

The cloud, like the Star, rises, moves forwards and stops to mark where to camp. In Matthew 2, it's stressed twice that the Star of the magi was seen ἐν τῇ ἀνατολῇ. Each time, like the fire-cloud, it leads to their movement in a new direction, first Jerusalem and then Bethlehem.

In linking the fire-cloud pillar with the Star, in *Wis.* 10.17 (a Greek Alexandrian text that so far has been difficult to date. The current consensus is sometime between 220 BCE and 50 CE), the cloud of Exodus is identified with wisdom, 'she [wisdom] guided them along a marvellous way, and became a shelter to them by day, and a starry flame through the night [καὶ εἰς φλόγα ἄστρων τὴν νύκτα]' and in 18.1–3 the author describes the conditions during the plague of darkness, Τοῖς δὲ ὁσίοις σου μέγιστον ἦν φῶς Ἀνθ᾽ ὧν πυριφλεγῆ στῦλον, ὁδηγὸν μεν ἀγνώστου ὁδοιπορί ας, ἥλιον δὲ ἀβλαβῆ φιλοτίμου ξενιτείας παρέσχες. ('*But for the holy ones there was very great light. Their enemies heard their voices but did not see their forms . . . Therefore you provided a flaming pillar of fire as a guide for your people's inknown journey, and a harmless sun for their glorious wandering.*')

Did Matthew possess knowledge of *Wisdom*? It's possible that Wisdom 2.13 can be found in Matthew 27.47 and Jesus' quotation of Psalm 22.9, but the cloud-fire tradition could as easily have been transmitted through oral tradition. In apocalyptic literature, angels also act as guides. Angelology expanded greatly in post-biblical apocalyptic works, especially in *1 Enoch*, which featured prominently in the Essene community at Qumran.

The idea that the Star was an angel was a feature of later rather than early Christian exegesis. John Chrysostom concluded that the Star was 'an unseen power altering its appearance' (*Homily on Matthew* 6.1)[21] and later identified the Star as an angel. After the magi had visited Herod, John writes (*Homila* 7.3), 'an angel took them up again and taught them all things'. Prudentius (348–c. 405 CE) refers to the star as a 'winged messenger, most like the rapid south wind' (*Apotheosis* 611–612) and, though not a major influence in Christian exegetical history, the *Arabic Gospel of the Infancy* 7 depicts a descending angel acting as guide.

Dale Allison has attempted to explain why the Star as angel solution was never prominent in Christian reception history. He sees the Second Council of Constantinople (Fifth Ecumenical Council) of 553 CE as the reason, being a time when belief in stars as living beings was erased from Christian thinking.

Origen agreed with the Hellenistic philosophical view that the heavens were alive and had a soul. Yet his view on the transmigration of souls led to it being declared 'anathema' by the Fifth Ecumenical Council. Article III of *The Anathemas against Origen* states, 'If anyone shall say that the sun, the moon and the stars are also reasonable beings and that they have only become what they are because they turned towards evil: let him be anathema.' This anathema may have led to the idea of the heavens being alive being removed from Christian theology, 'and with that the identification of Bethlehem's star with an angel exited the house of exegetical options.'[22]

Despite the evidence for angels as guides and falling stars, the Star in Matthew 2 doesn't appear to be a specific angel in its own right. As Herod's enquiries suggest the rising of a specific body 'in time and space' (plus a heavenly messenger already exists in the prior form of the unnamed ἄγγελος κυρίου—*angel of the Lord*) it's more likely the Star had a separate existence and purpose in the narrative.

We could apply Platonic philosophy and surmise that the Star (assuming it's a royal sign from God) was moved by an invisible attendant angel. Hence, if Matthew 2 was designed to be *anti*-astrological, what we the magi are not being led by astrology but by the power of God over the heavens. The idea of astral fate (with the stars as heavenly powers) caused problems for early Christian cosmology. Was Christ an agent of free will or under the influence of fate?

In Luke's infancy account, he names this ἄγγελος κυρίου (1.11, 19) Γαβριήλ—*Gabriel* (1.26ff) and Hegedus briefly notes the possibility that the later identification of the Star of Bethlehem as an angel was 'prompted by the appearance of an angel in the other canonical nativity account'.[23]

7 ἕως ἐλθὼν ἐστάθη ἐπάνω (*until [having come] it stood over the place*)

(Matthew 2.9)

In Christian art, the Star is usually portrayed as standing high over the nativity scene as in, for example, Giotto di Bondone's *Adoration of the Magi* (1304–1306; which may depict the 1301 return of Halley's Comet) and Stefano de Verona's *The Adoration of the Magi* (1435). However, in Jacobi di Cione's San Pier Maggiore Altarpiece (1370–1) and Paolo Veneziano's *The Birth of Christ* (c. 1355), the Star is only a few metres above Jesus' head.

Though we can't use medieval art as a reliable source, there's a textual variant of 2.9 in the (controversial) fifth-century uncial D that presents the Star ἐστάθη ἐπάνω τὸ παιδίον' instead of the vague majority reading ἐστάθη ἐπάνω οὗ ἦν τὸ παιδίον.

What does Matthew mean when he wrote that the Star '*stood over where the child was*'?

The word ἕως is here used as a conjunction *to denote the end of a period of time* 'until it stood above' ('until it came to a stop').

Matthew writes that the magi followed the Star ἕως ἐλθὼν ἐστάθη ἐπάνω οὗ ἦν τὸ παιδίον. Of ἐλθών (the aor. act. pple. nom. sg. mas. of ἔρχομαι) the BDAG entry calls this usage *the movement from one point to another* and, more to the point, 'to denote that a person, in order to do something, must first come to a certain place.' This is seen from Matthew's five uses of ἔρχομαι at 2.2, 8, 9, 11, 23.

The LSJ entry also refers to its general use *for any kind of motion* (which includes the *rising* of stars) and could explain why Teres picks on ἐλθών as a key word related to retrograde motion. To Teres, ἐλθών refers to 'the star's continuous course [among the fixed stars]'.[24]

The verb ἐστάθη ('stood') is the third person aorist passive indicative singular of the transitive verb ἵστημι 'I stand.' All the lexical sources provide scores of examples of the usage of ἵστημι (to make stand, set up, be set, placed, bring to a standstill), but the general usage is as *stand (still), stop, come to an end, come up, stand, appear, resist, stand firm or still, hold one's ground*. The LN places this word in domain 85.40 ('Existence in Space') and sub-domain B ('Put, Place') and notes that it, 'may very well imply a standing position, *but what is in focus is not the stance but the location.*' (My emphasis.)

The adverb ἐπάνω is here used as an improper preposition and is followed by a relative clause with a genitive relative pronoun. It's translated as 'above a place'. The BDAG refers to its usage in Matthew 2.9 as '*stopped over the place*'.

The verb ἐστάθη ('stood') is the third person aorist passive indicative singular of the transitive verb ἵστημι 'I stand.' All the lexical sources provide scores of examples of the usage of ἵστημι (to make stand, set up, be set, placed, bring to a standstill), but the general usage is as *stand (still), stop, come to an end, come up, stand, appear, resist, stand firm or still, hold one's ground*. The LN places this word in domain 85.40 ('Existence in Space') and sub-domain B ('Put, Place') and notes that it, 'may very well imply a standing position, *but what is in focus is not the stance but the location.*'[25]

The adverb ἐπάνω is here used as an improper preposition and is followed by a relative clause with a genitive relative pronoun. It's translated (with the genitive) 'above a place'. The BDAG refers to its usage in Matthew 2.9 as '*stopped over the place*'.[26]

Planetary stationing

The Greek tells us that the Star kept on going (*as a guide in front of the magi*) until it came to halt above a specific spot. Thus, the grammar appears relatively simple and as Fritz Reinecker said: 'It kept on going before them until arriving at Bethlehem *it took up its position...right over* [above] *the spot* where the child was.'[27]

Though Otto Neugebauer comments that, 'Through actual observation it's very difficult to say when and where a planet is accurately stationary'[28], many astronomers have argued that the Star became stationary over Bethlehem due to the end of its retrograde motion.

> After moving from west to east against the stellar background for some time they slow down and reach a stationary point where they appear to stand still, after which they move in a retrograde direction from east to west until they reach a secondary stationary point, after which they resume their forward motion.[29]

Further, Robbins, in his translation of *Tetrabiblos*, provides this clear definition of stationing 'the points in the motion of the planets at which they appear to stand still before beginning retrograde movement.'[30] This 'stationing' was highly significant in astrology and Ptolemy writes that (*Tetr.* 2.4):

> Of the prediction itself, one portion is regional; therein we must foresee for what countries or cities there is significance in the various eclipses or in the occasional regular stations [στάσεις] of the planets, that is, of Saturn, Jupiter and Mars, whenever they halt [ὅταν στηρίζωσι], for then they are significant.

Further (*Tetr.* 2.6):

> Planets when they are rising [ἀνατέλλοντες] or stationary [στηρίζοντες] produce intensifications in the events.

For Molnar (who sees Aries as the significant constellation for Judaea), the stationing over Bethlehem of Jupiter in Aries, told the magi to come to Jerusalem—it being the capital and best place to find information.

Again, the works of Ptolemy are used to provide the astronomical connection to Matthew via his work on retrogradation and Toomer, in his rendering of the prepositions Ptolemy uses in his *Star Catalogue*, records that he differentiates between ἐπάνω for 'above' and ὑπέρ (*used spatially only with the accusative*) for 'over.'[31] Neugebauer notes that Ptolemy also uses ἐπάνω to mean 'ahead (in longitude).'[32]

It seems that Ptolemy prefers to use the verb στηρίζω as the technical term for *stationary* planets (as does Geminus). Neugebauer and van Hoesen translate στηρίζω (στηριγμός) as 'stationing' of planets while the LSJ cite the active intransitive usage being 'of planetary phases' = *'pause, stand still.'* Perhaps Matthew wasn't aware of such a technical word as στηρίζω but it appears that he didn't have stationing in mind.

Though Matthew doesn't use στηρίζω, Bulmer-Thomas cites two examples from

Neugebauer's *Astronomical Cuneiform Texts* to argue that planetary stationing does indeed lie behind Matthew's text:

> Jupiter on the fast arc, from disappearance to appearance, add 29 days. From appearance to the (first) stationary point, add 4 days.' ii). 'From the (first) stationary point to opposition add 58 days. From opposition to the second stationary point add 2 months 4 days. From the second stationary point to disappearance add 4 months 10 days.[33]

Quoting the findings of Dr Bernard Yallop, Bulmer-Thomas matches the Star to the movements of Jupiter from 19 May–22 November, 5 BCE. Yallop writes, in a classic example of the use of astronomy to explain a biblical event:

> My opinion is that the description in the Gospel of the star standing over the stable could fit at any time between this stationary point and the next on 4BC January 20... It is not clear to me what it means in the Gospel when it says that the star stood over the place where He was born. It seems to me more likely that the moment would be more obvious to an observer when transit was early in the evening and not well after midnight. Any time between the two stationary points seems to me possible, with the extra bonus that the winter solstice occurred around December 21, and the setting of the sun would help to demonstrate that the planet was over the same place for several nights in a row at the same place.[34]

However, it's also been noted that, 'In no conceivable fashion could these planets have stood over any one town, much less a particular house.'[35] So not every astronomer is convinced.

Teres likewise interprets Matthew 2.9 in general astronomical terms as, 'the star, in its apparent backward motion, came to a standstill, seen from Jerusalem, just over [in the general direction of] Bethlehem' He notes Matthew's use of the indicative ἐστάθη to imply that it was an event that really happened. However, it's incorrect to call it a mood of certainty or reality as this would imply that 'one cannot lie or be mistaken in the indicative.'[36] It's a mood more of assertion or *presentation* of certainty: *Matthew believed it had happened whether it actually had or not.*

There's is a difference between the *use of* a particular mood, tense or technical term and there being a specific historical event (in this case, a planetary stationing). Use of the former doesn't imply the latter. Given that there's prior evidence in ancient literature for a preceding star/torch-like object, the coming to a stop of such an object doesn't imply astronomical stationing. The stopping of the Star *over* Jesus is inevitable for it is αὐτοῦ τὸν ἀστέρα (*his star*). Theologically it couldn't stop anywhere else and planetary stationing isn't needed as an explanation.

There's no indication in Matthew's text to conclude that the Star was *only visible high in the sky. Prot. Jas.* 21.3; St. Ephrem the Syrian's commentary on Tatian's *Diatessaron* and John Chrysostom's commentary on *Matthew* (*Hom. Matt.* 7.5) all recognise the Star as coming down low to rest over Jesus' head. If this were how the text was originally to be interpreted by Matthew's community, it would have a significant impact on the application of modern astronomy or astrology to explain the Star.

Comet?

Only a comet can be seen as being able to hang over a specific spot in any meaningful way. Indeed, Josephus (*War* 6.289) records that prior to the First Revolt against Rome (66–74 CE):

τοῦτο μὲν ὅτε ὑπὲρ τὴν πόλιν ἄστρον ἔστη ῥομφαί παραπλήσιον καὶ παρατείνας ἐπ᾽ ἐνιαυτὸν κομήτης

So it was when a star, resembling a sword, stood over the city, and a comet continued for a year.

Further, Cassius Dio (54.29) records that:

Τό τε ἄστρον ὁ κομήτης ὠνομασμένος ἐπὶ πολλὰς ἡμέρας ὑπὲρ αὐτοῦ τοῦ ἄστεως αἰωρηθεὶς ἐς λαμπάδας διελύθη.

The star called the comet hung for several days over the city and was finally dissolved into flashes resembling torches.

However, unlike Matthew, Josephus and Dio use the preposition ὑπὲρ for 'over' instead of ἐπάνω.

8 παιδίον (*child*) (Matthew 2.9, 11)

Matthew isn't known for his chronological clarity, but he does provide some clues regarding Jesus' age in Matthew 2. When the magi enter Joseph's house we're told that (Matthew 2.11), εἶδον τὸ παιδίον μετὰ Μαρίας (*they saw the child with Mary*) and later (2.16) we hear that Herod had ordered the death of πάντας παῖδας ... ἀπὸ διετοῦς καὶ κατωτέρω (*all the children... from two years and under*). J.C. Fenton says that, 'From 2:16 it seems that the Star had appeared two years earlier.'[37]

However, the noun παιδίον has a wide range of usage and can mean anything from a newborn baby up to a seven-year-old young child/infant (at least below the age of puberty). Luke uses two words: παιδίον and βρέφος, the latter referring specifically to an unborn baby or very small child. However, the distinction isn't completely clear as 2 Timothy 3.15 uses βρέφος in the same sense as παιδίον.

J.P. Meier notes, 'the often overlooked fact that Matthew never presents the Christ child of the Magi story as the *newborn* king of the Jews.'[38] Despite the fact that the New American Bible, revised New American Bible and Raymond Brown refer to the 'newborn king of the Jews' (Matthew 2.2) the Greek states, Ποῦ ἐστιν ὁ τεχθεὶς βασιλεὺς τῶν Ἰουδαίων.[39] The Revised Standard Version of the Bible translates this more accurately as, 'Where is he who has been born king of the Jews?' and the NRSV of 1989 as, 'Where is the child who has been born...?' Davies and Allison, on the other hand, regard the NAB as correct arguing that ὁ τεχθεὶς isn't independent of βασιλεὺς but in fact an attributive participle. They see the translation not as 'he who has been born' but as 'the (new)-born king of the Jews'.[40]

How old was Jesus when the magi arrived? In the LXX παιδίον is chiefly used for יֶלֶד (child, son, boy, youth), נַעַר (boy, lad, youth) and בֵּן (son, etc). Interestingly, in LXX 1 Chron. 17.23 it's used to refer to the *future* Davidic king, Καὶ νῦν, Κύριε, ὁ λόγος σου ὃν ἐλάλησας πρὸς τὸν παῖδά σου (*And now, O Lord, as for the word that you have spoken concerning your <u>servant</u>*). The fact that Herod has his soldiers kill all the children ἀπὸ διετοῦς καὶ κατωτέρω provides us with a limit for Jesus' age at 2.16. However, Robert Gundry observes that an infant would have been regarded as two years old *immediately upon entering* his second year, 'Therefore we should express the thought with the phrase 'one year and under' despite Matthew's reference to two years.'[41] He sees behind the 'two-year' reference Matthew's attempt to square Pharaoh's slaying of the male children at birth with the time it took the magi to reach Bethlehem.

Given that Matthew provides no clear chronology or explanations, we can't be sure how much time he believes passed between the magi's failure to return and Herod's action, nor how long Matthew perceived the magi's travel to Jerusalem to have been. Two years is a vague figure but it's clear Jesus wasn't a newborn. Either Matthew was being characteristically vague in his chronology or we're missing the implied knowledge of his intended audience.

* * *

In his book *The Star of Bethlehem*, Michael Molnar paraphrases what he believes Matthew is saying:

And behold the planet [ἀστέρα, ἀστήρ] which they had seen at its [morning] heliacal rising [ἐν τῇ ἀνατολῇ] went retrograde [προῆγεν] and became stationary above [ἐστάθη ἐπάνω] in the sky (which showed) where the child was.[42]

Likewise, Teres has Matthew using astronomical expressions (which he believes came from the magi themselves) to write a condensed astronomical account about 'evening' and 'morning' risings of Jupiter, with Herod questioning the magi while the Star was still visible, and the Star moving in its heavenly course, retrograding over Bethlehem's general direction. Teres considers that his grammatical analysis demonstrates that Matthew 2 is an authentic and original historical text, derived from the magi themselves and that it conforms with reality and what's known about Babylonian astrology.

Is this what Matthew was writing? Given the *technical* usage of the Greek, it's possible. However, we mustn't put together all the references to the Star into one paraphrase and then apply suitable technical (astrological) meanings to back it up. Nor can we assume it's a basic narrative derived from a more complex source (the magi themselves). The non-astrological usage of the lexica and their use as literary or poetic devices must also be taken into account.

Only giving examples from ancient astrological texts will generate a false interpretation of the source text. Indeed, the Star apparently disappeared from view for an unspecified period (perhaps up to two years). Molnar's neat paragraph may create a stronger astronomical case, but it doesn't match what Matthew wrote (or what he, as author, intended to write).

This is the fallacy of *selective and prejudiced use of evidence*, that is, the use of ancient astrological sources to explain ἀστήρ, ἠκρίβωσεν ... τὸν χρόνον τοῦ φαινομένου, προάγω, and ἐστάθη ἐπάνω as *planet(s), ascertained the helical rising of Jupiter, retrograde motion* and *planetary stationing* respectively. It's true that the small number of source citations could account for such a usage (though many use alternative vocabulary), but in Matthew 2 the usage appears much simpler and much less technical in its application. Matthew 2 would not work as a watered down horoscope. In this respect, linguistic analysis suffers from being selective and from trying too hard to squeeze an astrological meaning into a descriptive narrative.

Another fallacy in operation is the *false assumption about technical meanings* where:

The interpreter falsely assumes that a word always or nearly always has a certain technical meaning—a meaning usually derived either from a subset of the evidence or from the interpreter's personal systematic theology.[43]

If we replace 'theology' with 'astronomy' or 'astrology', we see this fallacy in action with regard to the lexis above, especially when lexical ambiguity presents room for such interpretation.

Matthew 2 is a *closed text*, one that was clear to the *implied reader* of Matthew's community but is ambiguous to modern readers. This is consistent with Matthew's method of leaving much to the implied cultural knowledge and traditions of this intended audience. By using ἀνατολῇ and having μάγοι *observe and follow* the Star to Jerusalem and onto Bethlehem, Matthew (as author) expects his community to have a specific response based on an assumed knowledge.

On Matthew's silence, Allison, writing again about Matthew 27.45, has recently commented, in a remark that applies equally well to Matthew 2, that it, 'enhances the aura of mystery, has become opportunity for commentators, who have done their best to fill in the blanks.'[44] Thus, a spectrum of interpretation exists in the modern literature ranging from poetic fiction to genuine astronomical account.

> An author can control his or her words and can intend them to express such-and-such an idea, but he or she cannot control the meaningfulness (or lack of it) those words will have for any particular reader or listener, let alone for a translator, who, in effect, creates a new text, a kind of fantasia on the original. Just as the original text stands between the author and even those who share that author's culture (including language), beckoning and yet bewildering, so the translator stands between even this illusory communication of meaning and a new set of readers who may be far removed in time, place, and culture from the original author.[45]

The eight words and phrases don't allow us to determine if Matthew is referring to a real celestial event. Conclusions as to the origin and meaning of the Star can't be drawn from a grammatical and lexical analysis alone. However, we can make these observations about the Star:

1. Given the lexical ambiguity and semantic uncertainty of the word ἀστήρ, we have to use other indicators to surmise its meaning. (Given the context of Matthew 2, ἀστήρ can't be translated as 'planet' or 'planetary conjunction').

2. Matthew couldn't *literally* be portraying the actions of any naturally occurring observable celestial event. However, this doesn't exclude a real event being described poetically (or retrospectively).

3. It can be concluded with more certainty that by using ἀνατολῇ Matthew *does mean* 'the rising of a star [over the eastern horizon]' and that *he meant to give the Star an independently observable beginning in time*. This 'rising' could be linked to the 'rising' messianic star of Balaam's oracle.

CHAPTER 4:
JEWISH AND EARLY CHRISTIAN
RESPONSES TO ASTROLOGY

The widespread nature of astrology in the ancient world made its contact with Judaism unavoidable, and there are numerous examples of the influences of pagan astral religion and astrology in Judaism.

> A few decades ago historians had no clear evidence that Jews composed astrological tracts about the time of Jesus; many good scholars thought that Jewish interest in the zodiac surfaced only late in medieval Jewish Mysticism.[1]

For example, M.R. Lehmann (in 1975) concluded that Jewish astrology was only evident in those sectarian writings 'at variance with normative Judaism'.[2] This is no longer the case as many texts (particularly those from the Dead Sea Scrolls and Pseudepigrapha) have considerably altered this view.

A brief introduction to ancient astrology

There was no distinction in the ancient world between ἀστρονομία (*astronomy*) and ἀστρολογία (*astrology*). Both could mean either *astronomy* or *astrology*.

Astrology can be divided into two two types: *natural* astrology, 'the calculation and foretelling of natural phenomena, as the measurement of time, fixing of Easter, prediction of tides and eclipses; also of meteorological phenomena' (the *celestial omen* astrology of ancient Mesopotamia) and *judicial* astrology, the art of reading horoscopes. Judicial astrology can be divided into four branches, which are evident by the late Classical period: *genethialogy*, *general*, *catarchic* and *interrogative* astrology. We'll focus on genethialogy and general astrology.

Genethialogy is concerned with the relationship between celestial positions at birth and an individual's destiny, requiring the use of horoscopes. The heavens along the ecliptic are divided into twelve 30° parts known as the ζωδιακός (*zodiac*) with each sign being the house for a planet. The zodiac is further sub-divided into 36 decans. Each planet and sign exerts particular and specific influences on the individual via their motion through the zodiac and through such events as conjunctions.

> From a particular spot on the earth's surface this motion appears as a succession of signs rising one after another above the eastern horizon. The sign that at any moment—say, the individual's birth—is just rising, is the horoscope... The astrologer, therefore, when informed of the exact moment and place of a native's birth, casts his horoscope by fixing the boundaries of the twelve places with respect to the moving ecliptic and calculates the momentary longitudes and latitudes of the planets. He then can predict various aspects of the native's life by examining the intricate relations of the zodiacal signs and their parts and the planets to the appropriate places and to each other.[3]

The following examples show how this gradual movement of the planets through the zodiac was seen to affect daily life on earth and how they were interpreted by astrologers.

Dorotheus of Sidon

An astrological poet of the first-century CE, his *Carmen Astrologicum* has survived only in a c. 800 CE Arabic translation of a third-century CE Persian text. This is from Book 1.27:

> If you find Saturn with the Moon in one of the cardines, then, even if he is the son of a king, it indicates his fall from fortunes and property. If with this Mars aspects [them], it will be a disaster. If Jupiter is with them in a cardine, then his property and his fortune will remain for some time, but after that will decline, even if Jupiter is aspecting.[4]

Claudius Ptolemy (c. 100–178 CE)

Ptolemy (*Tetrabiblos* 4.2) also discusses material fortune:

> In a special way, when Saturn is associated with material fortune, if he is in aspect with Jupiter, he is the cause of inheritances, particularly when this comes upon the upper angles and Jupiter is in a bicorporeal sign or holds the application of the moon.

The Star couldn't be astrological in the genethialogical sense, as it can't be a true ὡροσκόπος (*horoscope*) cast by the magi from a known birth date (though a 'magian horoscope' has been referred to by some critics).

General astrology is the analysis and practice of historical patterns and can be *chiliastic* (millennial) in concept. It's concerned with the calculated periodic movements of the planets through the zodiac plus their effects on the political and social spheres of people, cities and nations.

Astrology, astral religion and the Old Testament

Given the exile in Babylon and the syncretistic spread of Hellenism since the conquests of Alexander the Great, it would have been impossible for Jewish thought and tradition not to have been affected by the practice of astrology and astral worship.

Many passages in the Old Testament demonstrate that the lure of worshipping other gods not only existed but also had to be stopped. Both the first commandment and Deuteronomy 17.2–7 give a clear warning against the worship of (astral) gods. The fact that the Old Testament often had to condemn the worship of other gods and the heavens shows that not all Israelites were monotheistic. King Manasseh (698–642 BCE), son of Hezekiah, introduced Assyrian astral deities into the Israelite religion as well as the Canaanite goddess Asherah (2 Kings 21.3).

Later, Josiah, in his reforms of Judaism (c. 627–621 BCE), purified Manasseh's astral 'cultic aberrations' and 'put down' those who burnt incense to the planets and host of heaven (2 Kings 23.4–26). The practice of looking to the skies for omens is also mentioned in the Bible and likewise condemned (Jeremiah 10.2; Isaiah 47.12–14).

Yet Genesis 1.14–16 shows that God *controls* the stars and heavens. Heavenly bodies were seen as the servants of God and were often personified. Psalms 19, 74 and 104 refer to the sun, moon and seasons while Job 38.4–7 describes the heavenly court, speaking of the morning stars in parallel with the sons of Elohim, beings that were the same as the stars. However, Job shows his pride in not being tempted by such astral worship.

The view in the Bible, apart from polemics against foreign astral cults, was of the heavens as living beings, but beings that were subservient to, and created by, God and who knew their place. This is consistent with the view of the cosmos in the philosophical Judaism of Philo—hence his interpretation of the cosmos wasn't just the result of Hellenistic influence. It also appears in the Pseudepigrapha where in 1 *Enoch* 72 the heavens bear out the will of God.

Josephus

In his description of the Temple, Josephus mentions cultic items of apparently astrological significance; a Babylonian curtain of the heavens, the Menorah whose seven branches represented the seven planets or days of the week and a table of twelve loaves.

Josephus also refers to similar items in his later description of the Tabernacle. He again mentions twelve loaves, representing the twelve months of the year, and a candelabrum consisting of seventy portions, which represent the ten degrees (δεκαμοιρίας) of the seven planets. Josephus also refers to the zodiac in connection with the twelve stones on the high priest's tunic.

Josephus was writing under Roman patronage and for a primarily Gentile audience. Therefore, his portrayal of these items could have been coloured by an apologetic desire to present a Judaism much closer to Hellenistic astral religion than it was.

Astrology and the Dead Sea Scrolls

What's come as a surprise is the existence of astrological texts amongst the Dead Sea Scrolls, regarded by most scholars as being the work of the sectarian Essenes from Qumran. Commentary on the Essenes and DSS over the past fifty years has been vast but the most accepted view is that they were a group who existed from approximately the second century BCE to c. 70 CE and who perhaps grew out of contempt for Maccabean Temple practices, that is, when the Teacher of Righteousness rebelled against Jonathan Maccabaeus who, though from a non-hereditary priestly family, became High Priest in 152 BCE.

It seems that the writer of the Aramaic Targum of Job 4Q157 30.7 didn't feel comfortable with Job 38.4–7. When writing the Targum, theological changes were made whereby the anthropomorphic 'morning stars' were changed from 'singing' to 'shining all at once'.

Despite this nervousness of those biblical passages that seem to present a hint of astral religion, astrological texts *have* been found amongst the DSS (all from Cave 4). These documents (4Qcryptic), which date from the end of the first century, contain horoscopes or fragments of astrological physiognomies and demonstrate that the Essenes made use of the zodiac.

4Q186

Both this fragment, the only true horoscope from Qumran, and 4Q534 refer to the amount of darkness (evil) and light (goodness) a person holds within.

[...] unclean [...] granite [...] a man of [...] clean and his thighs are

long and thin, and his toes are thin and long, and he is of the Second
Vault. He has six (parts) spirit in the House of Light, and three in the
Pit of Darkness. And this is the time of birth on which he is brought
forth—on the festival of Taurus. He will be poor; and this is his beast-
Taurus. (4Q186, column 2)

The problems of 4Q186 can be solved by interpreting it in the light of a Greek
zodiacal text that refers to nine parts of the zodiacal body. How many parts are
over the horizon, the boundary of light and darkness at the moment of birth
determines a person's character. Recently it's been argued that these changing
divisions of light and dark are attributed by the 36 decans and for the moment
of conception, not birth. Both ideas are genethlialogic in nature.

4Q317 (4QAstrCrypt)
4Q317 consist of seventy-two fragments of text recording the phases of the
moon (which has been divided into fourteen sections) over a 364 day calendar,
for example: '[On the f]ifth [day] of it [the month] [tw]elve [fourteenths of the
moon] are covered and thus it enters the day'.

Such predictions based on the movement of the moon are known as a
selenedromion. This list of lunar phenomena is part of the Essenes' desire for
strict time-keeping.

4Q318
This fragment contains an Aramaic *brontologion* in the last four lines of column
eleven, that is, a method of predicting the future based on the sounds of thunder
heard on a specific day (a form of celestial omen divination also practised by the
Romans and Etruscans).

[If in Taurus] it thunders... [and] hard labour for the country and
sword [in the cour]t of the king and in the country of... to the Arabs
(?) [...] starvation and they will pillage one anoth[er]... If in Gemini it
thunders, terror and affliction (will be brought) by strangers and by...[5]

An alternative translation is:

[If] it thunders [on a day when the moon is in Taurus], (it signifies)
[vain] changes in the wo[rld (?)...] [and] suffering for the cities, and
destru[ction in] the royal [co]urt and in the city of dest[ruction (?)...
] there will be, and among the Arabs... famine. Nations will plunder

one ano[ther...] If it thunders on a day when the moon is in Gemini, (it signifies) fear and distress caused by foreigners and by [...]

The zodiac of this text begins with Taurus instead of the usual Aries 0°. 4Q318 also consists of a fragmentary calendar showing the passage of the moon through the zodiac during the year, 'On 1 and 2 Aries; on 3 and 4 Taurus; on 5 [and 6 and 7 Gemini]; on 8 and 9 [Cancer; on 10 and 11 L]eo'.

4Q534
This early text could also be a horoscope of the Royal Messiah:

> ... of his hand: two... a birthmark. And the hair will be red. And there will be lentils on... and small birthmarks on his thigh [and after] two years he will know (how to distinguish) one thing from another... His designs [will suceed], for he is the Elect of God. His birth and the breath of his spirit... and his designs shall be for ever...

Here we see a similarity to the Emmanuel prophecy of Isaiah 7.14 as used by Matthew (Matthew 1.23.) The fragment also refers to the child being two years old before, as Isaiah says, 'he may know how to refuse evil, and choose the good.'

Furthermore, a reference to Noah in *Enoch* (1 *Enoch* 37–71) uses the term 'Elect of God' to refer to a superhuman being. In the New Testament, some MSS of John 1.34 refer to ὁ εκλεκτος τοῦ θεοῦ (*the elect of God*). Noah was such a being in some Pseudepigrapha, such as the *Genesis Apocryphon* also found at Qumran (1Q20).

Astrology and Qumran
What can we conclude about the existence of such texts in Qumran? The astrological texts of the Dead Sea Scrolls can be seen more as literal devices than actual divinations but:

> It is surprising that they existed at all among what otherwise seem to be zealous holy warriors. This shows that they must have played a role in the everyday life of the people, as indeed they did in the Roman Empire generally...[6]

Although 4Q318 has been called 'the oldest witness to an actual Jewish handbook of astrology', these references to astrology contrast sharply with the strict tones of *The Temple Scroll* (11QT), where there appears the passage from

Deuteronomy 17.2–7 threatening anyone who worships the heavens with death, and the Pseudepigraphal condemnation of astrology of *Jubilees* and *1 Enoch*.[7]

Copies of *1 Enoch* and Jubilees have been found at Qumran. The presence of these two texts (on heavenly courses and solar calendars) are due to the Essene's obsession with chronology with regard to the appointed times of festivals and holidays and messianic eschatology. This may have been one reason for their split with Jerusalem. Thus, the reference to the 365-day calendar which appears in six columns of 4Q394 at the start of *Some of the Works of the Law*, a composition that explains their differences with the Jewish authorities.

However, these concerns over calendrical issues differ greatly from actual astrological practice. Martin Hengel suggests that, as the Essenes were separated from 'alien influences', their 'the adoption of astrological knowledge' must be early.[8] And Meir Bar Ilan concludes that the writers of the Dead Sea Scrolls believed in astrology like any other Hellenistic thinker (he interprets their astrology as being Mesopotamian in origin). The answer to a horoscope such as 4Q186 could lie in determining the light/dark spirit ratio of the person born, in accordance with the Rule of the Community.

Another possibility for the existence of horoscopes at Qumran lies in a remark by Josephus (*Ant.* 13.171–173) that:

τὸ δὲ τῶν Ἐσσηνῶν γένος πάντων τὴν εἱμαρμένην κυρίαν ἀποφαίνεται, καὶ μηδὲν ὃ μὴ κατ᾽ ἐκείνης ψῆφον ἀνθρώποις ἀπαντᾷ.

The sect of the Essenes, however, declares that Fate is the mistress of all things, and that nothing befalls men unless it be in accordance with her decree.

Josephus also records that the Essenes could foretell the future and make predictions. Though wrapped in popular Hellenistic language, the point here is that they saw everything as foreordained by God. As the Essenes were waiting for God to send his royal (Davidic) Messiah to lead Israel to redemption through war, perhaps the use of horoscopes amongst the community was connected to their belief in εἱμαρμένον (*fate*) and the chronology of Daniel and Jubilees, being an attempt to predict when God would act.

Astrology and the Pseudographa

The *Pseudepigrapha*, a numerous and diverse collection of Jewish and Hellenistic intertestamental texts (mostly composed between 200 BCE and 200 CE) also contain references to astrology but (given their wide range of beliefs and chronology) these passages are far from uniform and voice contradictory views.

1 Enoch 72–82

1 Enoch is known primarily from its Ethiopic version: in *1 Enoch* 1.8 (second century BCE), which discusses fallen angels. Astrology is seen as an evil taught by the angel Baraquyal. *1 Enoch* 3.72 uses zodiacal ideas, while *1 Enoch* 80.2–8 discusses the irregularities of the planets.

Enoch was found, in its Aramaic text, at Qumran and with a longer astronomical section than the Ethiopic version. Its copies date from 200 BCE to the early first century CE but most were copied earlier. Perhaps interest in Enoch waned over time.

Jubilees

The greatest condemnation of astrology in the Pseudepigrapha appears in the second-century BCE *Book of Jubilees*, a midrashic elaboration of Genesis 1 to Exodus 12. In 12.16–18, Abraham is shown the futility of astrology, and this tradition of Abraham is echoed in Josephus' *Antiquities* 1.154–168. In *Jubilees*, the story of Abraham in Genesis is smoothed and improved to present him as the exemplary Jewish hero in deed and action, while Josephus presents him as the exemplary example of the perfect Greek philosopher and teacher.

Sibylline Oracle 3.227–228[9]

Book three of the *Sibylline Oracles* (approx. 160–150 BCE) likewise speaks of the Jewish rejection of astrology. Written in Egypt, probably during the rule of Ptolemy VI Philometor, *Sib. Or.* 3.218–230 is a piece in praise of the Jews (my italics),

> There is a city... in the land of Ur of the Chaldeans,
> whence comes a race of most righteous men.
> They are always concerned with good counsel and noble works
> for they do not worry about the cyclic course of the sun
> or the moon or monstrous things under the earth
> nor the depth of the grim sea, Oceanus,
> nor portents of sneezes, nor birds of augurers,
> nor seers, nor sorcerers, nor soothsayers,
> nor the deceits of foolish words of ventriloquists.
> *Neither do they practice the astrological predictions of the Chaldeans*
> *nor astronomy. For all these things are erroneous,*
> *such as foolish men inquire into day by day,*
> *exercising themselves at a profitless task.*[10]

Testament of Solomon

This is a Greek text from between the first and third centuries CE (dating is difficult due to the complicated MS scripture) in which Solomon interrogates and thwarts various demons, who reside in constellations and signs of the zodiac. It's primarily a Christian text, though it preserves earlier Jewish traditions.

The 36 *decani* (here seen as astral-demons who cause mental/physical illness) appear at 18.1–42 and describe themselves as the zodiac. Solomon eventually gains control over these *decani* via a divine ring, and orders some to build the Temple. This astronomical/astrological knowledge is in the *Wisdom of Solomon*, a first-century BCE apocryphal text. In *Wisdom* 7.7–22 we have a description of Solomon's wisdom where (v19) he knows ἐνιαυτοῦ κύκλους καὶ ἄστρων θέσεις (*the circles of years and the positions of stars*).

Letter of Rehoboam

Solomon also appears in this little-known first or second-century CE letter, in which he instructs his son Rehoboam in astrological techniques and exorcism. Written in Koine Greek, the text presents a hierarchy of planetary gods, with God as the supreme ruler, and explains how to harness their powers.

Treatise of Shem

The *Treatise of Shem* is a Hebrew or Aramaic Alexandrian text dated to perhaps the 20s BCE.) Though there's little internal evidence for a Jewish origin, it'as been called, 'the only preserved Jewish Pseudepigraphical document that consistently advocates astrology.'[11]

The Treatise is a *calendologion* and a work of scientific astrology with few religious references, a type of practice rejected by the author of Jubilees, which describes the year according to the zodiacal sign in which it begins. It has twelve chapters corresponding to each sign of the zodiac. For example:

> (1) *If the year begins in Aries*: the year will be lean. (2) Even its fourfooted (animals) will die; and many clouds will neither be visible nor appear. (3) And grain will not reach (the necessary) height, but its corn will (reach good height) and will ripen. (4) And the river Nile will overflow (at) a good rate. (5) And the king of the Romans will not remain in one place. (6) And the stars of heaven will be dispersed as sparks of fire; and the moon will be eclipsed.[12]

Although the author believed that the zodiac could determine and predict the year and fate of those born in that year, he didn't claim that the stars themselves daily affected life on Earth.

Jewish Hellenistic historians and Abraham's astrological knowledge

Artapanus

Artapanus was an Egyptian Jew from the first or second century BCE. He describes Abraham as related to the giants, implying he learnt his astrological knowledge from them, and that he taught astrology in Egypt.

Ps. Eupolemus

The second or third-century BCE *Ps. Eupolemus* records that Abraham discovered astrology and the 'Chaldean science', which could mean astronomy or mathematics. Abraham then taught the Phoenicians and introduced the Egyptians to astrology (ἀστρολογίαν). He notes how the Greeks believe that Atlas had discovered astrology, but that Atlas was just another name for Enoch, implying that Jewish knowledge of astrology was older than the Egyptians and Babylonians.

Josephus

Josephus (whose source may have been Polyhistor's *On the Jews*) notes Abraham's observation of the celestial bodies and that he'd introduced astronomy and arithmetic to the Egyptians (from whence it reached the Greeks). He records that Berosus had called Abraham μέγας καὶ τὰ οὐράνια ἔμπειρος (*a great man versed in celestial lore*).

However, he doesn't state that Abraham had *discovered* astrology (he uses the term ἀστρονομία instead of ἀστρολογία), which could be due to the Roman death penalty for practising astrology at the time of the *Antiquities* composition. Josephus is also more concerned with presenting Abraham as the originator of monotheism than astrology/astronomy. This is an example of the *rewritten Bible*, a feature of intertestamental writings. For though Josephus states he will present Jewish scripture οὐδὲν προσθεὶς οὐδ᾽ αὖ παραλιπών (*neither adding nor omitting anything*), he does in fact add and omit accounts. This is to be expected given that he'is writing primarily for pagan Greeks.

Astrology as Jewish apologetic historiography

This second Abraham tradition is an example of those Hellenistic Jewish apologetic histories designed to show that what the Greeks revere (astrology and the alphabet) had been invented or known even earlier by the Jews. Efficiency in astrology was the product of a nation's long age:

[astrology and astronomy] was assumed to be the ultimate criterion of antiquity, since only the oldest nation(s) possessed the continuous records from the many centuries needed to observe celestial cycles and to discern their correspondences with events on earth.[13]

This perhaps explains Josephus' comment with regard to the long life spans of the antediluvian humans. Longer life meant greater knowledge.

The antiquity of the Egyptians and their influence on later Greek culture is much attested in classical literature. Therefore, such statements about Abraham shouldn't be treated as *specifically positive statements* about astrology but as part of the scheme to place the Jews at the beginning of antiquity. It perhaps links to the question of how the Jews re-interpreted their history as they grew more Hellenised.

Indeed, the late second or early first-century BCE Jewish historian Eupolemus writes that it was Moses who first taught the alphabet, which was received later by the Phoenicians and finally by the Greeks. Similarly, Philo, though disassociating Abraham from astrology, states that Moses learnt astrology and the Chaldean (Χαλδαῖος) science of the heavenly bodies in Egypt. Feldman sees two purposes behind this: establishing the antiquity of the Jews and the association of Moses with astrology. Hence, Philo reports that part of Moses' education included the different astrological systems of the Chaldeans and Egyptians.

Matthew's astrological milieu

The textual evidence that survives demonstrates that by the first century CE, the Jews had adapted astrology and astral thought into their beliefs and philosophy, despite scriptural and pseudepigraphical anti-astrological polemic. This is especially evident in the apologetic use of astrology to demonstrate the wisdom of Abraham and the antiquity and role of Judaism in bringing scientific knowledge to the Egyptians and Greeks.

We know little of the views of the illiterate majority and the general attitudes to astrological belief may have ranged from rejection to adoption with all shades in between. There existed a clearly observable syncretism between Judaism and Hellenistic astral religions.

Given the wide acceptance of astrology in the Near East and Greco-Roman world, it's likely that Matthew's Jewish community would have had no doctrinal problems with the concept and practice of astrology. Even Origen records that many of his congregation consulted astrologers. We could argue that members of Matthew's community did likewise.

Astrological speculation could well have been linked with Jesus' birth by Jewish Christians before Matthew wrote... Proof of astrological speculations among the Jews prior to the birth of Christianity, as now demonstrated by the recovery of the Treatise of Shem, coupled with the indisputable fact of a 'most unusual display' near the time of Jesus' birth, by no means prove that Matthew ii preserves reliable historical information; but it's now more difficult to claim that Matthew's star was created purely out of a myth. Some historical event may lie beneath the embellished traditions.[14]

The cautious possibility that some residual historical nucleus lies behind Matthew 2.1–12 is a common conclusion even from those who don't fully advocate the astrological hypothesis. However, an anti-astrological reading is possible and the Star could represent what's in the Dead Sea Scrolls and the Hebrew Scriptures, that is, it's a symbol of the messiah brought about by God's control over the heavens and fate, which foolish astrologers follow.

CHAPTER 5:
ASTRAL FATE IN THE PAGAN WORLD

In the first two hundred years of Christianity, the idea of the stars as agents was still accepted. However, this flexible and incohesive Christian view of the cosmos, still influenced by its Greco-Roman origins, would eventually be rejected in the third and fourth centuries as Christianity began to develop a stronger, more independent cosmology. With regard to the Star, none of the early commentators interpreted it astrologically.

This fluid approach to astrology, caused by the worldview of its Judaic and Greco-Roman origins, created a problem in Christian thought. This can be seen as early as Paul's letter to the Colossians (c. 54–61 CE) and his reference to τὰ στοιχεῖα τοῦ κόσμου ('supernatural forces/elemental spirits?') in connection with an unspecified philosophy/heresy.

This problem (which was to last centuries) was of *astral fate* versus *free will*, the difficulties raised by trying to reconcile the appearance of the Star in Matthew 2 with pagan astrological foreknowledge and causality. Was Matthew saying that astrology was valid? Was the Star a sign of the Messiah, a witness or an agent? Did Christ fall under the power of astral forces? The issue was of Christ's free will over and against the predictive power of the stars. Could Christ be removed from such astral determinism or was he too subject to fate in the new Christian cosmos?

'Astral fatalism, the conception that all things, especially all human things, are determined by the stars, became the science of late antiquity.'[1] This power over fate was one of the abilities of magicians, who could overcome fate through astrology, a form of prophecy. In this respect the μάγοι of Matthew 2 become not scientific astrologers but magician-astrologers—a common combination in the Greco-Roman world. The need for a release from these bonds of astral fatalism was the reason why many joined esoteric cults (such as that of Isis and Mithras), which offered a way of controlling this 'preordained' destiny.

The Star in patristic *Wirkungsgeschichte* and *Auslegungsgeschichte*

A text's reception history can tell us much about its origins. Dale Allison warns us of the dangers of 'impoverishing exegesis' by ignoring the past and treating it like a hard science, regarding old work as obsolete. He notes, 'As the literature in the field of biblical studies continues to grow at a dismaying rate, we may be increasingly tempted to ignore old writers.'[2]

A study of the Patristic sources can lead us to interpretations not in the modern literature or to the knowledge that what we thought was new is centuries old. For example, the Father's interpretation of the missionary account in Matthew 10.9–10 is a Moses typology derived from LXX Exodus 12. This reading appears in only one modern commentary on Mark and this modern reading is *a rediscovery*.

The desire to re-examine classical Christian exegesis appears in the *Blackwell Bible Commentaries* (2003–), *The Church's Bible* (2004–) and the *Ancient Christian Commentary on Scripture* (1998–). This last series (the only one at present to contain a commentary on Matthew) aims to provide Patristic exposition on the whole of the Old and New Testaments using sources that cover a period from Clement of Rome (c. 95 CE) to John of Damascus (c. 749 CE). The Matthew volume (covering Matthew 2.1–12) perhaps over-uses Chrysostom but is still a useful source of ancient interpretation.

The analysis of the history of a text's influences and effects has been labelled *Wirkungsgeschichte*, the study of what's happened to a text *after* its creation and after it's left its author's hands. We must also examine the history of the text's exegesis (*Auslegungsgeschichte*).

As the Fathers were much closer to the time when Matthew was composed than we are, it's possible they interpreted the text with the same implied knowledge as the first Gospel readers. However, the Fathers didn't apply modern criticism to the Gospels, and Patristic hermeneutics was a more literal, spiritual and allegorical affair.

There's a complexity in early Christian attitudes to astrology. For example, though the Syrian apologist Tatian (fl. 150 CE) in his *Oratio ad Graecos* 8–12 (a highly polemical attack on Greco-Roman mythology, astrology, and philosophy) saw astral fate as the work of demons, he never dismissed astrology as an existing working system of practice. Instead, Tatian saw Christians as merely apart and separate from astral fate. Thus, two systems were in existence: the stars and planets ruled the polytheists; Christ controlled the destiny of the baptised.

These polytheists also included Christians who had incorporated astrology into their worldviews, especially those who were regarded as heretical sects. The danger of idolatry and syncretism from Greco-Roman cults, as Paul had (perhaps) encountered in Colossae, was a major area of conflict for emerging Christianity. In fact, it was common for early Christian writings to use astrology in their polemic against Gnostic teachings. For example, Irenaeus (c. 120–200 CE) records that the μονομοῖραι (an astrological term for the single degrees of the zodiac) were revered by the Marcionites as gods.

Later, Hippolytus of Rome (170–236 CE) recorded the astrological doctrines of the Gnostic teacher Basilides (fl. c. 132–135 CE). Hippolytus also mentions in passing 'two heretics', Euphrates the Peraetic and Acembes the Carystian, who drew on Chaldean astrological principles, principles which Hippolytus was attempting to refute.

Astral fate and the 'end of astrology' I

Astral fatalism versus Christian free will, especially that of Christ, continued to occupy Christian thought on astrology. The Middle-Platonist philosopher Celsus wrote a treatise against the Christians called *On the True Doctrine* (c. 178 CE) in which he discussed the Star. He asks if the Star meant that pagan astrology was still valid in the new 'Christian cosmos'. Was Christ powerless under the greater cosmic power or agent of astral fate?

From a Gnostic perspective, Theodotus (a Valentinian) resolved the problem with the concept that astrology *used* to rule causality but that the coming of Christ had replaced this system with the beneficence of divine providence. However, Basilides, in the early second century, emphasised the *pre-existence* of a Christ who had been 'mentally preconceived at the time of the generation of the stars.' Theodotus and Basilides came from the position that the stars were causal agents and incorporated this into the doctrine of Christ's pre-existence.

Ignatius and Ephesians 19.2–3

Another solution was to argue that the advent of Christ had brought about an end to the power of astrology. Thus, Ignatius of Antioch (d. c. 107 or 115 CE) and later Theodotus interpreted the Star as the embodiment of Christ himself.

Indeed, the earliest known reference to the Star (outside Matthew) is an allusion which appears in Ignatius' *Letter to the Ephesians* 19.2–3, a text full of astral imagery:

2. πῶς οὖν ἐφανερώθη τοῖς αἰῶσιν; ἀστὴρ ἐν οὐρανῷ ἔλαμψεν ὑπερ πάντας τοὺς ἀστέρας, καὶ τὸ φῶς αὐτοῦ ἀνεκλάλητον ἦν καὶ ξενισμὸν παρεῖχεν ἡ καινότης αὐτοῦ. τὰ δὲ λοιπὰ πάντα ἄστρα ἅμα ἡλίῳ καὶ σελήνῃ χορὸς ἐγένετο τῷ ἀστέρι, αὐτὸς δὲ ἦν ὑπερβάλλων τὸ φῶς αὐτοῦ ὑπὲρ πάντα· ταραχή τε ἦν, πόθεν ἡ καινότης ἡ ἀνόμοιος αὐτοῖς. 3. ὅθεν ἐλύετο πᾶσα μαγεία καὶ πᾶς δεσμὸς ἠφανίζετο κακίας·

ἄγνοια καθηρεῖτο, παλαιὰ βασιλεία διεφθείρετο θεοῦ ἀνθρωπίνως φανερουμένου
εἰς καινότητα ἀϊδίου ζωῆς·

2. A star in the sky shone brighter than all the stars. Its light was indescribable and its novelty created astonishment. All the other stars, along with the sun and the moon, formed a chorus to that star, and its light surpassed all the others. And there was a disturbance over whence it had come, this novel thing, so different from the others [Matthew 2.3]. 3. Hence all magic was vanquished and every bondage of evil came to nought. Ignorance was destroyed and the ancient realm was brought to ruin, when God became manifest in a human way, for the newness of eternal life.

Hans Lietzmann interprets *Ephesians* 19.2–3 as a 'parable in mythological form' and views the star as a symbol of Christ defeating cosmic power (represented by the sun, moon and stars).[3] His view is that this star is *not* the same that Matthew depicts in 2.1–12. If this is the case, the earliest possible date for the first true reference to the Star outside of Matthew is pushed forward.

Earlier scholars tended to view 19.2–3 as a linear text that portrayed a kind of Gnostic redemption myth where a redemptive figure descended then ascended in victory. However, the star appears to represent more the disturbance of astral powers coupled with the notion of Christ's hidden descent than any glorious ascension as a star.

The Greek word αἰῶνες (*cosmic powers*) more likely refers to 'supernatural beings' than 'ages' (*Ephesians* 8.1). Therefore, Christ's descent was *outside* the influence of the stars. Ignatius refers to the 'bond' (πᾶς δεσμὸς) of astral destiny and magic being broken and destroyed and there are numerous examples in Indo-European thought where 'fate' and 'destiny' was seen as binding or depicted in the form of ropes, cords, webs or nets.

Theodotus (74.2) also argued that astrological law (ἀστροθεσίαν) had no effect over Jesus, *as he was the Star itself*:

Therefore the Lord came down, bringing to those on earth the peace that is from heaven... a strange and new star arose [ἀνέτιλεν ξένος ἀστὴρ καὶ καινός], doing away with the old astral decree [ἀστροθεσίαν (*old order of the constellations*)], shining with a new unearthly light, which revolved on a new path of salvation, as the Lord himself, a guide for all people, came down to earth to transfer from Fate to his providence those who believed in Christ.

Thus, Jesus' advent threw off the stars and rendered the astrology of the Greeks and Romans useless. In the Gnostic *Pistis Sophia* 1.15, Christ's descent to earth likewise throws the cosmos into disarray.

The irony is that the early Christians, 'appear to have drawn the model of Christ subverting astral destiny from Greco-Roman paradigms' (Isis and Mithras).[4]

Patristic reception in the third to fifth centuries

By the third and fourth centuries, anti-astrological treatises were beginning to appear with increasing frequency. Despite Zeno of Verona's Christian reading of the zodiac, the fourth century and later saw the appearance of *Quaestiones veteris et novi testamenti*, ascribed to either Ambrosiaster or Decimus Hilarianus Hilarius; book four of *Instructio ad competentes* by Nicetas of Remesiana entitled 'Against the use of a Horoscope' (c. 385 CE, now lost), and the lost books of Diodore of Tarsus (fl. 378–90 CE), *Against Astronomy, Astrology and Fate; On the Spheres and Seven Planetary Zones; On the Spheres According to Hipparch* and *On the Celestial Bodies: Against Aristotle*.

Astral fatalism continued to be a concern and was the subject of Gregory of Nyssa's *De Fato* (c. 382 CE); Augustine's *City of God*, Book 5 (c. 415 CE); Isidore of Pelusium (c. 400–449 CE) and Protclus of Constantinople (411–485 CE). Eusebius (c. 260–340 CE) in his *Contra Hieroclem* (a critique of Hierocles' comparison of Christ with Apollonius of Tyana) states that a divine holy man who is 'a puppet of destiny and the fates' isn't an impressive figure.

Astrology and prophecy

The Star of Bethlehem as a sign from God clearly places it in the scriptural prophetic tradition. Matthew had no problem with using astrologers in a narrative that included scriptural fulfilment but astrology now posed a greater threat to Christian prophecy for it rivalled God as the means of controlling the cosmos and the future.

Origen of Alexandria (185–254 CE), for example, maintained that, though the magi *were* astrologers, they had learnt of the coming of Christ through the oracle of Balaam. Origen explained 'to the Greeks' that (*Contra Celsum* 1.60) as the magi, having lost their powers of divination, and knowing the oracle of Balaam, travel to Jerusalem to learn of its significance. The author of the non-canonical infancy harmony *Gospel of Pseudo-Matthew*, as his solution, replaced the magi with 'prophets who were in Jerusalem.'[5]

Sign or agent?

In his *Commentary on Genesis*, Origen attempted another reply to the question raised by Celsus, 'Was Christ also subject to fate according to the movements of the stars at his birth?' Unlike Ignatius (who saw Christ as having overcome and replaced astral fatalism), Origen, who denied the claims of astrologers, adopted the position of Plotinus: the stars weren't responsible for fate; they were simply signs from God. The power of the stars was transferred to God.

Thus, against the astrological assumption that the ἀπόρροιαι (*effluences*) of the stars caused events below the moon, Origen, following Philo, Clement of Alexandria and Platonic tradition, saw the stars as *signs* of future events and not their *causes*.

Origen justified free will against astral fatalism by arguing (*Philocalia* 23.1– 21), 'it is not due to the stars, but rather to one's own desire, which God has foreseen rather than predestined.' To interpret the Star as a *sign from God*, rather than a causal agent of predeterminism, followed the dictum of *Astra inclinant, non necessitant*.

Augustine, though an avid follower of astrology in his youth, gave his altered opinion in *Contra Faustum Manichaeum* (398 CE) where he claimed that Christians:

> Also deny the influence of the stars upon the birth of any person; for we maintain that, by the just law of God, the free will of human beings, which chooses good or evil, is under no constraint of necessity. How much less do we subject to any constellation the incarnation of the eternal Creator and Lord of all![6]

To Augustine, the Star was merely a witness and guide with no astrological influence over Jesus. It was God who lay behind the Star and in *C. Faust* 2.5 he gave a full answer to the problem, concluding:

> So Christ was not born because it shone forth, but it shone forth because Christ was born; so if we must speak of it, we should say not that the star was fate for Christ, but that Christ was fate for the star.

'End of astrology' II

The attack (which had begun with Ignatius) on the validity of astrology as a system of knowledge also continued. Tertullian (c. 160–220 CE), in response to a Christian convert who wished to remain an astrologer, interpreted the Star as the last use of a system now to be rejected (*De idololatria* 9):

> Astrology now… is the science of the stars of Christ, not of Saturn and Mars or anyone else from the same class of people. That science was allowed just until the advent of the gospel, in order that after Christ's birth no one should henceforth interpret anyone's horoscope by the stars.

He interprets the magi's return home by a different route as signifying their rejection of astrology. To Tertullian, all astrologers, magi and philosophers were now akin to heretical sects.

Origen had also interpreted the coming of Christ as causing the end of magic and daemonic power. This notion of Christ or the star bringing about the end of magic and astrology can be seen in a variety of fourth-century writings. For example, Jerome (c. 347–420 CE), *Commentary on Isaiah* 13.47.12–15 and John Chrysostom (347–407 CE) states that (*Homilia* 6.1), 'he [Christ] set [us] free from the power of astrology.' Gregory of Nyssa (c. 331–396 CE) composed a poem, *On Foreknowledge*, in which the magi converted to Christianity when they saw Jesus. As a final example, the Latin Christian poet Prudentius (348–405 CE) visualised the signs of the zodiac recoiling in fear from the *new star* of the Messiah (*Apotheosis* 617–626).

Julius Firmicus Maternus

This polemic against astrology has led Michael Molnar to suggest that in the *Mathesis,* a treatise on Hellenistic astrology by Julius Firmicus Maternus (c. 334 CE), there lies 'hidden' evidence to show that Maternus knew of the Star and its astrological significance. Though it's perceived as a pagan work, Molnar claims that Maternus' conversion to Christianity, evident from his later *On the Error of Profane Religion* (c. 346 CE), took place while he was writing *Mathesis*.

In this text, Firmicus presents a horoscope that (according to Molnar) describes the celestial events of 17 April 6 BCE, the date Molnar put forward as that of the Star. On this date, the moon had occulted Jupiter during the day (when it couldn't be visibly seen), the result being 'unconquerable generals who govern the whole world.'

Molnar suggests that if Firmicus *were* a Christian this passage would be related to Christ and not to Augustus Caesar, perhaps the more obvious choice (for example, Manilius, *Astronomica* 1.385, had referred to Augustus as 'like a star who had fallen to the fortune of the world').

In this case, this text would represent a significant source for understanding the Star. Yet it's difficult to agree with these suggestions regarding Firmicus, even if only on textual grounds. It's a weak argument to suggest that *if* Firmicus were a Christian, it *must* refer to Christ.

Also against Molnar's argument is that in traditional exegesis of Matthew up to the fifth century and beyond, it appears that only Origen tried to provide any kind of practical, verifiable scientific explanation for the Star. He refers (*Contra Celsum* 1.58-59) to Chaeremon the Stoic's treatise *On Comets* and muses on the Star being some kind of celestial object *similar to a comet or meteor*, albeit one with divine origins and writes:

> The star that was seen in the east we consider to have been a new star, unlike any of the other well-known planetary bodies, either those in the firmament above or those among the lower orbs, but partaking of the nature of those celestial bodies which appear at times, such as comets, or those meteors which resemble beams of wood, or beards, or wine jars, or any of those other names by which the Greeks are accustomed to describe their varying appearances.

Beyond this (even Origen elsewhere speaks of the Star coming down (un-comet-like) to where Jesus lay), there's nothing other than that of a new star that came down from the heavens.

Ignatius referred to the Star's newness in *Epistle to the Ephesians* 19.2 (ἡ καινότης αὐτοῦ), as did Theodotus. Similar terminology can be seen in the Christian *Sib. Or.* 8.475–476 where 'The heavenly throne laughed and the world rejoiced./A wondrous, new-shining star was venerated by Magi' and in the *Homilia in evangelia* 10.4 of Gregory the Great.

Gregory of Nyssa referred to 'the new rising star' as did Ambrose (*Commentary on Luke* 2.48), 'the Magi saw a new star which had not been seen by any creature in the world; they saw a new creation and not only on earth but also in heaven.'[7] Augustine also continued the tradition when he spoke of a 'new star'.

The apocryphal *Infancy Gospel of James* likewise refers to the Star in terms of its uniqueness (and greatness). The magi state (*Prot. Jas.* 21.8):

Εἰδομεν ἀστέρα παμμεγέθη λάμψαντα ἐν τοῖς ἄστροις τούτοις καὶ ἀμβλύναντα αὐτούς, ὥστε τοὺς ἀστέρας μὴ φαίνεσθαι·

(*We saw a star of exceptional brilliance in the sky, and it so dimmed the other stars that they disappeared*).[8]

This is echoed in the much later *Gospel of Pseudo-Matthew* 13 (fifth to ninth century CE), which refers to 'A great star, larger than any that had been since the beginning of the world.'

Chrysostom interpreted the Star as being apart from the usual heavens (*Homelies on Matthew* 6.2–3). God had shown the magi, 'a large and unusual star, so that by means of its greatness and the beauty of its appearance, and manner of its course, they would be amazed.' Likewise, Ephraem (c. 306–373 CE) clearly describes the power of the Star to operate outside of the heavens.

Gregory of Nazianzus (329–389 CE), in *Poemata Arcana* 5, also rejected astrology and fate. Of the 'guiding' Star, he states that: 'This is not the kind of star dealt with by expounders of astrology, but rather a star without precedent which had never previously appeared... a star newly shining [ἀρτιφαῆ].'[9] Finally, Leo the Great, in his Epiphany sermons, mentioned the 'unusual star' and 'star of new splendour.'

In Patristic exegesis, and the apocryphal Infancy Narratives, the Star was interpreted as a bright, new object in the heavens, one that came to be seen as being under the astral influence of God or Christ, an object that heralded freedom from astral fatalism and evil powers, and the genesis of a new Christian cosmology. Hence, 'in the guiding of the Magi by the star [Jesus] appears as the conqueror of the evil powers even before his birth.'[10]

In examining the astrological background to Matthew 2 and assessing the early Christian reactions to the Star and astrology in general, there's no reason to suppose astrological thinking would have been anathema to Matthew's community. However, neither has any clear evidence of genethialogical meaning been found in the text.

This offers three possibilities:

1. That no genethialogical meaning is implied by the text.

2. That such an interpretation was lost soon after Matthew's composition.

3. Matthew 2.1–12 was rapidly re-interpreted to meet contemporary Christian responses to astrology.

The evidence shows that the first possibility is more likely.

CHAPTER 6:
THE ASTROLOGICAL HYPOTHESIS

There's no indication that the Star was seen as anything other than a miraculous new event, one brought about by God to proclaim the newly arrived Messiah. Nowhere is there any astronomical clue to suggest that the Star was a planet or grouping of planets.

Given the significance of the conflict between astral fate and Christian free will, perhaps the fact that no reference is made to any astrological conjunction suggests there was none, though we could argue it was the desire of early Christian theologians to distance Christ from astral fate that led to such silence.

Even if such knowledge were limited to Matthew's community, how did this interpretation disappear so quickly and completely from a Gospel pre-eminent in the early Church? Why did no evidence of the tradition emerge out of Antioch, the third largest city (in size and importance) of the Roman Empire 'a centre of the Christian movement' and 'the cradle of worldwide Christianity'?[1] Indeed, it was the city where (according to Luke) the disciples were first called Χριστιανούς (*Christian*). How did the Star evolve from a miraculous sign from God into the complex conjunction of planets favoured today?

Astronomical conjunctions

The OED defines a planetary conjunction as:

> An apparent proximity of two planets or more heavenly bodies; the position of these when they are in the same, or nearly the same, direction as viewed from earth.

Conjunctions can take place according to two different co-ordinate systems:

1. The 'right ascension' system, which is based on the equator of the body from which they're observed (a measurement from zero to 24 hours).

2. The 'celestial longitude,' the orbital plane of that body (a measurement from 0° to 360°).

Calculations can use only one of these systems (software usually uses only the celestial longitude system), and they can also be calculated as being viewed from the equator and ecliptic of the Earth (geocentric) or the Sun (heliocentric).

Conjunctions can be calculated centuries in advance due to the predictable nature of planetary orbits, and such calculations can readily be found in ancient texts. For example, Jupiter makes a complete circuit around the zodiac once every 11.862 years while Saturn takes longer and orbits once every 29.457 years. Eventually, every 19.859 years Jupiter passes by Saturn and the two are said to be in conjunction (they have the same apparent longitude or right ascension).

The most popular conjunction hypothesis centres on a particular triple conjunction, that of Jupiter (king) and Saturn (Israel) in 7 BCE. A *triple* conjunction occurs when Jupiter passes Saturn but then lags behind (retrograde) and passes by again (prograde) three times in short succession.

Such triple conjunctions occur on average every 180 years (the intervals aren't periodic and range from 44 to 377 years. Thus, the triple conjunctions will have occurred only 20 times between 601 BCE and 3000 CE). However, the triple conjunction that took place in the constellation of Pisces in 7 BCE occurs only once every 1440 years.

Sassanian Persia (226–652 CE) and early Islamic astrology

The Islamic expansion of c. 750–850 CE saw much assimilation of Indo-Persian astrological thought and Indo-Persian astrology and astronomy was highly influential on the first Islamic astrologers (of whom many were Persian). The eventual intellectual decline of Islamic thought in the thirteenth century was countered by the rise of European learning during the Renaissance and Enlightenment.

During the Sassanian period of Iran a doctrine of *historical horoscopes* appeared. (*general* astrology, a system based on a millennial theory whereby the conjunctions (Arabic, *Kirān*) of Jupiter and Saturn were mixed with the four triplicities of Hellenistic astrology. This chiliastic style doctrine can be described as follows:

1. The two planets are in conjunction approximately every 20 years (*small conjunction*).

2. Consecutive conjunctions will move westward 117° through each constellation. The zodiac is linked in groups of three (each 120°

apart from each other) that form an equilateral triangle. Known as a triplicity (or trigon), each was ruled by one of the four elements. Such small conjunctions indicated small changes in political, economic or military status.

3. For the next 240 or 260 years, the following twelve conjunctions take place in the same triplicity before the thirteenth shifts into the next. This was known as the 'shift in transit' (*intiqal al-mamarr*) and this two hundred and forty year period was called a *middle conjunction*. Such a change signified a possible change in the reigning dynasty.

4. After approximately 960 years (four middle conjunctions throughout the millennium), the conjunctions will have moved through all four triplicities and returned to start the cycle again (*big conjunction*). Such changes heralded the arrival of prophets.

By calculating the horoscope for each small, middle and large conjunction, the origins of major earthly events could be explained.

Persian religion spoke of *thousand year* cycles of history and David Pingree, speaking of 'the Zoroastrian millenarianism of Sassanid Iran', refers to:

> The revolutions of the world-years; the cosmic cycles—i.e., the mighty, big, middle, and small varieties of the *kisma*, the *intihā*', and the *fardārs* of the planets; the mighty years of the planets; and the planetary lords of the millennia, centuries, decades, and single years. [2]

Peter Whitfield, however, sees a much earlier source, namely the belief of Pythagoras and Plato that numerical symmetry was evidence of a pattern in nature.

Origin of the astrological hypothesis

This form of political astrology became extremely popular during the later medieval and Renaissance periods but what is important is Pingree's conclusion that this *non-Hellenistic* doctrine of recording history was Sassanian in origin and their main, 'if not only', contribution to astrology. Was this new Sassanian stream the origin of the astrological hypothesis? If so, this provides a starting point for the type of historical judicial astrology used in solutions to the Star.

'Abbāsid continuation of Sassanian historical astro-political ideology

The early periods of Islamic expansion saw an enormous interest in translating the Zoroastrian Persian texts of the Sassanians. This translation movement began during the 'Abbāsid revolution (c. 720–54) and was to last the next two centuries, as the attempt by the new caliphs to legitimise their rule over the predominantly Persianised Arabs and Zoroastrian Persians. The early caliphs al-Mansūr (r754–75) and his son al-Mahdī (r775–85) were motivated to appease all by adopting this Persian culture, proclaiming the 'Abbāsid dynasty the heirs of both the Prophet Muhammad *and* all the preceding Mesopotamian empires.

With no indication of a pre-Islamic astrology in Arab society, astrology rapidly emerges as a dominant system during the rule of al-Mansūr, a ruler who had many astrologers in his retinue and had texts translated from Middle Persian that dealt with political astrology or astrological history, primarily to incorporate Sassanian/Zoroastrian imperial ideology. Indeed, Abū-Sahl ibn-Nawbat's *Kitāb an-Nahmutān* (*Book of Nahmutān on the Nativities*), a text on astrological history, translated from an earlier Sassanian source, is 'one of the first, if not the very first book of its kind in Arabic.'[3]

Māshā'allāh (c. 730–c. 815)

With the rapid rise of Sassanian political astrology in early Islamic ideology, it wasn't long before the doctrine of cyclic periods was applied to biblical history and Christ himself (regarded as a great Prophet by Muslims.) The earliest known reference to conjunctions in connection to the birth of Christ (and the earliest history based on the millennial theory) comes from the eighth-century Persian-Jewish astrologer, Māshā'allāh.

Around 800 CE Māshā'allāh produced, based on Greek, Indian and Sassanid traditions, *Kitāb fī al-qirānāt wa al-adyān wa al-milal* ('Book on Conjunctions, Faiths, and Religions') in which he explained the significance of Jupiter and Saturn conjunctions in the major events of humanity's history, claiming, via horoscopes, that the biblical flood (11 February 3380 BCE), birth of Jesus and the birth of Muhammad (19 March 630 CE) were all predicted by such conjunctions.

Māshā'allāh cast three horoscopes for the birth and nativity of Christ:

1. The eighth (small) conjunction [since the shift from the air to water triplicity which caused the Deluge] of the middle conjunction in which the birth of Christ occurred.

2. The conjunction following the above, the small conjunction indicating the birth of Christ.

3. The birth of Christ.

These horoscopes, however, weren't made for the time of the conjunction but the time of 'year-transfer' (*tahwil al-sana*). This was the vernal equinox of the year in which the cycle of conjunctions had completed its 960-year journey, and predictions were made by casting the horoscope for this date. For the third of Christ's horoscopes, cast for 22 March 12 BCE, Māshā'allāh found that:

> He will be born in ten months of this year [December], and that because the transfer is nocturnal and the moon is with Mars [in conjunction] in the ninth, it indicates violence [crucifixion] he will meet, and fear about him being killed in a high place, because the two are conjunct in the highest of signs...

Abu Ma'shar (787–886 CE)

The effects of conjunctions were also studied by Abu Ma'shar, the most influential of the Islamic astrologers (although he's also been branded a fake who copied his work from his contemporary al-Kindi) and a strong link in the transmission of Hellenistic and Indo-Iranian astronomy into the West. His work on conjunctions—translated from Arabic into Latin as *De magnis conjunctionibus* ('On Great Conjunctions')—was (like that of Māshā'allāh) founded on the doctrine that rare conjunctions of Jupiter and Saturn (with the influence of Mars and the Sun) influenced human events.

In this work, he names the cycles of 20, 240 and 960 years the Great, Major and Maximal conjunctions (or great, greater and greatest). He also claimed (unlike Māshā'allāh; he connected the birth of the cosmos with conjunctions in Cancer and Capricorn) that the world had been created when the seven planets were in conjunction in the first degree of Aries and that its end would come when they were again in conjunction in the last degree of Pisces. He had calculated, using the Saturn-Jupiter theory, the date of the Deluge to 3101 BCE. He also connected Jesus with Virgo (*The Great Introduction to Astrology* 6.1):

> In its first decan there arises a girl, whom Teucer calls Isis; she is a beautiful, pure young woman with long hair and nice to behold; she has two ears of wheat in her hand, and sits on a throne on which cushions lie; she cares for a little boy and gives him broth to eat in a place that is called the atrium; some people call this child Isu [Jesus].[4]

Virgo is often portrayed holding a branch in her left hand and an ear of wheat in her right. This wheat is a symbol of the harvest, as the sun passed through Virgo in September-October. The brightest star in Virgo is called *Spica* (Latin, 'ear of wheat, corn') the *'bright and golden Ear of Corn'*. Thus, Virgo was the symbol of the harvest throughout the ancient world. Virgo can be identified as Ceres, the goddess of the fields and growing crops and also with Demeter, the earth-goddess. Isis, who taught women to grind corn, is regarded by Apollodorus and Herodotus as being Demeter. The connection between Isis and Horus with the Virgin and Christ-Child is well documented and doesn't need to be re-examined here.

Astrology and the Star in Medieval and Renaissance thought

Islamic civilisation and its influence on medieval Judaism led to the knowledge of astronomy, logic, philosophy and mathematics entering Christian Europe during the ninth to thirteenth centuries. During this Golden Age of Arabic learning, Greek thought was translated first into Arabic and then Hebrew. This learning was later translated into Latin and other European languages during the twelfth and thirteenth centuries by thinkers such as Adelbard of Bath and Roger Bacon. The fall of Constantinople in 1453 and the exodus of scholars to the West was also a factor.

The Indo-Iranian astrology of Islam reached eastern Byzantium culture towards the end of the eighth century through the works of pseudo-Stephanus of Alexandria and Theophilus of Edessa with more being translated into Greek during the Comenan period (late eleventh to twelfth century). From the eleventh century, especially in Muslim Spain (where Judaism came under Islamic influence), we find Jewish messianic speculation making more and more use of astrology to predict the coming of the Messiah.

According to A.H. Silver, Solomon ibn Gabirol's (1021–1051 CE) attempt to calculate the date of the Redemption using the Jupiter-Saturn conjunction doctrine was 'the first instance recorded of an attempt to calculate the end by means of astrology.' Although their status as 'kings' dominated Christian thought, it was during the late Medieval period that the magi become more closely linked with astrology.

Abraham bar Hiyya (1070–1136?) and Maimonides (1135/8–1204)

In the twelfth century, the Spanish-Jewish mathematician and astrologer Abraham bar Hiyya (one of the first to write comprehensive and complex calculations) also used astrology to predict the return of the Messiah. In fact, he'd calculated an entire history of Israel from the exodus to his present day using the doctrine of historical astrology. Bar Hiyya presented five types of conjunction:

1. Minor conjunctions (19⅞ years)

2. Intermediary conjunctions (60 years)

3. Major conjunctions (238 years)

4. Great conjunction (953 years)

5. Grand conjunction (2859 years)

Ben Hiyya interpreted Pisces as the significant sign for Israel, and calculated that 1358 CE would see Redemption take place. Maimonides, however, refuted such theories. In his letter to the Jews of Yemen (1172), he rejected astrological calculations in respect to the coming Messiah and refers to such a prophecy made in Andalusia (Muslim Spain) and the political dangers involved. Later, in his letter to Marseilles (1194), he called astrology 'un-scientific and stupid.'

Pisces as the sign of Israel

Pisces has become a common constellation to represent Israel in the astrological theory. Michael Molnar suggests that the connection between Pisces and the Star gained support during the Renaissance when it was realised that during the dawn of the first century the vernal equinox had moved from Aries into Pisces. Georgic de Santillana and Hertha von Dechend comment that the coming of Pisces had been an event long looked forward to with the triple conjunction of Saturn and Jupiter in 6 BCE being the Star and herald of this new age.

However, the idea that Pisces represented the Jews could have been based on interpretations of Christian symbolism. The fish was an important symbol in early Christianity as seen from its frequent use in second-century burial catacombs, such as the Capella Greca and the Sacrament Chapels of the catacomb of St Callistus.

Historical astrology in the Latin West

The Sassanian doctrine of an 'astrology of history' determined by conjunctions continued among medieval Jewish and Christian astrologers. Roger Bacon (1214–1294) in *Opus majus* noted Abu Ma'shar's Virgo computation, as did Albertus Magus (1208–1280) in his *Speculum astronomiae*; Henry of Melius dated the Deluge to 3382 BCE via a conjunction in Cancer; and Dante Alighieri (1265–1321) showed knowledge of the doctrine.

Belief in the existence of a conjunction at the time of Jesus' birth is recorded towards the end of the thirteenth century in the *Annals of the Abbey of Worcester*, where the Saturn and Jupiter conjunction of 31 December 1285 is recorded:

> Saturnus et Jupiter eodem anno errant in conjunctione in Aquario, **quod non contigit post Incarnationem**, nec multo tempore secondum astronomicos iterum eveniet ut aestimatur.[5]

> *Saturn and Jupiter wander in the same year in conjunction in Aquarius,* ***which did not happen after the Incarnation,*** *nor after a long time Astronomical results will again be estimated.*

In the fourteenth century, Peter of Abano (1210–c. 1315) discusses in *Conciliator* (1303) the great conjunctions of Jupiter and Saturn with regard to historical figures, and was the first to call Aries the sign in which new kingdoms and religions (i.e. Christ) arise; and Antonius de Montulmo (c. 1396) wrote an astrological treatise entitled *On the Judgement of Nativities* that later influenced Johannes Müller.

Pierre d'Ailly (1350–1420)

The French Cardinal of Cambrai, Pierre d'Ailly, influenced by the doctrine of historical horoscopes in Bacon's *Opus Majus*, wrote a trio of texts (c.1414) in which he demonstrated that dates of major historical events and biblical chronology could be determined by astronomical calculations.

Like the Islamic and early medieval astrologers before him, d'Ailly delineated four types of Saturn-Jupiter conjunction: the *coniunctio maxima* (960 years), the *coniunctio maior* (240 years), the *coniunctio magna* (60 years) and the *coniunctio minor* (20 years). By studying astrological history, d'Ailly attempted to combine his astrology with the traditional Christian view of history, using Saturn-Jupiter conjunctions to settle chronological problems relating to the span of history between the creation, the birth of Christ and the Apocalypse.

D'Ailly had also constructed a horoscope of Christ set for 24 December 1 BCE with Virgo rising. Though this traditional date for Jesus' birth is drawn from Dionysius Exiguus' (525 CE) *anno domini* system, d'Ailly did refer to the conjunction of Jupiter and Saturn in Aries six years previously (7 BCE). This conjunction had been presided over by Mercury, the ruler of Virgo, indicating a virgin would give birth to a 'great prophet'. D'Ailly noted in *Concordia astronomie cum theologia* (1414) that God would have had a hand in Christ's horoscope as well as nature, but 'Despite his caveats, however, we are left with the strong impression that astrology could have predicted... the birth of Christ.'[6] An impression the early Church Fathers wouldn't have approved of!

Isaac Abravanel (1437–1508)

Isaac Abravanel, in Book 12 of his commentary on Daniel, *Ma'ayene Hay-Yeshu'ah* ('The Wells of Salvation', 1496-7) used *five* types of conjunction, each of which had a progressively more powerful effect on world events:

1. Small conjunctions every 20 years

2. Middle conjunctions every 60 years

3. Great conjunctions every 239 years

4. Large conjunctions every 953 years

5. Mighty conjunctions every 2860 years

Mighty conjunctions (the greatest in cosmic significance) always took place (he believed) in Pisces and heralded the birth of great prophets *and the Messiah*. Abrabanel calculated that a mighty conjunction had taken place in 1396 BCE, three years before Moses' birth, and that the next mighty conjunction, in 1491, would bring the Messiah. To complicate matters, he also asserted that the Messiah would come in 1502–3 and that the true redemption would be in 1534 or 1542.

His *Ma'ayene Hay-Yeshu'ah* became influential on the subsequent usage of astrology and 'others had only to alter the dates [of the text] and find other conjunctions favourable to their own calculations, to utilise all the fundamental arguments adduced by Abravanel.'[7] Indeed, such a process of finding 'favourable conjunctions' appears to be a common method used by those searching for the Star.

Johannes Müller (Regiomontanus; 1436–1476) and Jakob von Speyer

In his 1454 almanac, mathematician and astronomer Johannes Müller calculated his own horoscope for Christ, the Deluge and creation of the world based on the works of d'Ailly and Henry of Melius. Later, on 15 February 1465 while in Italy, he began a correspondence with the Court Astronomer of Prince Frederic d'Urbino, Jakob von Speyer on matters of astronomy. He began by asking twenty-four questions, including: 'When will the next conjunction of Saturn, Jupiter and Mars occur?' Speyer's reply arrived on 6 April in which he asked several questions of his own, four of which concerned conjunctions:

1. Given that that appearance of Christ is regarded as a consequence of the Grand Conjunction of the three superior planets [Jupiter,

Saturn and Mars], find the year of His birth and of His appearance…

2.   What conjunction determined His death and the manner of His death?

3.   On what day of the month and day of the week did He die?

4.   When was the time of the real conjunction of the superior planets in 1425, and what was its meaning, especially with regard to the awaited new prophet? When will he appear and where was he born? (The 1425 conjunctions of Jupiter, Saturn and Mars were in Scorpio 30 August and 14 and 22 October.)

5.   When will the next conjunction of the three superior planets take place at Urbino, based on their true motions as taken from the tables?

The first question again refers to the 'Grand Conjunction' theory of the Star, but Speyer is evidently not aware of any specific date for this event. Müller's answer was that it wasn't a question of astronomy but of astrology (a subject he'd come to believe wasn't as worthy as astronomy).

In his answer, Müller observed the earlier works of Abu Ma'shar, Masha'alla, Antonius de Montulmo and Pierre d'Ailly without giving any opinion himself. For question four, he denied it signified the advent of a prophet as the change in triplicity had occurred in 1365 and not 1425.

Criticism of historical horoscopes
Acceptance of the doctrine of historical horoscopes wasn't universal.

Marsilio Ficino (1433–1499)
Towards the end of the fifteenth century, in a letter to the Duke of Urbino dated 6 January 1481, Marsilio Ficino noted that though astrologers speak of 'the laws of Christianity' beginning with 'a conjunction of Jupiter and Saturn' he wonders why, if these planets 'always come back to the same conjunctions every 960 years and conjoin four times during the interval in one or more of the zodiacal signs', Mosaic and Christian law only appeared on earth once or have not been destroyed 'since there has been a very large number of unfavourable conjunctions between Saturn and Jupiter for a long time already.'[8]

Giovanni Pico della Mirandola (1463–1494)
Neo-Platonist philosopher Giovanni Pico della Mirandola, wrote an all-encompassing

polemic against astrology called *Disputationes adversus astrologiam* (1495) in which he described the Star as a unique event initiated by God for a specific purpose. Book Five was devoted to the heaven's influence on religion with regard to the Jupiter-Saturn conjunctions and here Pico notes the disagreements over the interpretation of great conjunctions and refutes d'Ailly's theory that the doctrine of conjunctions could be used to explain historical events. Of astrologers, Pico writes (my emphasis) that they:

> Run through so many thousands of years, as if they were speaking of something which is taken for granted. 'Here', they say, 'is the constellation which produced the flood. This one gave birth to Muhammad. *That one preceded the birth of Christ...*'[9]

He also rejected the theory of Abraham Judaeus (that is, ben Hiyya) regarding the conjunctions occurring at the time of Moses' and Jesus' birth.

Johannes Kepler (1571–1630) and the conjunction of 7 BCE

The Renaissance and Enlightenment saw the beginning of a change in the interpretation of the Star. A gradual shift towards a more modern astronomical view began as the belief in astrology declined and technological advancements (such as the invention of the telescope) led to a greater understanding of the solar system. However, it wasn't until the nineteenth century that astronomy eclipses astrology with regard to the Star.

> Astrological doctrines about the recurrence of planetary conjunctions and their influence upon the course of affairs had helped to form the concept of a historical 'period'. [10]

Thus, astrologers such as William Lilly (1602–1681) and John Gadbury (1627–1704) continued to use conjunctions to predict and explain historical events.

It wasn't just astrologers: John Milton (1608–1674) in *Paradise Regained* has Satan refer to conjunctions while speaking of Christ's horoscope. Even Isaac Newton (in *The Chronology of Ancient Kingdoms Amended* [1728]) used astronomy to reconstruct lost chronologies of the past.

Though Cyprian Leowitz (1524–1574) had, in his 1564 volume on conjunctions compared the forthcoming 1583 conjunction with the one which had preceded Christ's birth, it was Johannes Kepler, successor to Tycho Brahe (1546–1601) as court astronomer to Emperor Rudolf II, who became the catalyst for all future interpretations of the Star, being the first to associate the triple conjunction of 7 BCE with Christ's birth. By doing so, he influenced nearly every following commentator on the Star and has been called the inaugurator of a 'cottage industry that has manufactured astronomical explanations for the Christmas star.'[11]

Rudolf II had asked Kepler to comment on the single conjunction of Jupiter and Saturn of 1603 (which marked the shift into the fire triplicity). This was followed by a triangular massing of Mars, with Saturn and Jupiter (which were still in conjunction) in October 1604.

Kepler saw this 1604 conjunction as the first in a new 800-year cycle. As it was believed that the world was about 5,600 years old and that Christ had been born five trigons (5 x 804 years) after the Creation (with the seventh denoting Charlemagne's rule 804 years after Christ's birth), he associated this eighth 804-year shift to his sponsor, Rudolph II (see Table 3).

TABLE 3: KEPLER'S CHART OF WORLD HISTORY[12]

Periodi.	Anni ante Christum.	A rerum origine.	Personae insignes.	Res coincidentes : tu lector cave a trigonis effectas dixeris.
1	4000	000	Adam.	Creatio mundi.
2	3200	800	Enoch.	Latrocinia, urbes, artes, tyrannis.
3	2400	1600	Noah.	Diluvium.
4	1600	2400	Moses.	Exitus ex Aegypto. Lex.
5	800	3200	Esaias.	Aera Graecorum, Babyloniorum, Romanorum.
6	Post Christum	4000	Christus Dominus.	Monarchia Romana. Reformatio orbis.
7	800	4800	Carolus Magnus.	Imperium Occidentis et Saracenorum.
8	1600	5600	Rodolphus II.	Vita, fata et vota nostra, qui haec disserimus.
9	2400	6400		Ubi tunc nos et modo florentissima nostra Germania? Et quinam successores nostri? an et memores nostri erunt? Siquidem mundus duraverit.

Popular opinion at the time regarding these 'fiery trigon' conjunctions had formed the prediction that a comet would also appear. Instead of a comet, a nova appeared in the constellation of Ophinucus, which was observed by Kepler on 17 October 1604, and he compared this event to the nova that Brahe had observed in 1572. His observations were published in his 1606 *De stella nova in pede serpentarii.* Kepler believed that the conjunctions had caused the nova to appear and this led to his theory that a similar event lay behind the Star. In 1605, while writing *De stella nova*, he'd come across a book written by Laurence Suslyga of Poland in which he'd argued for Jesus having been born in 4 BCE. Kepler wrote:

If the author was correct, in order to reckon the Age of Christ, four years must be added to the Epoch of Christianity now in use. It would follow, therefore, that Christ was born one or two years after the great conjunction of the three Superior Planets in the first part of *Aries* or in the end of *Pisces*, occurring for the sixth time since the foundation of the world [c. 4000 BCE]. Hence the star which led the Magi to the manger of Christ, if it occurred two years before the birth of Christ, could be compared with our star.[13]

Using Suslyga's theory, he added an appendix to *De stella nova* in which he argued that 5 BCE was the year the magi arrived to worship Jesus. This was the first of several texts written by Kepler about biblical chronology, though this work left him open to criticism: 'We shall honor the great achievements of that great astronomer by leaving to its slumber the astrological piffle of one of his off moments.'[14]

According to Kepler, there'd been a triple conjunction of Jupiter and Saturn in Pisces in June, August and December 7 BCE. On 6 February BCE, Mars had come into conjunction with Saturn in Pisces and a month later had come into conjunction with Jupiter in Aries, with the Sun also in close conjunction with Mars. In a later 1614 work, Kepler details how the conjunction might have led to the appearance of the Star:

> The Magi were of Chaldea, where was born astrology, of which this is a dictum: Great conjunctions of the planets in cardinal points, especially in the equinoctial points of Aries and Libra, signify a universal change of affairs; and a cometary star appearing at the same time tells of the rise of a king... Granted, then, that the new star of the Magi was first seen not only at the same time as Saturn and Jupiter were beheld each in the other's vicinity, namely in June B.C. 7, but also in the same part of the sky as the planets... what else could the Chaldeans conclude from their, and still existing, rules of their art, but that some event of the greatest moment was imminent?[15]

He still concluded that the new star was divine in origin and not an ordinary celestial event. This view (that it was the new star alone that was divine) would become obscured and all that most remembered was that Kepler had linked a 7 BCE conjunction with the Star.

New critical thinking and the New Testament

The nineteenth century saw a quantum leap occur in biblical scholarship. Belief in the divinely inspired infallibility of the Bible and historical accuracy of the Gospels (especially John) was gradually eroded as the New Testament began to be examined critically and historically (to the horror of those who feared it would be the end of orthodox Christianity.)

Spreading from Protestant Germany, the nineteenth century saw the rise of critical, scientific thinking, which led to advances in the dating of New Testament writings, the nature of 'biblical' Greek, a more critical text of the New Testament, the Synoptic Problem and the development of new tools and methodologies.

The post-Enlightenment liberal thinker of the nineteenth century sought a miracle-free Jesus and many biblical critics rejected the Star as a fictional (mythic) invention. Kim Paffenroth notes the 'extremely loud and eloquent silence' in Ernest Renan's (1823–1892) influential and popular, *La Vie de Jesus* and similarly in D.F. Strauss' (1808–1874) *A New Life of Jesus* (a revision of his 1835 *Life of Jesus*), and offers the following quotes: 'The general legendary character of this narrative... stamp(s) on the story the impress of poetic or mythic fiction' and 'it is necessary to distinguish what is objectively real in the narrative from what arises from the subjective stand-point of the author of Matthew's Gospel.'[16]

Despite the tendency to remove the supernatural and the miraculous from the Gospels, many scholars were *not* silent and dismissive on the subject of the Star. However, by this time, though still based on the doctrine of historical conjunctions, the emphasis had shifted from calculating horoscopes to a more scientific approach.

CHAPTER 7:
INTERPRETING THE STAR IN THE AGE OF SCIENCE

Nineteenth century

In 1821, Bishop Frederick Münter of Zealand, Denmark discussed Kepler's theory regarding the Star and referred to Abravanel's *Ma'ayene Hay-Yeshu'ah* and the Jupiter-Saturn conjunctions in Pisces. But it was from the German Ludwig Ideler that the mistaken belief arose that Kepler regarded only the triple conjunction as the Star of Bethlehem and not the supposed nova, for he incorrectly attributed to Kepler the conjunction-as-star theory of Münter. Ideler's interpretation of the conjunction theory was as follows (emphasis mine):

> Both planets [Jupiter and Saturn] came in conjunction for the first time A.U. 747, May 20, in the 20ᵗʰ degree of Pisces. They stood then on the heaven before sunrise and were only one degree apart. Jupiter passed Saturn to the north. In the middle of September both came in opposition to the sun at midnight in the south. The difference in longitude was one degree and a half. Both were retrograde and again approached each other. On the 27ᵗʰ October a second conjunction took place in the sixteenth degree of Pisces, and on the 12ᵗʰ of November, when Jupiter moved eastward, a third in the fifteenth degree of the same sign. *In the last constellations, also the difference in the longitude was only about one degree, so that to a weak eye both planets might appear as one star. If the Jewish astrologers attached great expectations to conjunction of the two upper planets in the sign of the Pisces, this one must all have appeared to them most significant.* [1]

Thus, the mistaken belief was perpetuated.

In 1830, J.F. Encke (1791–1865) also described the Jupiter-Saturn conjunction as the Star and, though ultimately providing a mythological origin, D.F. Strauss in *The Life of Christ Critically Examined* (1835–6) likewise noted the 7 BCE conjunction saying the idea, 'was put forth by Kepler, and has been approved by several astronomers and theologians.'[2] In 1847, R. Anger published a thorough

examination of the Star and concluded that the 7 BCE triple conjunction in Pisces
had the closest connection. Anger couldn't trace the idea further back than the
eleventh century, though Friedrich Lichtenstein (also accepting the conjunction
theory) commented that the tradition was probably older than surviving records
indicated. In 1856, C. Pritchard (though agreeing with Ideler's conclusions) re-
calculated what he saw to be an 'astronomical error' in his theory and assigned
slightly later dates. To Pritchard also, the spectacle of the two planets so close
together was what had brought the magi.

Kepler's 'astrological' solution for the Star would become/became the
dominant solution during the nineteenth century. For example, George C.
McWhorter notes the 'three fold conjunction of the planets Jupiter and Saturn
which synchronised with the then approaching birth of Christ...';[3] Johannes H.A.
Ebrard concurred with Kepler; Henry Alford accepted the natural explanation
that the Star was the 7 BCE triple conjunction; W.T. Lynn, though seeing the
star as a miracle, accepted that the 7 and 6 BCE conjunctions may still have
had significance; E.S. Taylor quoted Alford regarding the triple conjunction; A.
Trotter wrote on the triple conjunction; and Henry van Dyke called the 7 BCE
theory of Kepler a 'fairy tale of science' that may confirm Matthew 2.1–12.[4]

In 1891, Frederic Farrar likewise noted the views of Kepler on the Star.
However, he advised caution with regard to any astronomical interpretation:

> We are, in fact, driven to the conclusion that the astronomical
> researches which have proved the reality of this remarkable planetary
> conjunction are only valuable as showing the possibility that it may
> have prepared the Magi for the early occurrence of some great event.[5]

He considered that the conjunction was too vague for use in any dating of Jesus'
birth and, 'only likely to lead to highly uncertain or entirely erroneous results.'[6]

In his two-volume work of 1883, Alfred Edersheim discusses the conjunction
theory and notes Münter's theory regarding the 7 BCE conjunction. However, he
rejects this idea in favour of the comet theory. He's also dismissive of Münter's
quotation of Abravanel stating, 'it is manifestly unfair to infer the state of Jewish
belief at the time of Christ from a haphazard astrological conceit of a Rabbi of
the fifteenth century.'[7]

Edersheim does draw attention to the *Aggadoth Mashiach* (Messiah-
Haggadah) which reads:

> A Star shall come out of Jacob [Num 24:17]. There is a Boraita in the
> name of the Rabbis: The heptad in which the Son of David cometh—in

the *first* year, there will not be sufficient nourishment; in the *second* year the arrows of famine are launched; in the *third*, a great famine; in the *fourth*, neither famine nor plenty; in the *fifth*, great abundance, and *the Star shall shine forth from the East, and this is the Star of the Messiah*. And it will shine from the East for fifteen days, and if it be prolonged, it will be for the good of Israel; in the *sixth*, sayings and announcements; in the seventh, wars, and at the close of the *seventh* [a highly significant number in the ancient world] the Messiah is to be expected.[8]

It's interesting to note how here the Star appears *two years* before the expected Messiah.

Despite the dominance of Kepler's view, there were exceptions. In 1892, J.M. Stockwell interpreted the Star as being the close approach of Venus and Jupiter on 8 May 6 BCE. Here, Jupiter was 32′ north of Venus, visible, 'as a star in the east a couple of hours before sunrise.' His astrological conclusion was that this was, 'perhaps, the strongest corroboration of the truth of the biblical narrative concerning the origin of the Christian dispensation that has yet to be found, having a purely scientific basis.'[9] Stockwell's theory was later criticised by J. Swift who, in 1893, counter-argued that a Venus-Jupiter conjunction wouldn't have accounted for the magi's second sighting of the Star.

In Volume One (1898) of the new *Dictionary of the Bible*, Turner, in his article on the chronology of the New Testament refers to the triple conjunction of Jupiter and Saturn in 7 BCE, citing Abravanel's view on Pisces and the Messiah. Ramsay uses Turner's article in his 1898 study of Luke, where, in his short discussion of the Star, he also cites the earlier conjunction of 6 BCE (which Turner doesn't).

Twentieth century

The twentieth century witnessed an significant increase in literature exploring the astrological theory, most since the 1970s, no doubt helped by the rapid advances in astronomical theory and the development of increasingly more sophisticated and powerful computers which can accurately calculate and display the position of the stars and planets at any given point in history. The rapid expansion since the early 1990s of the worldwide web has seen a proliferation of internet sites referring or devoted to the Star. Planetariums have contributed much to the debate on the origins and dating of the Star and related articles have been printed in *The Planetarian*, the trade journal of the industry.

1900–1949

The twentieth century begins with P.V.M. Benecke's article on the magi in Volume 3 of the *Dictionary of the Bible* (1900). Benecke, after discussing the usual conjunction theories, concluded there must have been an astronomical reason for the magi's visit but that the exact cause hadn't yet been ascertained.

In 1908, E. Walter Maunder continued the error of noting Kepler's interpretation of the 7 BCE conjunction of Jupiter and Saturn in Pisces, but quickly dismissed it: 'Ingenious as the suggestion was, it may be dismissed as unworthy of serious consideration.'[10] Early twentieth-century writers who *did* give serious consideration include the Germans J. Hontheim (1908), H.H. Kritzinger (1911), Franz Boll (1917) and O. Gerhardt (1922).

In 1930 J. Gresham Machen noted the 7 BCE conjunction in Pisces, referring to it as the 'most famous' hypothesis and (again) attributing it to Kepler. Likewise, in 1937, R.S. Richardson referred to the triple 7 BCE conjunction theory, but attributed its origin to Ideler and said that the hypothesis was 'found wanting.'[11]

1950s

In 1956, Werner Keller argued for the triple conjunction, presenting this historical reconstruction:

> On May 29 in the year 7 B.C. the first encounter of the two planets was observed from the roof of the School of Astrology at Sippar. At that time of year the heat was already unbearable in Mesopotamia. Summer is no time for long- and difficult journeys. Besides that they knew about the second conjunction on October 3. They could predict this encounter in advance as accurately as future eclipses of the sun and moon. The fact that October 3 was the Jewish Day of Atonement may have been taken as an admonition, and at that point they may have started out on their journey. Travel on the caravan routes even on camels, the swiftest means of transport, was a leisurely affair. If we think in terms of a journey lasting about six weeks, the Wise Men would arrive in Jerusalem toward the end of November.[12]

In 1959, the astrologer John Addey calculated a retrospective horoscope of Christ.[13] Arguing for the 7 BCE triple conjunction (giving the dates of 22 May, 15 October and 30 November 30), and using Luke 2 as the 'historical evidence', he gave a birth date of 22 August 7 BCE. This is one of the few horoscopes for Christ produced in the twentieth century. Taking the third of the three conjunctions as the Star, Addey described how he saw the historical events unfolding, with

Joseph arriving in Bethlehem around August and the magi arriving around late November or early December, after Jesus had been circumcised and presented at the Temple.

The 'Sword over Jerusalem'

In 1959, H.W. Montefiore suggested that Josephus' account of the star and sword hanging over the Temple prior to its destruction in 70 BCE (*War* 6.289) recalls both Jesus' prophecy that it would be destroyed and the Star. The Star, he conjectures, was probably the triple 7 BCE conjunction coupled with a comet in five BCE and the magi were Babylonian astrologers lured by the prophecy that a ruler would be born in the east plus the *Messiah-Haggadah* tradition that a star would appear two years before his birth.

1960s

In 1968 Roger Sinnott broke with the traditional chronology for Herod's death (though he doesn't mention the eclipse) and concluded that the Star was the conjunction of Jupiter and Venus in Leo, 17 June 2 BCE. (This idea of a 2 BCE date was later studied and popularised in the late seventies by E.L. Martin.)

Sinnott arrived at his answer by combining the chronology of Luke (i.e. the known Quirinius census date of 6 CE) and Matthew to give a birth range of 12 BCE–7 CE, removing those conjunctions which would have been either too brief or not in a tight 'imaginary' three-degree circle at least 15 degrees from the sun. On 17 June 2 BCE the two planets had effectively been fused into one, and he cites Numbers 24.17 and Genesis 49.9–10 as the basis of the magi's interpretation of such a sign in Leo.

However, in a 1991 letter published in *The Observatory*, Bidelman notes that such Jupiter-Venus conjunctions were common, with 28 in the century prior to Jesus' birth and ten between 1976 and 2005 alone. Despite this, the 2 BCE date has had much support from modern astronomers and planetarium shows.

1970s

In 1977, Clark, Parkinson and Stephenson published an article that favoured the nova of 5 BCE. Noting (incorrectly) the idea that Kepler suggested the 7 BCE conjunction as the Star, they concluded that attempts to link any astrological significance to the birth of a Messiah 'are fraught with inconsistencies.'[14]

Calculating the relative distance between the two planets during their closest approaches (27 May, 6 October and 1 December they say, 'there is no possibility that the two planets could be close enough to appear merged together to form a single, bright object.'[15] Although they refute the astrological theory, it's on the basis of scientific calculation and not biblical critical considerations.

In response to the nova theory, Ian Elliott (of the Dunkirk Observatory, Ireland) presented an article in 1978 that argued, once again, for the 7 BCE. conjunction. In this article, Elliott takes a literal view and interprets a harmonised account of Matthew and Luke as being historically accurate.

He argues that shepherds would need to protect flocks from predators during the March-November grazing period, suggesting an autumn conjunction. Elliott further cites Hughes regarding the duration of time taken for the magi to traverse the desert and interprets Herod's murder of those two years old and under being caused by his confusion over the magi's account of *two* events—7 May BCE. (Jupiter and Saturn) and 8 February BCE (Mars, Jupiter and Saturn).

1980s

In 1980, Carl Wenning, a Planetarian, also dismissed the triple conjunction solution and instead argued for a biblical solution: the Shekhinah (*sh'khinah*) Glory. The term doesn't occur in the Bible, but emerged as a common Talmudic term for a personified divine attribute—the manifestation of God's presence on Earth.

In 1983, Anthony Barrett argued for a comet as the Star, however, an anonymous reviewer pointed out that in the USA, most planetariums which present special 'Star of Bethlehem' shows concentrate on the triple conjunction of Jupiter and Saturn in 7 BC as the best astronomical explanation.

'Chronos, Kairos, Christos' Festschrift (CKC)

The year 1989 saw the publication of a *Festschrift* that, though rarely cited in Star bibliographies, contains eight articles which address the issue of New Testament chronology and of Matthew 2 and the magi in particular. The focus of this collection, Jack Finegan, had published the *Handbook of Biblical Chronology* in 1964 (revised 1998), which contains a wealth of invaluable information and detailed references with regard to the birth of Jesus and the Star.

However, of Finegan's *Handbook*, John Meier warned that, '[it] lacks a thorough application of historical criticism, especially form and redaction criticism, to the Gospel texts' and that there's too much use of patristic and rabbinic literature, 'without sufficient questioning of the sources and reliability of the claims made.'[16] He applies the same criticisms to *CKC* and the later *CKC* II, noting that at times its treatment of the New Testament 'approaches fundamentalism.'[17] Meier's cautions could be applied to many of the monographs or articles that deal with the Star.

D'Occhieppo and the 7 BCE Conjunction.

According to Ferrari d'Occhieppo, the 7 BCE Jupiter/Saturn conjunction in Pisces is the Star and he gives Jesus a birth date of 15 September. D'Occhieppo believes that Babylonian mathematical astrology lies behind the Star and takes as his starting point the view that the story in Matthew 2.1–12 is historically accurate and could even be a technical text originating from the magi themselves, suggesting that 2.1–12 appears to be an insertion.

D'Occhieppo considers that the Babylonian calculations of dates and phases of the planets (especially the rising and movements of Saturn, Jupiter and Mars) as in cuneiform tablets can be seen in Matthew's text. For example, Babylonian almanacs exist for Seleucid Era 305 (7/6 BCE) that forecast the movements of Jupiter and Saturn (though the conjunctions themselves aren't mentioned).

He notes how the 126 BCE 'weak' Jupiter-Saturn conjunction (not a true conjunction as Jupiter's retrograde phase ended too far from Saturn) in Pisces occurred in the same year as the birth of the Hasmonean king, Alexander Jannaeus, and reasons that if a weak conjunction could 'produce' a great Hasmonean king, observers of the stronger 7 BCE event might be justified in, 'the expectation of an extraordinary happy and glorious King of the Jews who might fulfil the ancient prophecies of a truly Messianic age.'[18]

D'Occhieppo describes in detail how the magi would have seen the conjunction as they travelled and how they would have used its position in the sky to find Jesus in Bethlehem. For example, he describes how on late afternoon 12 November 7 BCE, Jupiter would have been at its second stationary point, 50 degrees above the horizon in the direction of Bethlehem, hence their great joy. To explain the Star 'standing still', he concludes that a band of *zodiacal light* had pointed out Jesus:

> When the sky grew darker, Saturn became visible near Jupiter. About half an hour later, the diffuse cone of zodiacal light appeared, with Jupiter being close to its top. One could imagine that it was the star that sent a broad light beam towards the earth... Thus, it appeared as if the star stood still... but also above a certain place on the earth, which was (scientifically speaking, by mere chance) just that part of the village where the child was dwelling...[19]

Supporting this unusual phenomena, Gustav Teres notes d'Occieppo's personal account of an event in January 1941 where he saw a triple conjunction of Jupiter and Saturn in Aries, before which the zodiacal light allowed him to see the contours of houses two kilometres distant.

D'Occieppo also appeals to the apocryphal *Infancy Gospel of James*, arguing that its use of 'ΑΣΤΕΡΑΣ' strengthens his argument and that this suggests the episode of the magi derived from, 'a very old and reliable tradition' with Joseph privy to a technical report by the magi. Quoting the *Papyrus Bodmer V* edition (and changing the original uncial to [unaccented] minuscule) he translates ειδον αστερα εν τη ανατολη προηγαν αυτους εως εισηλθαν εν τω σπηλαιω as 'They saw the stars in the ascent and they [i.e. the stars] went before then until they entered the cave.'[20]

There are two concerns with this interpretation. First, the textual history is complex and the Bodmer papyrus is just one reading of one early fourth-century manuscript (other critical editions give the singular). Second, there's a danger in appealing to later apocryphal texts (especially apocryphal infancy gospels) as reliable sources.

A more difficult problem is that it requires astrology to be a genuine scientific method of divination to work. Otherwise how could the magi have accurately interpreted the signs? Yet he writes:

> Even though astrology must be acknowledged as a legitimate part of
> the philosophy of the Magi... I do not accept the validity of astrology
> as a science since it does not have an observable, repeatable base.[21]

If d'Occhieppo doesn't accept the validity of astrology, how can we accept the validity of his argument? Perhaps a clue lies in his statement that the zodiacal light over Bethlehem 'was mere chance.' If the astrology isn't valid, the odds of a planetary conjunction, leading magi all the way to Bethlehem at the time Jesus was born *simply by pure chance* must be as near to impossible as we can get.

Percy Seymour and the validity of astrology

One astronomer who does believe in the scientific validity of astrology is Percy Seymour. His presentation of a scientific explanation for astrology has also led him to speculate on the origin of the Star. In 1988, he argued that the Star was Jupiter on Tuesday 15 September 7 BCE when it was in conjunction with Saturn in Pisces.

He repeats the well known 'King', 'planet of the Jews', 'area of Palestine' symbolism of Jupiter, Saturn and Pisces respectively as the sign which triggered the magi's journey. Despite not being an original theory, his scientific interpretation of the astrological influences makes his hypothesis unique among astronomers. Later in 1998, he published a much-expanded version of his theory in which he examined and refuted the hypothesis of many conjunction theorists.

His views on scientific astrology aside, his theory suffers from a failure to employ the received opinion of biblical scholarship. For example, by taking elements from both Matthew and Luke, Seymour refers to Jesus being born in a stable and describes how those in Bethlehem for the census would have helped the magi to find it.

1990s

A 1996 article published in *The Times* again presents the June 2 BCE conjunction hypothesis:

> Astronomers may have solved the mystery of the biblical Star of Bethlehem. A powerful computer programmed [by NASA] to replay 'the history of the universe' has shown how the paths of planets in our solar system crossed to create a bright celestial body at about the time Christ is thought to have been born. According to the program, the 'star' appeared in June of the year 2BC and, far from being a miracle, was actually one of the brightest objects in the unpolluted skies 2,000 years ago.[22]

This is typical of how the popular media present astronomers as having solved the 'mystery' of the Star. In the same year, Adrian Gilbert, following the symbolic hypothesis of Stansbury Hagar (1918), suggested that the nativity was a narrative representation of the celestial events of 27 July 7 BCE: the conjunction of Jupiter and Saturn in Leo as the sun rose with Regulus. He argues that the entire night sky had been written into the nativity stories of both Matthew and Luke as a *symbolic literary horoscope*: the sun in Leo (Jesus in the manger); the zodiac (stable of animals); Taurus (ox), Aries (ram); and Jupiter, Saturn and Mars (three magi) in Pisces, all lying along the ecliptic. Hagar had likewise interpreted the nativity as a 'scientific account in literary form' of an *asterism* (form or collection of stars) 'which annually marked for astronomers the approach of the [late December] solstice'.[23] More recently, Bernadette Brady (2013) suggested a similar solution to Luke's inclusion of shepherds and cattle.

A political interpretation of the 7 BCE conjunction has been suggested by Kocku von Stuckrad (1999). His argument is that the 'great triple conjunctions' of 126 BCE, 7 BCE and 134 CE were all used for political means, especially when linked to Balaam's star prophecy. Referring to the Sassanian doctrine of historical conjunctions, Stuckrad combines these events with the now typical symbolism of Jupiter as the king planet and Saturn as the star of the Jewish people to produce the following relationship with Jewish politics:

126 BCE: This weak conjunction took place at the birth of the Hasmonean kingdom under Alexander Jannaeus (103-176 BCE). Von Stuckrad speculates that the use of stars on the Hasmonean bronze coins was a symbol of their divine election and fulfilment of Numbers 24.17.

7 BCE: Herod's killing of his wife, sons and other 'enemies' during 7-6 BCE becomes a 'reasonable answer to the planetary threat' of the 7 BCE triple conjunction in Pisces. (No such astrological reason is suggested by Josephus.) Of the Christian interpretation of this conjunction, Stuckrad writes:

> The Christian version of the triple conjunction's 'true meaning' was near at hand. From this perspective, the birth of the Messiah was accompanied by a heavenly sign and the great conjunction was moulded into the 'Star of Bethlehem', thus ensuring the belief in Jesus' divine origin. [24]

As there's nothing to suggest that a conjunction lay behind the Star, Von Stuckard's response weakly notes that 'From the second century on patristic literature discussed its theological implications.'

134 CE: The third conjunction (a *single* conjunction, not a triple) took place during the Bar Kokhba revolt of 132-135). Coins were minted in 133/134 depicting what has been interpreted by some as a star above a representation of the Temple.

Finally, 1999 also saw the publication of *The Star of Bethlehem: An Astronomer's View* by Mark Kidger. Though Kidger's conclusion was that the Star was ultimately a nova, it was an event supported by proceeding conjunctions, occulations and planetary massings:

Event	Interpretation
(1) Triple conjunction of Jupiter and Saturn in Pisces 7 BCE	Pisces = sign of the Jews Jupiter = royalty Royal event in Judaea. Magi await a second sign
(2) Massing of Jupiter, Saturn and Mars in Pisces, February 6 BCE	Second sign
(3) Pairings of moon and Jupiter (occultation) plus Mars and Saturn in Pisces, 5 BCE	Foretells a royal birth in Judaea
(4) Nova in February/March 5 BCE	Star of Bethlehem

He concluded that 'they [the Magi] already knew when Jesus would be born and so could react at the correct time' due to the previous three events.[25] Kidger interprets the Star as a real historical event, but one that is both celestial *and* miraculous. However, Shelley Jordan states what is true of a large number of astronomers writing about the Star:

> In the end, Kidger has solved the problem of the Star for himself alone. In his massive assumptive leap, the Star has somehow been transfigured from a solitary bright object's rising and setting to a series of rather sophisticated observations of astronomical events. Nothing in Matthew justifies or supports this imaginative, even flagrantly astrological, solution.[26]

Kidger's assumption is that:

> We have an advantage over the Magi because, with the benefit of hindsight, we know the date of the nativity was around March-April 5 BC. We can thus filter out all the events that were not visible within a small interval of time.[27]

Jacqueline Mitton clearly defines the primary problem, one that astrological theories can't avoid:

> Kidger has unwittingly constructed an argument that does more to defend astrology than to trumpet a success for historical astronomy… If the Magi were indeed able to read so much correct information from the heavens, is it not time we all took astrology more seriously?[28]

The Star in the new millenium

At the time of writing, the twenty-first century has seen no significant new research on the conjunction hypothesis.

In 2000, Gustav Teres, Adjunct Astronomer of the Vatican Observatory, published a detailed study of the Star in which he strongly supported the 7 BCE conjunction of Jupiter and Saturn in Pisces as presented by his two major influences, Hughes and d'Occhieppo. Angela Tilby, in the companion book to the BBC's 2001 documentary series *Son of God* notes the occultation theory of Molnar (who appeared in the series) as well as the standard 7 BCE. Jupiter-Saturn conjunction in Pisces. She concludes that these theories, 'do indicate possible contemporary events that point to [the Star] being more plausible than has sometimes been thought.'[29]

In Simo Parpola's 2001 *Biblical Review* article, we again find Babylonian astrology used to present the 7 BCE theory. Parpola does add one new interpretation for the third conjunction (1 December).

> About three weeks before the winter solstice, when the Babylonians held their annual celebration of the victory of their saviour god, Nabū, over the forces of darkness. The magi may well have associated the birth of the child they were looking for with this festival, for the Mesopotamian king was commonly regarded as an incarnation of Nabū. Interestingly, the Babylonians proclaimed Nabū's victory as 'good tidings' (*bussurāti*) to all the people.[30]

Parpola correctly points out that Kepler saw a nova as the Star. However, this same basic error still persists for in *Gods in the Sky* (also a three-part Channel 4 series in 2002) Chapman, a member of the Royal Astronomical Society, states:

> The Star of Bethlehem... is now generally believed to relate to a brilliant conjunction (a close apparent mutual approach) of the planets Jupiter, Saturn and Mars in February 6BC. Indeed, in 1606 the German astronomer Johannes Kepler first suggested this possible explanation for the nativity star, for another such planetary conjunction had occurred in 1604.[31]

In December 2005, the *Independent* and *Daily Post* ran articles citing Professor M. Bode, an astronomer from Liverpool John Moores University, who has argued for the 3 and 2 BCE Jupiter and Venus conjunctions in Leo. The articles infer that this is a new theory.

Finally, in 2007, astrophysicist Professor G. Matthews (of Notre Dame University) presented the 17 April 6 BCE conjunction in Aries of Jupiter, Saturn with the Sun and the Moon (with Mars and Venus nearby).

CHAPTER 8:
MAJOR EXPONENTS OF THE CONJUNCTION THEORY

David Hughes

David Hughes of Sheffield University is probably the most quoted astronomer on the subject of the Star. Numerous journal articles, internet sites and books mention or quote him (or thank him for his assistance) and the popular press quote his opinions whenever required.

Assuming that the combined accounts of Matthew and Luke are historically accurate, his theory is that the 7 BCE triple conjunctions, via Babylonian astrology, represents Matthew's star. In his 1976 *Nature* article, Hughes presents two scenarios.

TABLE 4: HUGHES' TWO SCENARIOS

SCENARIO ONE	SCENARIO TWO
1. 29 May 7 BCE, first conjunction. Visible for two hours in morning.	1. Conjunction of 7 BCE attracts magi's attention. Hughes refers to Epiphanius' (315–403 CE) claim that the Star shone two years before the magi arrived.
2. Magi set out end of June. Both planets would have been visible during their journey.	2. Comet of March 5 BCE starts their journey.
3. 29 September the second conjunction confirms the magi's predictions.	3. Magi visit Herod.
4. Jesus born early October. Events of Luke 2 take place (Temple visit and Shepherds in fields).	4. Nova of April 4 BCE, magi arrive in Bethlehem. Hughes writes: 'But why would Joseph and Mary stay in Bethlehem for 2 yrs when they had only gone there to be taxed?'
5. Meeting with Herod.	
6. 4 December, third conjunction, 'pointing was south to Bethlehem.'	

In his later 1979 book on the subject, Hughes adjusted his dating and notes the first conjunction as beginning 27 May, the second 6 October and the third 1 December. By 1999, the date of this first conjunction has been corrected again as, he argues, the magi:

> Could have watched the first conjunction from Babylon in May of 7 BC, but delayed travelling until the end of the long, hot summer. On their way to Jerusalem, they could have witnesses the astrologically important moment when Jupiter and Saturn were rising at the instant of sunset.[1]

In 1979, Hughes argued that Jesus was born on Tuesday 15 September 7 BCE during the acronychal rising of Jupiter and Saturn. This led Hughes to present the sequence given in Table 5 based on an amended Scenario One and the combined chronology of Matthew and Luke.

TABLE 5: HUGHES' THIRD SCENARIO

SCENARIO THREE
1. The magi, 'have decided amongst themselves that the new Messiah of the Jews is to be born on Tuesday, September 15, 7 B.C.E.'
2. Magi set out at end of summer.
3. Magi view acronychal rising which occurs at Jesus' birth.
4. Sunday 24 September and Wednesday 25 October: Jesus' circumcision and purification.
5. 'The interlacing of the nativity accounts of Matthew and Luke indicates that the Magi visited the holy family some time after the purification.'
6. Mid-November second stationary points of Jupiter and Saturn. Hughes wonders if this led the Magi to rejoice (Matthew 2.10)
7. Magi journey to Bethlehem from Jerusalem around November 11–19.
8. Third conjunction of December 1.

E.L. Martin

> It isn't often that we see the demise of an astronomical theory that dates back to pre-telescopic times. Yet a theory first proposed by none other than the famous astronomer Johannes Kepler himself, and generally accepted as correct for more than 3½ centuries, is now being discarded … [by] new historical research of Dr Ernest L. Martin.[2]

Martin has put forward a 2 BCE date for the birth of Jesus. Interestingly, the majority of early Church Fathers also dated the birth of Jesus to this time. Indeed, two chronologies in Josephus, could be exploited to provide both 4 BCE *and* 1 BCE. dates for Herod's death, though the latter date hasn't received general acceptance.

Table 6 presents Martin's description of the numerous celestial events and conjunctions that took place between 3–2 BCE and the astrological interpretations he uses to link them to Christ's birth.

TABLE 6: CHRONOLOGY OF CELESTIAL EVENTS

DATE	CELESTIAL EVENT	MARTIN'S INTERPRETATION
1 Aug 3 BCE	Jupiter visible on eastern horizon	Rev. 22.16
12 Aug 3 BCE	5 am—Close conjunction between Jupiter and Venus (0.23° apart). Sun (Supreme Father), Moon (Mother) and Mercury (Messenger) all grouped in Leo.	Jupiter (Father of the Gods and Greater Good Fortune) in union with Venus (Lesser Good Fortune). Associated with coming birth. Leo symbol of tribe of Judah (Rev. 5.5)
18 Aug 3 BCE	Mercury leaves Sun to become the morning star.	
1 Sept 3 BCE	Venus and Mercury in conjunction in Leo (0.36° apart) Sun enters Virgo.	Venus was Ishtar— Goddess of Fertility. Christ descendant of Judah (Leo), introduced by messenger (Mark 1.2)
14 Sept 3 BCE	Jupiter in first conjunction with Regulus in Leo (0.63° or 0.33° apart)	Regulus (chief star of Leo) and was known as the King Star. Connected with birth of kings. King planet linked with king star in Leo, sign of Judah.
1 Dec 3 BCE	Jupiter begins retrograde motion	
20 Dec 3 BCE	Venus evening star in the west (moves slowly east)	

17 Feb 2 BCE	Jupiter in second conjunction with Regulus (1.19° or 0.85° apart)	
8 May 2 BCE	Jupiter in third conjunction with Regulus (1.06° or 0.72° apart)	
17 June 2 BCE	Conjunction of Venus and Jupiter in Leo during full moon (0.2° apart)	Planets appear as one star.
27 Aug 2 BCE	Jupiter is morning star. Mars in conjunction with Jupiter in Leo (0.14° or 0.09° apart). Jupiter then moves westward.	
25 Dec 25 BCE	Jupiter stationary in Virgo due to retrogression. Jupiter stationary 65° above southern horizon. Sun also in winter solstice.	Jesus = newborn sun (Mal. 4.2) born of Virgin.

Martin interprets Jupiter as the Star due to its major role in these events, especially as its 25 December stationary point, 'would have shown the planet shining down on Bethlehem!'[3] To fit these celestial events into the nativity, he harmonised the stories of Luke and Matthew to create a chronology:

1. Mary and Joseph travel to Bethlehem for the census (the oath to Augustus under Quirinius in Syria as recorded by Tertullian).

2. (11 September 3 BCE) Jesus born in the stable on Day of Trumpets. According to Martin, this is also the date given by John in Revelation 12.1–5.

3. (18 September 3 BCE) Jesus circumcised.

4. (20/21 October 3 BCE) Jesus dedicated in the Temple.

5. (3 October BCE) Family return to Nazareth (Luke 2.39).

6. (Spring/summer 2 BCE) Family return again to Bethlehem (Matthew 2.11).

7. (25 December 2 BCE) Jupiter stationary in Virgo.

8. (December 2 BCE) Jesus a toddler. Magi appear with gifts. Family move to Egypt.

9. Massacre of the Innocents.

10. (approx 28 January 1 BCE) Herod dies.

John Thorley, who uses Martin's theory in his own chronological reconstruction of Christ's life, notes how the years 6 BCE to 4 CE are a period, 'by a quirk of fate,' poorly recorded by Roman historians. Trying to confirm the chronology of Luke, Thorley sees Martin's chronology and 2 BCE hypotheses as the key to this period of Christ's life.

We have seen how the 2 BCE conjunction has found support in hundreds of Planetarium shows. In 1980, J. Mosley of the Griffith Observatory wrote:

> If and when the majority of classical scholars conclude that Christ was born in or near 2 B.C., reference to the events of 7 B.C will be dropped altogether. It is after all, not important to astronomers that it was one conjunction or the other—what *is* important is that astronomers have something to contribute, that the 'Star' was an identifiable astronomical phenomenon, and that planetariums are justified in re-examining it each Christmas.[4]

Thus, Martin is confident in his solution and dismissive of those he terms 'religious' and who wish to maintain that the Star was a miracle. Despite the favour this theory has found, it isn't without its critics. For example, Douglas Johnson has disputed this 'false' theory on chronological grounds (Herod's death) in two articles published in *The Planetarium* and he cites two further scholars who have likewise refuted Martin's hypothesis. Johnson's own solution is the standard theory of the 7 BCE triple conjunctions in Pisces.

Apart from the common problems of astrology needing to be a valid observable science for this hypothesis to work, and the harmonisation of Matthew and Luke, the theory will continue to suffer as a credible hypothesis due to the accepted scholarly opinion that Herod died in 4 BCE. Indeed, of the various efforts to demonstrate a later date for Herod's death, the best summary conclusion is that of Meier who states the attempts to refute the 4 BCE date, 'must be pronounced a failure.'[5]

Michael Molnar

Molnar ranks alongside Hughes in being one of the most popular citations in the media. Indeed, he's cited in the 2005 revised third edition of the *The Oxford Dictionary of the Christian Church* as a 'modern suggestion'. Molnar's methodology is to dismiss the general scanning of the period of Christ's birth for portents. We must find instead confirmation in the ancient sources, thus, his claim that Firmicus Maternus presents Christ's horoscope in his fourth-century text, *Mathesis*.

Molnar's theory (though no different from any other astrological interpretation) has broken from the standard 7 BCE conjunction mould for he sees the Star as the invisible *occultation* (obstruction of a planet by the moon) of Jupiter in 6 BCE. Molnar's theory requires a large amount of sophisticated astrological theory and interpretation, so only the general mechanics of his hypothesis will be examined.

Coins of Antioch

In 1992, Molnar observed that certain coins minted in Antioch depicted Aries on the reverse with either a star or a star with crescent moon (Figure 4). On a 13–14 CE coin, he interprets the ram and star symbols to represent a conjunction of Jupiter and Mars in Aries, 7 CE, cementing Syria's new power as ruler of Judaea, Samaria and Idumaea which had taken place a year earlier.

A minting in c. 55–57 CE shows Aries with both a star and crescent which Molnar speculates as representing the lunar occultation of Venus in Aries 27 April 51 CE. However, such crescents were common on Neronian coinage. Molnar suggests that:

> The coin appears to be typical Roman propaganda following a period of bitter conflict between the Jews and Samaritans. Very likely Quadratus [the Syrian Legate] hoped the unrest was permanently quelled, as foretold by the celestial sign of peace and harmony.[6]

There's no supporting evidence to back his conclusion and the statement is pure conjecture.

Aries and the Star

The connection between the sign of Aries and Judaea is the key to Molnar's theory. Noting that Syrian coins appear to depict celestial events involving Aries, which appear linked to Judaea, he then looked for any event that would include Aries and match the events told in Matthew 2.

Molnar's 1999 monograph is an expansion of his 1992 and 1995 articles.

Using Greek astrology and noting that the moon played an important role in royal and imperial horoscopes, his theory is as follows:

- 20 March 6 BCE: One minute after sunset in Jerusalem, the moon occults Jupiter in Aries. Occultation ends half an hour later. Though hidden by bright sky, Molnar assumes the magi had knowledge to predict it and notes how astrological aspects of this event show similarities with the horoscopes of Tiberius, Augustus and Hadrian. This event convinces the magi that a king had been born in Judaea.

- 17 April 6 BCE: Second lunar occultation of Jupiter in Aries occurs during Jupiter's heliacal rising. As this happened after noon, only mathematical calculations would have alerted astrologers to its occurrence.

- 23 August 6 BCE: Jupiter becomes stationary in Taurus then reverses direction (retrograde motion) and moves westward.

- 19 December 6 BCE: Jupiter's second stationary point, this time in Aries

Applying this to Matthew 2.1–12, Molnar interpreted the passage to read:

And behold the planet [Jupiter] which they [the magi] had seen at its heliacal rising [17 April] went retrograde [23 Aug] and became stationary [19 December] above in the sky (which showed) where the child was.[7]

Molnar argues that Matthew's two references to the Star rising in the east demonstrate how portentous for Jupiter an eastern rising was in astrology. The fact that only predetermined mathematical calculations indicates that the occulations had taken place explains everyone's failure to have seen the event. Molnar also puts the Massacre of the Innocents in 4 BCE, giving the two year gap.

The Star in Luke?

Molnar also attempts to link these events with Luke 2.13–14, with the 'heavenly hosts' (morning stars) and sheep being another form of describing Jupiter in Aries. He describes a situation where the coins of Antioch caused the local Christians to believe that they portrayed the messianic star of Jesus. Luke heard these stories and, as the first Aries coins appeared in 6 CE, he placed Jesus' birth at the time of Quirinius' Syrian census. Molnar describes this scenario as 'more plausible' than the idea that Luke confused the events of Herod's death in 4 BCE with the annexation and taxation of 6 CE.

κριός (Aries)—Zodiacal Sign and Astrological Geography

Molnar argues that the astrological symbolism of occultations and heliacal risings in Greek astrology means that these events in Aries provide the best astrological interpretation for the Star. As Aries is so important to this hypothesis, we must examine Molnar's claim that this sign, and not Pisces, is the symbol of the Jews.

As Pisces had been interpreted since the early medieval period as the sign of the Jews, what evidence does Molnar provide for Aries? Here we enter the sub-discipline of astrological chorography, *the influence of the stars over specific regions and cities*. Molnar points to Ptolemy who notes the influence of the sign in which a planet stops:

> Of the prediction itself, one portion is regional; therein we must foresee for what countries or cities there is significance in the various eclipses or in the regular stations of the planets, that is, of Saturn, Jupiter, and Mars, whenever they halt, for then they are significant... The inhabitants of Coele Syria, Idumaea, and Judaea are more closely familiar to Aries and Mars, and therefore these people are in general bold, godless, and scheming.[8]

He notes the works of Manilius (*Astronomica,* 4.744–54) and Vettius Valens (*Anthology* 1.2) neither of whom refers to Judaea specifically but to 'Syria down to northern Egypt' and 'Coele Syria and its adjacent lands', both areas which would have included Judaea. Molnar also suggests that Nero's foretold return to power specifically in the east was due to Aries' appearance in his horoscope.

Molnar states that Valen's 'ethnographic system' is based 'apparently' on a work of Hipparchus (c. 150 BCE) and states that:

> We have an independent confirmation that during the centuries spanning Christ's birth, astrologers claimed that Herod's kingdom was symbolised by Aries. We conclude that Aries is the zodiacal sign that held the Magi's Star.[9]

Molnar notes how William Lilly (1647) likewise associated Judaea and Syria with Aries and, though not cited by Molnar, I have also found a reference to Aries and 'Palestine' in another seventeenth-century work by Pierre Bayle: 'Aries... reigns over Palestine, Armenia, the Red Sea, Burgundy and the cities of Metz and Marseilles.'[10] However, such late sources can't be classed as authorities.

A significant secondary work not cited by Molnar in his bibliography is a study by Bruce Metzger on astrological geography in relation to Acts 2.9–11 (the list of nations). Metzger compares the list of nations referred to by Luke in Acts 2.9–11 to a later fourth-century list in an astrological text by Alexandrinus entitled *Elementa Apotelesmatica*. Though concluding that there's no discernable relation between Paulus and Acts, he does make several useful points with regard to astrological geography that affect Molnar's Aries hypothesis.

There existed numerous systems of astrological geography, each of which varied in their use of signs for countries. Alexandrinus' list is the simplest but he makes no mention of Judaea.

TABLE 7: ASTROLOGICAL GEOGRAPHY OF ARIES

Paulus Alexandrinus	Dorotheus of Sidon	Acts 2.7–11	Manilius	Hephaistio of Thebes (c. 380 CE)	Ptolemy
Persia	Babylon	Parthians	Hellespont	Babylonia	Britain
	Arabia	Medes	Propontis	Thrace	Gaul
		Elamites	Syria	Armenia	Germania
			Persia	Persia	Bastarnia
			Egypt	Cappadocia	Syria
				Mesopotamia Syria	Palestine
				Red Sea	Idumaea
					Judaea

The nature of astrological geography, with its development and variations over time, means that caution must be exercised in ascribing one country to a sign.

The same conclusions have been drawn by Ernest Lucas with regard to Franz Cumont's suggestion that the four animals from Daniel 7.2–7 (= Babylon, Media, Persia and Greece) is the result of influence on the author of the systems of both Teucer of Babylon (a source not mentioned by Molnar) and Ptolemy. Here, Aries refers to Persia.

Molnar's theory has received a great deal of positive acclaim from astronomers and the media. For example, Owen Gingerich (senior astronomer emeritus at the Smithsonian Astrophysical Observatory and Research Professor of Astronomy and the History of Science at Harvard University) said, 'I take Molnar's work quite seriously. Anything he comes up with along these lines has to be considered as being very likely correct.'[11]

He isn't without his critics. Seymour doubts the ability of the ancient astrologers to have calculated the events so accurately. Though Molnar provides evidence that mathematical sciences were quite advanced, Seymour agrees only that conjunctions of slow-moving bodies such a Jupiter and Saturn were possible at the time.

David Hughes likewise notes it would have been impossible for ancient astronomers to observe lunar occultations, and argues that an occultation of the moon in front of Jupiter signifies the *death* of a great ruler, not his birth.

Although astronomical events were frequently depicted on ancient coinage, the combined star and crescent was a common symbol. The ram and star image on Antioch's coin *may* have symbolised a astronomical event but they were also the Babylonian signs for Ishtar, Venus (eight-pointed star) and the moon god, Sin (crescent). In addition, the star was also employed as a symbolic motif enforcing the zodiacal nature of the image portrayed.

This star and zodiac combination, plus the evidence that Aries was the sign of Syria, makes is more probable that the leaping ram and star was a local symbol for Antioch, especially as the leaping ram and star was used on her coinage down to the third century CE.

There are further problems with Molnar's hypothesis, such as his use of Firmicus Maternus' *Mathesis* and Hellenistic astrology. Despite the alleged mathematical ability of the ancient astrologers, even if it's granted that this theory uses contemporary astrology and horoscopes to apparently convincing effect, there are no astrological texts dating from the period of Matthew's composition. Even *Mathesis* dates from the fourth century (c. 337 CE) with no evidence for its existence prior to the eleventh. (This isn't a major weakness. A text's age can be irrelevant for it could preserve an accurate and uncorrupted copy from an earlier age.)

Jim Tester calls the *Mathesis* complicated, muddled, confused and jumbled, and argues that 'nobody could actually have practised astrology with only the *Mathesis* to hand.'[12] Molnar's theory also suffers from the usual problems. Beck presents the fundamental problem; though he 'applauds' the move from the standard 'visually impressive' event to the 'astrologically significant configuration' he concludes that the hypothesis would have been more credible if Molnar had been, 'less concerned with salvaging the historicity of the story of the quest of the Magi.'[13]

It's also an example of a theory that appears to defend astrology while failing to understand the Synoptic Problem relating to the relationship between Matthew and Luke. However, Molnar does appear to have found evidence for political astrology in Antioch, the home of Matthew's community.

Mark Kidger

In 1999, Kidger, a researcher at the Institutio de Astrofisica de Canaria, published *The Star of Bethlehem: An Astronomer's View* and writes:

We have an advantage over the Magi because, with the benefit of hindsight, we know the date of the nativity was around March-April 5BC. We can thus filter out all the events that were not visible within a small interval of time.[14]

This is a wild assumption, as we don't know when Jesus was born and we especially can't narrow it down to a month. To present such a statement *as fact* can only result in a suspect conclusion. This conclusion is absurdly complicated and bears no relation to the Matthew's text. Kidger's conclusion is that the Star was a nova but combined with prior conjunctions, occulations and planetary massings.

TABLE 8: THE STAR ACCORDING TO KIDGER

Event	Interpretation
(1) Triple conjunction of Jupiter and Saturn in Pisces 7 BCE.	Pisces = sign of the Jews Jupiter = royalty. Royal event in Judaea. Magi await a second sign.
2. Massing of Jupiter, Saturn and Mars in Pisces, February 6 BCE.	Kidger says little, only that it was the second sign and astrologically significant.
3. Pairings of moon and Jupiter (occultation) plus Mars and Saturn in Pisces, 5 BCE.	Which 'clearly' foretold a royal birth in Judaea.
4. Nova in February/March 5 BCE.	

Kidger views Event 4 as *the* Star simply from, 'the coincidence of the dates', but backtracks through events 1-3 as there must have been something else to distinguish this ordinary event from any other, therefore he concludes that, 'they [the Magi] already knew when Jesus would be born and so could react at the correct time.'[15]

Kidger interprets the Star as a real historical event, but one that is celestial *and* miraculous. However, the usual problems remain:

In the end, Kidger has solved the problem of the Star for himself alone. In his massive assumptive leap, the Star has somehow been transfigured from a solitary bright object's rising and setting to a series of rather sophisticated observations of astronomical events. Nothing in Matthew justifies or supports this imaginative, even flagrantly astrological, solution.[16]

Jacqueline Mitton clearly states the second problem, one that astrological
theories can't avoid:

> Kidger has unwittingly constructed an argument that does more to
> defend astrology than to trumpet a success for historical astronomy...
> If the Magi were indeed able to read so much correct information from
> the heavens, is it not time we all took astrology more seriously? [17]

This inability to isolate astrology from astronomy when discussing the Star is
a common failing. Yet Kidger continues to present this version of events in his
recent 2005 *Astronomical Enigmas* and his 'groundbreaking' theory has been
championed by Robert Matthews in the December 2005 issue of *Focus*, the BBC
science and technology magazine.

CHAPTER 9:
CURRENT STATE OF THE ASTROLOGICAL HYPOTHESIS IN BIBLICAL STUDIES

Twentieth century

The first 1957 edition of the *Oxford Dictionary of the Christian Church* states of the Star that, 'such rationalizations of the story have now been generally abandoned.' This clearly wasn't the case! Ethelbert Stauffer (1960) referred to the Star as the 7 BCE conjunction of Saturn and Jupiter as did J.C. Fenton (1963) who states, 'The planet Jupiter apparently crossed the paths of Venus and Saturn in 7BC, and there may be some reference to this in Matthew.'[1] David Hill (1972) also mentions the 7 BCE Jupiter and Saturn conjunction.

George Soares Prabhu (1976) inevitably refers to astronomical solutions in his study of Old Testament motifs in 2.9b–12. He notes the 7 BCE conjunction with regard to d'Occhieppo but observes that:

> Astronomers, alas (and Ferrari d'Occhieppo is no exception) tend to approach a biblical text bristling with unsuspected exegetical difficulties, with the same blithe naïveté that exegetes betray when dabbling in statistics or astronomy.[2]

He still cautiously concludes that 2.1–12, due to:

> Its strangeness, and the absence of any real parallels in the Old Testament or in rabbinic literature, is more likely to have some historical nucleus, even if Num 22-24 and Is 60 have had a large part in its shaping.[3]

In 1977, Raymond Brown published his exhaustive study and commentary of the nativity stories in both Matthew and Luke (updated in 1993). In his discussion of the planetary conjunction theory, he refers only to the rare triple event of 7–6 BCE. Despite the dispute over Pisces, he does state that it was a constellation 'sometimes associated with the last days and with the Hebrews',

but in the end concludes that such claims can only remain speculative at best.[4]
His overall conclusion with regard to the Star was:

> Given such a plethora of imaginative suggestions, I must judge that
> there is no greater consensus now than there was when the [Birth of
> the Messiah] was written as to what astronomy/astrology can tell us
> about the star.[5]

Brian Nolan (1979), in his study of Davidic Christology in Matthew 1–2, refers
specifically to d'Occhieppo's theory of the 7 BCE conjunction of Jupiter and
Saturn in Pisces as possible extra-biblical background. Interpreting Jupiter as
a royal planet (Babylonian Marduk) Nolan notes that this 'significant' planet,
'was eminently suited to herald the king Messiah.'

F.W. Beare (1981) is dismissive of the astrological hypothesis. Yet he can't
avoid referring to some 'popular remembrance' (in this case, of Halley's Comet
in 12 BCE) lurking beneath the story. Of astrology, he writes:

> It is quite silly for anyone… to put any faith in astrology. And it would
> be equally absurd to suppose that magicians of the first century were
> any more able to read in the stars the signs of coming events in human
> history on earth than are the columnists who give advice in our own
> newspaper.[6]

Daniel Harrington continued the 7 BCE conjunction idea in his 1982 commentary
and James Charlesworth (1983), in his introduction to the *Treatise of Shem*,
likewise points to the astrological significance of Jupiter (kingship) and Saturn
(Israel) with regard to Matthew 2.

C.E.B. Cranfield (1988), believing that Stauffer's claim 'stands on solid
ground', argues for the historical plausibility of the conjunction of 7 BCE and the
events of Matthew 2. W.D. Davies and Dale Allison (1988), in their near exhaustive
commentary on Matthew, after discussing the many sources in scripture and
Roman historical texts, also note the Jupiter and Saturn conjunctions. However,
they're more cautious and conclude that it's only possible, 'that Christians, after
the event, remembered an unusual celestial happening and connected it with
Jesus' birth.'[7]

Ulrich Luz (1990), in his discussion of the historicity of Matthew 2, does
accept that the 7 BCE Saturn and Jupiter conjunction could fit the events
described. He notes, however, that the two planets were never close enough
to form one star and that Matthew's use of ἀστήρ means individual star and

not a group. Yet Luz concludes that such attempts to explain the Star 'rarely help' to explain the narrative. He concludes that a memory of some striking phenomenon could have existed in Matthew's community.

Donald Hagner (1993), who sees the Infancy Narrative as 'historical at its core', notes the 7 BCE conjunction (as well as the comet and supernova theory) though he draws no firm conclusion. He states that:

> In this phenomenon, whatever it was, the magi-astrologers perceived the sign of the fulfilment of the Jewish eschatological expectation concerning the coming king and so would have set off on their journey toward Jerusalem.[8]

Towards the end of the millennium, the *Jesus Seminar* (1998), while giving a black designation to Matthew 2.1–12, noted (along with the comet theory) the wide support for Kepler's 7–6 BCE conjunction in Pisces.[9]

Twenty-first century

Michael Green (2000), though citing numerous solutions, also puts forward the 7 BCE triple conjunction as the most likely of solutions noting, 'If this is in fact what arrested the attention of these star-gazing Magi, it isn't difficult to see how they would have interpreted it.'[10] Warren Carter (2000), referencing Raymond Brown, notes the comet, supernova and planetary conjunction of Jupiter and Saturn.

J.Neville Birdsall (2002) states that, 'no early quotation, allusion or comment ever read the words in an astrological sense.'[11] Yet he too can't fully dismiss the Star tradition. He suggests that an anti-astrological 'underplay' may have affected the tradition prior to its inclusion in Matthew with only the 'surviving and fossilised' phrase ἐν τῇ ἀνατολῇ (*in the east/at its rising*) having any direct link to the 'Magian horoscope.' N.T. Wright (2002) also suggests that the 'most likely' explanation is the 7 BCE conjunction.

Michael J. Wilkins (2003), though he ultimately favours an angel, cites the two *CKC Festschrifts*, David Hughes and Mark Kidger as his references with regard to the conjunction theories. Barbara Reid (2005) also refers to the 7–6 BCE conjunction, though she makes no firm conclusions. Likewise, according to John Nolland (2005), 'one might speculate' that the triple conjunction in Pisces of 7–6 BCE could have been taken to herald a royal birth associated with the Jews but in the end there's nothing in Matthew 2 which would lead to the identity of the Star.[12]

Finally, R.T. France (2007) notes the comet, conjunction and nova theories but suggests that the miraculous Star is perhaps more appropriate. However, he does conclude that, 'there is no improbability' of a real celestial event being the basis for the magi's 'initial deductions.'[13]

* * *

Though critics don't generally commit to any particular astronomical event or speak only of some *general phenomena* of astrological significance, the 7–6 BCE conjunctions remain the most common reference.

There's a trend for critics, even if not accepting a historical origin outright, to conclude cautiously that a historical origin *may* lie behind Matthew 2.1–12. Such caution, from a *historical* point-of-view. is correct and may be all that can be asserted.

Could the Star of Bethlehem have been astrological in origin?

The conjunction theory, with its symbolism of planets and constellations, is difficult to dismiss completely for it does appear to work well as a hypothesis: the planets Saturn and Jupiter (in Pisces or Aries) could be interpreted as depicting the birth of a ruler in Judea. Combine this with Matthew's use of μάγοι and Matthew's use of the astronomical term ἐν τῇ ἀνατολῇ, it becomes harder to refute such a conclusion.

When we add to the theory the ability of a planet both to appear to reverse course (go retrograde) and to appear stationary, this too becomes compatible with Matthew's claim that the Star changed direction and stood still over Bethlehem. It could even explain why Herod didn't 'see' the Star—only a trained astrologer would have known what to look for in the night sky and how to interpret it. The number of potential astrological events in the 7–2 BCE period perhaps also shed light on Herod's command to kill all those two years old and under.

It's for these reasons that the conjunction hypothesis remains the most accepted source for the Star, with one form or another being quoted in the media as the most likely solution or even as fact. But this hypothesis suffers from several serious problems (historical and scientific) that make this popular solution unlikely to have been what Matthew was portraying.

'The test of any hypothesis… is not that it resolves all doubts but that it offers the most consistent explanation, leaving few anomalies.'[14] Thus, in this section, we'll examine seven anomalies (in no particular order) that render this hypothesis (despite its initial appeal) inconsistent:

(Anomolies 1 to 3 also apply to the astronomical hypothesis. Two further anomalies—Matthew's idiosyncratic use of portents and the late first century BCE messianic, socio-political background—apply to both the astrological and astronomical hypothesis.)

1. Astrological conjunctions don't match Matthew's account

Matthew couldn't be *literally* portraying the actions of any real celestial event and ἀστήρ shouldn't be translated as 'planet(s).' The Star can't be a symbolic representation of a horoscope, for it's described as a *real physical body* acting as a guide and can't be interpreted as Hellenistic genethialogical judicial astrology.

2. Assumption that Matthew and Luke are writing two halves of the same story, which can harmonise into one smooth chronology

When historians are faced with two conflicting presentations of the same event, their usual methodology is to compare the account with existing historical records. As no eyewitness historical records exist for the birth of Jesus, and all later Patristic and apocryphal documents are based on Matthew and Luke's account, we're left with the problem of having only two early texts, both written 80–90 years after the events they're describing, that don't agree. We have no possible way of verifying their historical accuracy.

As N.T. Wright has pointed out, 'with most ancient history... we cannot verify independently what is reported in only one source. If that gives grounds for ruling it out, most of ancient history goes with it.'[15] However, Matthew 1–2 and Luke 1–2 purport to be two accounts *of the same event* and it appears that Matthew and Luke are not writing the same historical narrative but using a common core infancy tradition based on a mixture of historical nucleus and developing Christology. The two Infancy Narratives can't be harmonised into a single historical account.

3. Uncontrolled historical reconstruction

There are many examples of wild and speculative historical reconstructions to describe the actions, motivations and events that are devoid of any substantive evidence.

Given that only two differing New Testament texts have been transmitted which narrate the nativity, and that their historical verification is virtually impossible, speculation is all that's available. Such historical speculation and reconstruction is natural and allowable if presented cautiously and backed by solid research (it's what history is about) but it's rarely cautious when astronomers discuss the nativity, and tenuous arguments are often presented with no solid evidence. What we find is more *eis*egesis than exegesis. Some critics draw historical conclusions from what Soares Prabhu calls, 'evidence whose meagreness would leave a professional historian aghast.'[16]

The *fallacy of motivation* is evident in these theories, whereby the aims and reasoning of biblical characters are presented as fact without access to any solid primary evidence of their thoughts and with nothing more than the few passages of Matthew 2.1–12 and Josephus' accounts of Herod. It's sheer folly to attempt to reconstruct the psychologies of literary figures. To N.T. Wright, 'psychological theories of this sort—about people two thousand years ago in a different culture—are at best unprovable and at worst wildly fantastic.'[17] He observes that:

> Any jigsaw puzzle can be solved if we are allowed to create new pieces for it at a whim. But we should not imagine that historical scholarship built on this principle is of any great value.[18]

The most that can be offered (if we assume the account contains historical data) is the vague and cautious conclusion that *something* astronomical *may* have happened. We're left with open conclusions that can never be verified historically. To state that X, based on no solid evidence, *must be true* is a severe historical fallacy that seriously undermines any conclusions drawn from it.

4. No reference to an astrological conjunction of planets evident in Early Christian interpretation

The evidence has revealed no astrological interpretations among any of the Patristic commentaries on Matthew. Yet we must be aware of the dangers of arguing from negative evidence, the *fallacy of the negative proof*, which occurs when, 'a historian declares that, "there is no evidence that X is the case" and then proceeds to affirm or assume that not-X is the case.'[19]

Knowing something exists is different from knowing that something does not. Without studying *every* text, document or codex written by the early Church Fathers and Christian critics (an impossibility given what's been lost over time) it would be incorrect to claim that *nothing* astrological was written about Matthew 2.1–12 during this early period.

We can only go by the available evidence. Given the widespread and accepted usage of astrology in Jewish and Greco-Roman culture in the period of Matthew's writing and the centuries that follow, it can't be denied that the Patristic sources examined in this thesis never interpreted the Star as anything other than *a single, miraculous sign from God*, a new object outside the powers of the heavens.

If any early writings *did* make such an astrological claim, they must have been in a minority, exerting no influence on the wider 'miraculous' interpretation. In addition, socio-historical conditions provide support for concluding that 'no supporting evidence' equals 'no historical Star'.

5. Early medieval period as starting point for the doctrine of historical conjunctions (the triple conjunction theory only dates to 1604)

The astrological theory can't be accounted for prior to the early medieval period, and even then, only in the Sassanian-Islamic doctrine of historical horoscopes (general astrology). This doctrine, despite the use of Jupiter and Saturn, is a very different system from the Babylonian style astrology of the modern astrological conjunction hypothesis. The link between the two (and the origin of the modern theory) is the influence of the 1604 triple conjunction on Kepler's nova interpretation of the Star (Kepler being influenced by the 800-year grand conjunction doctrine).

6. Requirement of astrology to be a valid, observable science

It appears to be standard methodology for astronomers to search in the general confines of Jesus' birth dates, note what retrograde and stationary events might match Matthew 2, then appeal to contemporary astrological techniques and symbolism to explain the magi's reason for seeking him out. Ironically, given the nature of the astrological hypothesis, this appeal to astrology causes one of its most significant anomalies.

Astronomers generally assume that astrology is a baseless pseudo-science and not a verifiable scientific theory. But for the astrological hypothesis to work as a valid solution, and for the historical events that they believe Matthew (and Luke) is reporting to have occurred, *it's vital for astrology to both work successfully and be a valid observable phenomenon*. Otherwise, the whole basis of the hypothesis collapses.

If we instead tried to argue that Matthew was using astrology to provide a historical basis for his claim that the Star symbolised the Messiah, this would remove all elements of the historical accuracy that the hypothesis requires. Therefore, as those astronomers who propose the conjunction hypothesis treat Matthew and Luke as historically accurate, an inherent contradiction occurs as the science of astronomy tries to explain the seemingly accurate usage of a system that it rejects. Referring to Roman horoscopes, Ramsay MacMullen writes (my italics):

> Either ancient astrology had an accuracy lost, alas, to the modern world, or half the Roman aristocracy were at one time or another

promised great things; or, still a third possibility, *the stories of imperial horoscopes were invented after the event*. That last is surely the answer.[20]

7. Parsimony and the Occam factor

Though perhaps the weakest argument against the astrological theory, the principle of parsimony—with its condition that 'entities should not be multiplied beyond necessity' (a phrase attributed to William of Occam, 1285–1349)—can be used to demonstrate that the conjunction theory is *too complicated* and requires too many events and leaps of logic to be correct.

Many of the solutions fail the test of a good hypothesis. They, 'suggest explanations for all the data at the cost of producing a highly complex and convoluted hypothesis.'[21]

That astronomers rely on such complex solutions suggests there's a problem in correctly reading the text and that we must look for a simpler solution that better fits Mathew's theology and *Sitz im Leben*. We could counter argue that horoscopes and astrology *are* complex, but, again, the text doesn't suggest such a solution (anomaly 1).

* * *

The above inconsistencies demonstrate that there are more than just a few doubts remaining over an astrological origin for the Star. Even being cautious not to step into the trap of the fallacy of negative proof, what remains are deep flaws that the hypothesis fails to address successfully.

CHAPTER 10:
THE STAR AS A COMET (κομήτης)

The most common artistic image of the Star is as a comet-like object, moving through the sky with its tail trailing behind it. Such stars appear in works by Francesco d'Antonio (1394–1433), Giotto di Bondone (1267–1337), Antonio Busca (1625–1684), Gentile da Fabriario (1370–1427), Juan de Flandes (1496–1519) and Jean de Saint-Igny (1590–1647). Only Giotto is known to have used a real comet for his source.

In the first century, Greco-Roman world the most accepted view of comets derived from Aristotle (384–322 BCE), who saw them as sub-lunar objects in the upper atmosphere but below the heavenly spheres of sun, moon, planets and fixed stars.

Aristotle notes that Anaxagoras (500–428 BCE) and Democritus (460–370 BCE) interpreted comets as a group of planets touching each other; the Pythagoreans saw them as planets that did not rise far over the horizon, hence their infrequent sightings; Hippocrates of Chios (470–410 BCE) believed likewise but attributed their infrequency to their close proximity to the sun. Aristotle's own view (*Metaphysics* 344a–b) was that comets were caused by the rotating heavens of air and fire, 'so whenever the circular motion stirs this stuff up in any way, it bursts into flame at the point where it is most flammable'.

Fire became a popular explanation. Seneca (4–65 CE) agreed with Epigenes of Byzantium (*Naturales quaestiones* 7.30) who regarded comets as the product of whirlwind induced fires. Apollonius of Myndos, however, held the more modern view that they were distinctive bodies (*Naturales quaestiones* 7.17).

Being 'below the sphere of the heavens' provided an answer as to why comets appeared so close to the Earth and why many ancient writers described them as standing or a hanging over specific areas. Therefore, a comet *could* represent the Star, moving slowly through the sky from the east, and *hanging* over Bethlehem. But there's a problem with this theory—comets were primarily interpreted as negative signs.

Comets have always been linked to destruction or change. A well-known example from British history is the return of Halley's Comet on 24 April 1066 (as immortalised on the Bayeux Tapestry of 1070–1080) symbolising the doom of Harold II. The historian Holinshed in *The Chronicles of England, Scotland and Ireland* (1577) referred to a 'blazing star' in 1402 that foretold the defeat of Lord Grey:

> In the month of March appeared a blasing starre, first betweene the east part of the firmament and the north, flashing foorth fire and flames round about it, and, lastlie, shooting foorth fierie beams towards the north; foreshewing (as was thought) the great effusion of bloud that followed...[1]

Such fear appears in the comet reports of 1531, 1556, 1577–78 and 1580. In England, the astrologer and mathematician Thomas Digges (1546–1595) was requested to provide his opinion of the comet to the Privy Council and Dr Dee spent three days at court providing advice and assurance to Elizabeth I.

Returning to the ancient world, the *Sibylline Oracles* contain numerous references to earth shattering celestial events. In *Sibylline Oracle* 8.190–193, during the days of 'evil and doom':

> All the stars will fall directly into the sea,
> all in turn, and men will call a shining comet
> 'the star,' a sign of much impending toil,
> war, and slaughter.

Sibylline Oracle 3.334 (c. 163–145 BCE) states: 'in the west a star shall shine, which they shall call '*Comētēs*,' a sign to mortals of sword, famine, and death, destruction of leaders and of great illustrious men.'[2] R.H. Charles suggests this was the comet mentioned by Seneca (*Naturales quaestiones* 7.15) and which appeared at the death of Demetrius I of Syria (d. 151 BCE). However, the oracle refers to many men and not just one.

Al Wolters interprets the *Sibylline Oracle* comet as referring to the return of Halley's Comet between 24 September and 10 November (and again after 3 December; Halley's Comet always appears twice, before and after perihelion, as it swings around the sun), 164 BCE, which he associates with the death of Antiochus IV Epiphanes, the Maccabean Revolt and the dedication of the Temple in December 164 BCE. Wayne Horowitz argues that the perceived effects of this 164 BCE comet (and a second in 163 BCE), coming as they did during the Maccabean victory, were applied by the Jews during the First Revolt (66–73 CE) to the comet of 66 CE.

Manilius describes how comets cause plague, wars and treachery and how the comet of 9 CE occurred when three legions under Varus were destroyed by the Germans. Pliny (*Naturalis Historia* 2.92) writes of the portents of comets:

Sed cometes in occasura parte caeli est, terrificum magna ex parte sidus atque non leviter piatum, ut civili motu Octavio consule [43 BCE] iterumque Pompei et Caesaris [49 BCE] bello, in nostro vero aevo circa veneficium quo Claudius Caesar imperium reliquit Domitio Neroni [54 BCE], ac deinde principatu eius adsiduum prope ac saevum.

But sometimes there is a comet in the western sky, usually a terrifying star and not easily expiated: for instance, during the civil disorder in the consulship of Octavius, and again during the war between Pompey and Caesar, or in our day about the time of the poisoning which secured the bequest of the empire by Claudius Caesar to Domitius Nero, and thereafter during Nero's principate shining almost continuously and with a terrible glare.

This 'almost' continuous comet was probably the two that appeared between July to September 65 CE and January–April 66 CE.

Cicero (*Nat. D.* 2.14) describes comets, along with other natural phenomena, as bringers of 'dire disasters':

tum facibus visis caelestibus, tum stellis iis quas Graeci cometas nostri cincinnatas vocant, quae nuper bello Octaviano magnarum fuerunt calamitatum praenuntiae.

and also the appearance of meteoric lights and what are called by the Greeks 'comets' and in our language 'long-haired stars'. Such as recently during the Octavian war appeared as harbingers of dire disasters.

Despite the majority of negative comet reports, there are positive interpretations. The Alexandrian Stoic, Chaeremon (fl. 30–65 CE), who tutored Nero, wrote in his treatise *On Comets* that they could also herald good events. Marsilio Ficino (1433–1499), who believed the Star was a comet, cited both in his *De stella magnorum*.

Chaeremon was undoubtedly trying to placate Nero during the appearance of the 60 CE and 64 CE comets. Indeed, Origen's contemporary, Synesius of Cyrene, bishop of Ptolemais (370–430 CE), wrote in his early work, *Praise of Baldness*, that:

It is not even pious, in my opinion to call these stars, but if you wish to call them so, this much at least is clear, that hair is an evil, inasmuch as even in a star it produces perishable form. And whenever these comets appear, they are an evil portent... They assuredly foretell public disasters, enslavements of nations, desolations of cities, death of kings.[3]

Seneca likewise tried to turn the comet of 60 CE into a good omen by saying that it was a sign of prosperity under Nero and one that took away the bad reputation (*infamia*) of comets. However, Nero, ever paranoid and fully aware of the popular belief that comets indicated change, acted on the appearance of the 60 CE comet and Suetonius records an event that mirrors Herod's response to the magi:

Nec minore saevitia foris et in exteros grassatus est. Stella crinita, quae summis potestatibus exitium portendere vulgo putatur, per continuas noctes oriri coeperat. Anxius e are, ut ex Balbillo astrologo didicit, solere reges talia ostenta caede aliqua illustri expiare atque a semet in capita procerum depellere, nobilissimo cuique exitium destinavit ; enimvero multo magis et quasi per iustam causam daubas coniurationibus provulgatis...(*Ner.* 6.36)

Those outside his family he assailed with no less cruelty. It chanced that a comet had begun to appear several successive nights, a thing which is commonly believed to portend the death of great rulers. Worried by this, and learning from the astrologer Bilbillus that kings usually averted such omens by the death of some distinguished man, thus turning them from themselves upon the heads of the nobles, he resolved on the death of all the eminent men of the state ; but the more firmly, and with some semblence of justice, after the discovery of two conspirancies...

Nero's reign also saw the return of Halley's Comet in 66 CE, during the beginning of the First Jewish Revolt, during the visit of King Tiridates, who paid homage to Nero with accompanying magi and who returned home via a different route.

Comets as positive omens

Sibylline Oracle 5.240–241

In book five of the *Sibylline Oracles* (the book which contains the return of Nero and the advent of a saviour figure), we find the following in a section that's been entitled 'Praise and exaltation of the Jews' (5.238–241):

> There was once among men a shining light of the sun
> when the harmonious ray of the prophets was being spread abroad,
> a tongue dripping a beautiful drink for all mortals with honeyed sweetness;
> it made manifest, offered and effected gentle things for all.[4]

Comet of Mithridates

Another possible reference to comets as good omens is the two mentioned by Justin Martyr (c. 100–c165 CE) in his history of Mithridates VI Eupator, King of Pontus (who died in 63 BCE while Pompey was marching on Petra). Justin (*Epitome of Pompeius Trogus* 37.2.1), quoting from the earlier *Historiae Philippicae* of Pompeius Trogus, wrote:

> His future greatness was also predicted by celestial portents. For both in the year in which he was begotten [133 BCE] and in that which he first began to reign [120 BCE], a star, a comet, so shone on each occasion for seventy days the whole sky seemed to be on fire.

Chinese records clarify that comets *did* appear in the years referred to by Justin. The *Shih Chi* by Ssu-ma Ch'ien mentions a comet which appeared in the years of Yuanguang of the Western Han Dynasty (134–129 BCE) in the constellation of Fang (Scorpio), visible from Mithridates' birthplace in Sinope, and another comet in the years of Yuanshou (122–117 BCE).

The *Ch'ien-Han shu* (*History of the [Western] Han Dynasty*; c. 82 CE) may also describe the comet of 120 BCE. These two comets correspond to numbers 31 and 32 in John Williams' catalogue and Pliny notes that Hipparchus (161–126 BCE) had recorded a star which appeared in 134 BCE in the constellation of Scorpio. Without the Chinese records, such passages would have remained legends.

Signs of change

Michael Molnar argues that, far from being an example of a 'good omen', these comets were viewed as an omen of 'violent revolution' whose focus was altered by Mithridates to 'signify his struggle to evict the Romans from Asia Minor.'[5]

Hence, the appearance of comets heralded change and were bad or good omens depending on the observer's point of view.

The Chinese called some comets *sao-hsing* ('broom stars') and Chinese texts refer to the tails of these comets sweeping away the old traditions and order. A comment in the *Han-Shu* (regarding the comet of 5 BCE) states:

> Sui are the means of eliminating the old and inaugurating the new...
> The appearance of sui was a sign of change; the long period of its
> appearance was due to the importance of the incident [to come].

While Fang Hsüan-Ling (c. 635 CE) in the Chinese History of the Chin Dynasty (*Chin Shu*) records:

> The body is a sort of star while the tail resembles a broom... The
> appearance of a comet predicts military activities and great floods.
> Brooms govern the sweeping away of old things and the assimilation
> of new.

In a note to the appearance of Halley's Comet in 12 BCE, the *Han Shu* (1518) notes that a *hsing-po* had also appeared during the 'destruction of the Ch'in dynasty'.[6]

According to Colin Humphreys:

> The assumed astrological significance of comets to ancient civilizations
> is clear: they were interpreted as portents of gloom and death for the
> established order, but they were equally regarded as heralds of victory
> in war and the birth of new kings who would change the existing order.[7]

This image of the comet as a symbol of change (old Herodian/Roman rule to new rule of Christ) perhaps lends the comet theory the most credibility as a candidate for the Star.

'Comet' of 130 CE

In 130 CE, Antinous, a favourite companion of Hadrian (117–38 CE), drowned in the Nile (was sacrificed?) while accompanying the Emperor on a visit to Egypt. Hadrian stated (69.11.4) that he saw a star (ἀστέρα), which he took to be Antinous, 'and gladly lent an ear to the fictitious tales woven by his associates to the effect that the star had really come into being from the spirit of Antinous'.

Was this a comet? A.A. Barrett comments that this may refer to a nova and

Alexander von Humboldt (1769–1859) had recorded that a nova had appeared in 130 CE. However, Knut Lundmark queries as suspect any claim for a nova at this date and F.R. Stephenson records only a nova (*k'o-hsing*) in December–January 125–126 CE. Gary Kronk, in his *Catalog of Comets*, only records observations in 128, 132 and 133 CE. However, he does cite the 130 CE event in his list of 'Uncertain Objects'.

The constellation of Antonius was named at this time, being made up of six 'unformed' stars that made up the lower part of Aquila. Ptolemy notes its existence in his *Almagest* and Aquila would have been visible over Egypt in 130 CE. A nova might have appeared in Aquila in 4 BCE. Was the 130 CE event a second flare up of that nova?

Sidus iulium

One positive interpretation requires closer examination—this is Pliny's remark (*Naturalis Historia* 2.93) that, 'Cometes in uno totius orbis loco colitur in templo Romae' (*Comets is [are] worshiped in one place in the whole world, in the temple of Rome*).

The title *sidus Iulium* refers to two comets; one that had appeared at Caesar's death in 44 BCE when he received divine honours, and perhaps a second later in 17 BCE when Octavian was staging games in Caesar's honour. Dedicated to Julius' patron, *Venus Genetrix* (ancestress of both the Iulii and the Roman people), this second comet had appeared on the first day of the games (20 July) while a priest was sacrificing to Venus.

The comet was interpreted by Octavian and hence Roman poets as Caesar's soul ascending into heaven. The *Aeneid*, written in contemporary honour of Augustus, contains further allusions to Venus, stars and flames.

The stars could represent gods or deified rulers, and that the Stoic acceptance of this doctrine was dominant in Rome. Stefan Weinstock comments that this belief lay behind the unusual interpretation of the comets, though Robert Gurval sees the comet and star of Caesar as a slow developing tradition in Augustinian politics.

Observations

John Ramsey concludes his catalogue of 73 comets by observing that their Western interpretation as omens of war dates only from late date of the mid to late first century BCE, perhaps due to the plagues and civil war in the Empire. Indeed, Bradley Schaefer, in his study of thirty-five comet omens from the Roman and Byzantine periods (central and eastern Mediterranean regions), concludes that only two were positive. Every comet which appeared between 42 BCE and

14 CE was interpreted by historians as referring to death or defeat. Hence, Keener suggests that Herod saw the Star as the 'cosmic signal' of a new ruler 'indicating his own demise.'[8]

Comets of 5 and 4 BCE

5 BCE

The 5 BCE comet is recorded by Ma Duanlin (c. 1240–1280 CE) in his *Wenxian tongkao*:

> In the reign of Emperor Ai-Ti [6–1 BCE], the second year [5 BCE] of the epoch *Ch'ien-p'ing* [6–3 BCE], the second month [5 March–10 April], a comet [*hui-hsing*, sweeping star] appeared in *Ch'ien-niu* [Capricorn region] for about 70 days.[9]

The *Ch'ien-Han Chu* also records that it lasted for more than 70 days.

4 BCE

The 4 BCE. second comet is recorded in the medieval *Tung Keen Kang Muh* (1368 CE), 'In the third year of the same epoch, the third month, there was a comet in Ho-ku' and the *Chronicle of Silla* in the Korean *Samguk Sagi* (1145 CE), a 'sparkling star' appeared on a 'chi-yu day [Kronk notes that this date is impossible as the 'chi-yu' day came on the first and third months giving a date of 23 February or 24 April] second month, 54th year of Hyok-ko-se of Silla'. [10] This comet is also recorded in the *Ch'ien-Han Shu*, 'In the third month of Chi-yu... A comet appeared in the Ho-ku.' The Ho-ku/Aquila area of sky would have been visible in Judea and Babylon for most of the year.

The eighteenth-century cataloguer Alexandre Pingré had associated this comet with the birth of Jesus. However, Gary Kronk regards this ancient observation as indicating a 'misdated account' of the 5(4) BCE comet and that Pingré's Chinese translations had combined the two.

Applying the comets to Matthew 2

The problem with these two events is the different words used to describe comets in the Chinese records. There's confusion surrounding the word used to describe the second sighting. The Chinese 'Po hsing' refers to a comet without a tail and may have been a nova (a *K'o-hsing*). Though Kronk regards them as examples of the same event, opinion is divided on whether the 4 and 5 BCE events were novae or comets.

The existence of numismatic evidence, in the shape of Roman and Celtic coins from the very late first century BCE and early first century CE that depict a 'star' in Aquila, could tip the evidence towards a 4 BCE nova, as, perhaps, does a fresco from the Priscilla catacombs in Rome. Given such evidence, I interpret the 4 BCE event as a nova and the 5 BCE event as a comet.

Comet of 5 BCE
The shepherds watching their flocks in spring (Luke 2.8) matches up the Star with the Chinese account of a 19 May 19 to 16 June appearance.

Noting that the 5 BCE comet, as described in the Chinese records as appearing in Capricorn, C. J. Humphries suggests that in March-April this constellation, as seen from Arabia and its neighbours, was first visible in the morning twilight, hence 'seen at its rising'. Ptolemy and Pliny note that the direction a comet travels had significance. According to Ptolemy, this comet would have signified misfortune for Spain, Gaul and Germany, following Manilius' reckoning of lands influenced by Capricorn.

This comet was also visible for 70 days allowing a travel time of one to two months for the magi. Therefore, a maximum distance of 900 miles, from Babylon across the desert via the Fertile Crescent, would have been possible within two months. This appears to be compatible with the duration and movement of the comet as recorded by the Chinese.

Humphreys doesn't regard this comet as the *only* source for the Star. It's just the third and decisive event that convinced the magi that a great king had been born. Making the source of the Star as complex as the 3–2 BCE sequence, he combines the triple conjunction of Saturn and Jupiter in 7 BCE with the later massing, in Pisces, of Mars, Jupiter and Saturn in 6 BCE. This would have told the magi that a messiah-king would be born in Israel with the later appearance of the comet in Capricorn, the horns as the symbol of power and kings (rams and goats were symbols of power and leadership) telling them it had taken place.

Halley's Comet 12 BCE and 66 CE

The most widely known comet today is Halley's, and as early as 1913, it had been associated with the Star. Centuries before its 'discovery' (no doubt only by fortuitous timing), Giotto di Bondone is believed to have used its 1302 return as the source for his depiction of the Star in his *The Adoration of the Magi* at the Scrovengi Chapel, Padua.

This comet had been observed for millennia before Halley accurately predicted its cycle in 1705. For example, a Babylonian tablet (c. 164 BCE), now at the British Museum, describes observations of the comet; Rabbi Joshua, while journeying by sea to Rome with Rabbi Gamaliel (c. 95 CE) noted that 'A certain star rises once in seventy years and leads the sailors astray, and I suspected it might rise and lead us astray' while Isaiah 14.12 may refer to Halley in 540 BCE (interestingly, this is one year before Cyrus conquered Babylon).[11]

12–11 BCE Nativity?

A number of studies have attempted to reassess the chronology of Christ's life with all of them agreeing on a 12 BCE date for the nativity. All conclude that the Star was the 12 BCE return of Halley's Comet.

Jerry Vardaman

We know, according to the *Ch'ien Han-Shu* (1518), that Halley was visible for 56 days between August 26 and October 20, 12 BCE. It was during this visit that Dio recorded (54.29.8), 'The star called the comet hung for several days over the city and was finally dissolved into flashes resembling torches'.

Vardaman places Christ's birth in 12 BCE (and death in 21 CE) through a reassessment of the standard New Testament chronology via seven pieces of evidence:

1. Josephus' account (*Antiquities* 18.63–64) which places Jesus' ministry (according to Vardaman's interpretation) to around 15–19 CE.

2. Jesus had to have been born by 5 BCE if he was ἀρχόμενος ὡσεὶ ἐτῶν τριάκοντα ([beginning] *about thirty years old*) at the time of his ministry (Luke 3.23).

3. Luke originally wrote 'in the *second* year of Tiberius' (Luke 3.1), which had became corrupted to πεντεκαιδεκάτῳ (*fifteenth*) due to a scribal confusion between the numbers β and ιε′ giving John's baptistery the date of 13–14 CE.

4. That Quirinius was governor of Syria after the death of Agrippa in 12 BCE during the 12–11 BCE census year decreed by Augustus. As Luke refers to his πρώτη (*first*) census, this second was that mentioned in Acts 5.36, 37.

5. Paul's conversion must have been c. 27 CE.

6. Christ's death in 21 CE was a census year.

Vardaman gives 24 August to 17 October as the dates of Halley's passing and regards Mary and Joseph's movement to Bethlehem as being part of the Tabernacle season, citing John 1.14–18, καὶ ὁ λόγος σὰρξ ἐγένετο καὶ ἐσκήνωσεν ἐν ἡμῖν (*And the Word became flesh and lived [Tabernacled] among us...*).

Nikos Kokkinos
Kokkinos lies at the opposite end of New Testament chronology, placing the death of John the Baptist in 35 CE and the crucifixion in 36 CE. As he suggests Christ was nearing fifty when he died, he gives a 12 BCE date for his birth. According to Kokkinos, Luke mistakenly applied a tax assessment during Herod the Great's rule to Quirinius' later 6 CE Roman census.

Taking the details from Matthew 2 that the Star moved and hung/stopped in the sky and that comets can be bright, last for months and seem to appear stopped in the sky, Kokkinos concludes that the only phenomenon which fits the appearance and time is Halley's.

The 12 BCE theory requires a chronology that isn't accepted by the majority of scholars. John Meier comments that Kokkinos has missed Josephus' 'sloppy ordering of events in the latter part of the *Antiquities*' and that Vardaman's 'strange theory', for example, doesn't accurately translate Luke's use of ἀρχόμενος (Luke 3.23).[12]

An interesting idea is that that the Star was a response to the comet of 66 CE, especially with its connection to the First Revolt, Nero, the visit of Tiridates and messianism. This solution removes any historical phenomenon at the time of Christ's birth.

Josephus mentions a comet and sword that had appeared prior to the First Revolt against Rome. G. J. Goldberg suggests that the ἄστρον ἔστη ῥομφαί παραπλήσιον (*star resembling a sword*) and the κομήτης represent the visibility of the same comet's *two* tails and Chinese records do describe such comets, which they interpreted as heralds of war and destruction.

According to Chinese accounts, Halley's Comet was visible between 20 February and 10 April. Since Josephus records the comet as lasting for a year (ἐνιαυτὸς can mean 'period of one year'), Josephus is perhaps describing the two comets of 65 and 66, especially as they were also confused as one phenomenon by Pliny. As Figure 13 shows, a comet and 'sword-like' star might appear identical.

R, M. Jenkins
To Jenkins, the nativity is a work of Midrash and not a historical account. His reason for choosing the 66 CE comet is that it would have inspired Matthew to use it as the symbol of the Messiah, perhaps based on Numbers 24.17.

Jenkins interprets the movement of Halley's Comet as best matching the account of the Star in Matthew 2 and presents these details:

- On its first appearance, it rose in the eastern sky before dawn.
- At its brightest, it was visible through most of the night.
- It moved westward.
- Towards the end of its visibility, it was nearly stationary, as it had stopped moving west.
- It ended high in the southern sky, dimming rapidly.

Though Jenkins' conclusion is that the Star could have been anything from pure fiction to a conjunction to the 12 BCE return of Halley, he does refer to King Tiridates' celebrated visit to pay homage to Nero in 66 CE. The association between this high status visit of gift-bearing Parthian 'magi' paying customary political 'homage' (προσκυνεῖν, Matthew 2.2) and Matthew 2 has been made by many biblical commentators.

William Phipps

Phipps tries to link the comet to Numbers 24.17 via the *New English Bible* translation, which translates the Hebrew as a 'comet arising out of Israel' and the Dead Sea Scrolls references to Numbers 24.17 in 1QM associating said 'comet' with the coming messiah. Yet 1QM uses the word כּוֹכָב and LXX Numbers 24.17 speaks of ἀνατελεῖ ἄστρον ἐξ Ἰακώβ (*star out of Jacob*) so we can't conclude so easily that the passage refers to a comet.

G. J. Goldberg

Goldberg takes further the idea that Matthew was using Halley's 66 CE return, by applying a metaphorical and prophetic meaning to the comet. He connects the standing, sword-like comet with the standing sword wielding angels of Numbers 22.31 and 1 Chronicles 21.16 linking Matthew 2 with Davidic messianism, Numbers 24.17 and the report by Josephus that a χρησμὸς ἀμφίβολος (*ambiguous oracle*) prophesied a world ruler emerging from Judea.

His conclusion is that Matthew used a standing star over Christ in direct response to *War* (c. 75 CE) and the First Revolt, and that the evangelist believed the true Star of the Messiah had appeared decades earlier at Christ's birth. Though an interesting theory, it presupposes that Matthew knew Josephus (possible in the case of Luke), which can't be proven.

It also asks too much of the politically biased and ambiguous nature of Josephus' writings. Josephus' account of the star and comet were only a final 'and also' in a typical list of omens and portents, a digression from the world ruler prediction and not specifically related to it.

Wayne Horowitz

Horowitz, basing his short article on the evidence provided by Wolters (that the 164 BCE return of Halley's Comet was taken as a sign from God during the great victory of the Maccabean revolt), suggests that the 66 CE comet, was also interpreted as a similar sign from God. He asks, 'if the advocates of the Judean revolt against Rome in A.D. 66 knew of the tradition that a comet, or comets, appeared at the time of the Judean victory over Antiochus IV generations earlier.'[13]

To Josephus, the politico-religious fanaticism of the zealots were to blame for leading the Jews into war, along with various Roman insults, the dispute over Caesarea, and the ever possible threat of Temple desecration.

Was the Star a comet?

It's true that a comet comes closest to matching Matthew's description of the Star's movements, but problems remain:

1. Its appearance as a messianic herald would have generated fear and speculation, and Josephus (ever detailed in his account of Herod's reign) records none. If the events of Matthew 2 *were* historical, we should see some independent evidence for them.

2. Though Matthew does write that Herod and Jerusalem were troubled (ἐταράχθη) this is more to do with the magi's statement of a recently born βασιλεὺς τῶν Ἰουδαίων than any visible comet and Matthew's account depicts Herod, along with the whole of Jerusalem and Judea, as *ignorant* of any celestial phenomena.

3. The fact that Matthew used the word ἀστήρ and not κομήτης or ἄστρον ὁ κομήτης weighs against the comet theory.

4. The Star moves in a manner not possible in nature, *not even of a comet.*

These problems are removed if we conclude that the Star was a poetic symbol.

CHAPTER 11:
THE STAR AS A NOVA

Another popular solution to the Star is that it was a nova or supernova that had suddenly appeared in the sky as a 'new' star.

When the 1572 nova appeared, William Covell wrote that, 'All the world marked [the new star]... all the astronomers admired it, and remained yet astonished'. The later fiery trigon conjunction of 1583 seemed to vindicate the nova as the herald of a new epoch, a divine signal of world transformation.

It also generated a dispute over when the last nova had appeared. Cardan (1501–1576) and Valesius of Covarruvias (physician to Philip II of Spain) proposed that it was the reappearance of the Star, an ever existing object made visible by thinning air.

A 5 BCE nova?

Debate continues over which of the 4 and 5 BCE objects was a comet/nova. The Han Dynasty *Ch'ien-Han-Shu* records a comet in 4 BCE, which was visible in Ho-Ku/Aquila. Though appearing in *William's Comet Catalogue*, no motion is recorded. Was this stationary a nova and not a comet? Zhentao Xu, David W. Pankenier and Yaotiao Jiang only record the *po-hsing* of April 24, 4 BCE as a nova, and in 1924, a nova appeared close to the *Ch'ien* Aquilae location, suggesting that this was a second flare-up of the object recorded in 4 BCE.

K. Lundmark interprets the 5 BCE object as a nova, observing that its 70 day duration allowed time for the magi to travel from the east to Jerusalem. Stephenson likewise interprets the *hui-hsing* of 5 BCE as a nova, as does Jack Scarola who presents a detailed, if highly speculative, chronological account of how the magi travelled to Bethlehem. In addition, D.H. Clark, J.H. Parkinson and F.R. Stephenson also argue for a 5 BCE nova, though their conclusions have been disputed by C. Cullen.

The 'nova' of the Priscilla Catacomb

Attention has been drawn to evidence hidden in early Christian catacomb art. In the Christian catacomb of Priscilla in Rome there's a fresco depicting the scene of a shepherd with sheep among apple trees. C.M. Beehler concludes that this was painted *over* an earlier picture of the Madonna and child before which is a figure (perhaps Balaam) pointing upwards towards one of the 'apples'. Beehler regards the apples as stars from a crude star chart, painted over at a later date to hide their astrological meaning.

The red 'apples' and outline of the tree are visible to the middle and right. It's placed at the lower side of an archway. Near the top of the archway is a fresco of the good shepherd. Beehler sees, between these two frescoes, a star chart, with the figure of Balaam pointing to a particular star close above Jesus' head. Though the chart is distorted, she identifies it as the constellation of Aquila (the location of the *po-hsing* recorded in 4 BCE) and that this star represents the 5 BCE nova.

Beehler's drawing shows how she's matched this collection of apples/stars to Aquila. Comparing this to a modern star chart, we can see how Beehler has applied its cross-like shape with what sits sideways above the sheep on the right.

A 4 BCE nova in Aquila?

R.S. McIvor has provided evidence for what he believes represents a nova in Aquila, dating it to 4 not 5 BCE. Certain Roman coins of Tiberius (14–19 CE) and Domitian (81–96 CE) depict a large eagle standing on a globe. Likewise, Celtic coins minted by Tasciovanus (c. 20 BCE to 10 CE), Eppillus (c. 10–25 CE) and Caratacus (35–c. 43 CE) show an eagle and star. These three were all from Celtic dynasties that occupied southern England, and this period (10–40 CE), prior to the Icenian revolt of 61 CE, saw Roman influence on Celtic design.

McIvor interprets this eagle as the symbol for Aquila, due to the ancient interpretation of its star arrangement, and the 'star' as representing the nova. However, we must be aware of the highly symbolic nature of coinage. For example, Aquila (the eagle) was a bird consecrated to Jupiter and also the principal standard of the Roman Legions. The globus was a symbol of the world and represented the dominant rule of the Empire, thus the eagle on a globe was a symbol of the supreme power of Imperial Rome.

The 'nova' symbol on the Eppillus and Caratacus coins could be the common annulet-with-pellet mintmark or symbol. These 'pellet within ring' motifs, a symbol of continuity or eternity and Roman knighthood, appear on numerous Celtic coins, the majority of which feature horses or chariots.

The 4 BCE date is also given by A.J. Morehouse who has argued for the Star being, instead, a *supernova* in Aquila, which could explain its prominent existence on the Celtic and Roman coinage. Morehouse puts forward the Hulse-Taylor Pulsar (PSR 1913+16b), discovered in 1974, as the result of this event.

Supernova in 8 BCE

Recently, the astronomer F.J. Tipler has argued for the Star being a supernova in Andromeda. He begins by taking Matthew 2.1–12 to be a literal account, regarding the Star as being 'uniquely testable'.

Using Matthew 2.2 and 2.9, he calculates that the supernova occurred close to Jesus' birth on 22 March 8 BCE, a date associated with Augustus' known 8 BCE census of Roman citizens. He links this supernova theory with the popular acronychal rising of Jupiter and Saturn, presenting a second possible date of 21 September 6 BCE (with 25 December being the celebration of Christ's conception.)

Tipler's solution requires a Matthew-Luke harmony and a date arbitrarily based on the closest census prior to the death of Herod.

Kepler and the nova of 7 BCE

During Kepler's observations of the conjunctions in the constellation of Ophiuchus, he witnessed the appearance of a supernova between Jupiter and Saturn on 10 October 1604. This nova remained visible for 366 days and it Kepler believed it had been produced by the conjunction. As he considered this conjunction took place every 800 years, he calculated that such an event had also taken place in 7 BCE and that this too had produced a nova, the Star. However, Kepler still believed that the star which guided the magi was a miraculous event, something new.

Did this 7 BCE nova actually occur? If so, was it recorded? A study of records listing historical supernovae doesn't refer to any novae in 7 BCE so Kepler's theory of a nova at that time can't be supported. However, some researchers believe they have discovered this 7 BCE 'nova' in the form of a variable star known as Mira Ceti Maxima.

Variable stars: Mira

Variable stars are those that change in visual magnitude (brightness) over regular/ irregular periods of days or years. They can suddenly appear, as they grow bright then fade back into invisibility with the degree of change varying from star to star. The current system of describing star brightness was defined by Norman Pogson in 1856 (based on Hipparchus' star catalogue of 129 BCE). In this system, the brighter the object, the smaller the magnitude level:

Sun	-26.72
Full moon	-12.5
Venus	-4.74
Jupiter	-2.1
Sirius	-1.46
Canopus	-0.72
Rigel	0.12
Pole Star	2.0
Andromeda Galaxy	5.0

All variable stars are today known as 'Mira' types after Mira Ceti, a star in the southern constellation of Cetus (Whale or Sea Monster) and the first variable to be discovered. It's been argued that Mira Ceti was the Star. Mira's variable range is +10 to +3 and it was its brightening that gave it the appearance of a nova.

As the 1596 and 1609 observations were both when Mira was close to Jupiter, C. Sigismondi's argument is that Mira had been observed near the triple conjunction of Jupiter and Saturn in 7–6 BCE and was what had been hypothesised by Kepler. Indeed, in 1609 its discoverer, Fabricius, notes in a letter to Kepler:

> What is to be noticed, Jupiter was almost in the same place that the one of [15]96. I can't enough contemplate the admirable Work of God, and see here, my Kepler, that my [star] among new stars and comets is real, it is not created ex novo, but they are sometimes deprived of the light, and nevertheless, they complete in this way their motions.[1]

The magi, studying the predicted conjunctions, would likewise have observed Mira near Jupiter.

Analysing the average maxima of Mira, Sigismondi *et al* concluded it was most likely to be at its brightest every twenty-one years. Their criterion for applying Mira to the Star was that it had to be visible to the naked eye but not noticeable unless looked for and to have vanished and become visible a second time.

The Star's movement is explained away as the simple 'motion of the observers to a point-like source at infinity.' Thus, the unatural movement of Jesus' Star (Matthew 2.9) is explained away as natural stellar parallax.

M.B. Richardson's argument for Mira requires the magi to be Zoroastrians. As they worshipped fire, this would have drawn their attention to the sudden appearance of Mira in 6 BCE, a deep yellowy red star. He also associates Mira with Gayomart/Gayomard, the Zoroastrian god of birth.

Mira would have been seen by the magi in the east rising heliacally but when would this have taken place? On 19 April 6 BCE ideal conditions existed for its appearance. If the magi visited Bethlehem on 31 May 6 BCE, via Mar Elias and Rachel's tomb, at 3.50 am Mira would have been at magnitude 1.3 just above Bethlehem. At 4.16 am, it would have stood over the present day Basilica.

Interestingly, and Richardson is unique in offering this interpretation, when he speaks of the star being 'above' he means that it's on the horizon, standing over Jesus *from the side* and not when it was in the heavens at its zenith. Yet this doesn't equate with Matthew's depiction of the star at 2.9 nor his use of ἐστάθη ἐπάνω.

If Mira reaches maximum brightness approximately every twenty-one years, why wasn't it discovered until 1596? Its discovery seems to have taken place when conjunctions of Jupiter were being observed so why wasn't it observed and recorded by Babylonian astrologers in 7–6 BCE?

There are those who argue for ancient observations of variable stars. C. Sigismondi *et al* note the interpretation by Manitius, in the Greek-German astronomical appendix of the 1894 edition of Hipparchus, of the star 'epi tes lopsias' ('over the finbacks'—whale, sea monster) as Mira. D. Hoffleit argues that the first four variable stars discovered in the West (Mira, Chi Cygni, R Hya and R Leonis) were all recorded earlier by Chinese/Korean observers as 'guest stars' (novas) and the variable light of the star Agol (an eclipsing binary) was also noted in ancient Arabic astrology.

Mira being seen during the conjunctions of Jupiter and Saturn in 1596 and 1609 this doesn't imply that it was also seen in 6 BCE. The lack of Chinese nova records for this year tips the evidence towards Mira not being observed in antiquity.

Even if it was observed and recorded by astronomers, why was it regarded as significant enough to be 'followed' in the first place? Mira could be seen in the sky every twenty-one years. They also fail to provide a convincing reason for its supposed two appearances. Stating that 'Jupiter and Saturn…could help the Magi to see Mira twice…' doesn't constitute a strong enough argument.

A faint star that reached its brightest every twenty-one years (even if it were observed just once) is hardly a credible candidate for the Star as Matthew portrays it.

* * *

Could the Star have been a nova? Though this is a common solution, it's extremely unlikely as a nova couldn't have behaved in the manner in which Matthew describes the Star. Also, novae weren't seen as important astrological events by any major Western astrologers of the Roman Period. No mention of such objects appears in the astrological treatises of Ptolemy, Dortheus, Hephaestion, Firmicus or Valen. Ignatius used language and imagery that *could* imply a nova, but this 'star' more likely represents Christ himself or his existence outside the influence of astral fate.

Whether comet or nova, an event of some kind took place in Aquila, as the numismatic evidence (and perhaps the Priscilla fresco) portrays. It's possible that a local memory of this phenomenon was Matthew's source.

CHAPTER 12:
THE STAR AS A METEOR

According to Patrick Moore, the Star was one or two meteors that passed over in the direction of Jerusalem/Bethlehem. He imagines the magi seeing a brilliant meteor streaking across the sky from east to west, leaving a visible trail in the sky that would have remained for hours. It was a random, brilliant event, localised and moving in a specific direction.

Meteor showers are caused by the Earth's movement through cometary debris. This debris burns out at a height of fifty miles as it moves through the atmosphere and the break up and deceleration of dust particles result in a bright trail across the sky as friction heats them up. All meteors come from a specific point in the sky known as the radiant and showers are named after the constellation the radiant lies in, for example, the Leonids (Leo), Lyrids (Lyra) and Taurids (Taurus).

The density of showers is known as the zenithal hourly rate (ZHR). This is the number of meteors seen by the naked eye while the radiant is at its zenith. Weak showers have less than five while the Perseids and Gemenids can have over seventy per hour. Showers can be erratic, however, and Leonid meteor storms with a ZHR of thousands occurred in 1833, 1866, 1966 and 2000.

Though Chinese records of meteor falls show that such short lived events were regarded as important enough to be catalogued, it's in the cuneiform omen literature of the first and second millennium BCE that we observe their power as omens.

The Akkadian (Babylonian and Assyrian) word used for meteor was *kakkabu* and in Sumerogram, MUL. Both could mean star, constellation or planet. However, when associated with meteors, *kakkabu* occurs with *sarāru* (to flash) *maqātu* (to fall). Two examples demonstrate the oracular nature of meteors and meteorites.

Letter from court astromancer

> If a great star (MUL GAL) flashes in the east and goes down in the
> west, and its train is greatly extended(?) and lies (there)(?), the army
> of the enemy will be destroyed in battle... Two great stars flashed one
> after the other in the middle watch.[1]

Faint meteor omens from the Enūma Anu Enlil

> If a meteor flashes from the middle of the sky and disappears (on the
> horizon) in the west: a mighty rebellion will break out in the land.
> (Ishtar 63 iv 9)

> If a meteor flashes from south to north: in six months ... will rise, and
> the king of Amurru will be ruined. (Ishtar 63 iv 10)[2]

Could a flashing meteor have been the source of Matthew's star? The problem is
that (despite their sudden fiery appearances) they are short-lived events.

> A bright meteor you see for one or two seconds and in exceptional
> cases as much as 10 seconds. It would have appeared and disappeared
> so quickly the wise men would have had to have jet propelled camels
> to have followed it.[3]

Ancient oriental accounts of meteor showers don't record any taking place in
7–1 BCE. Susumu Imoto and Ichiro Hasegawa only give dates of 15 BCE, 12 BCE
and 36 CE, but Moore is talking about random meteors and not showers. The
main problem is that meteors couldn't act in the way Matthew describes. Moore
agrees that 'this would certainly be very un-meteoritic behaviour,' but accounts
for this by allowing Matthew 'a sufficient degree of poetic licence.'[4]

According to Moore, the appearance of the second meteor 'would certainly
be taken as a sign that something unusual was about to happen in the direction
indicated.'[5] David Hughes agrees that such an event, if it appeared as a fireball,
would have convinced the magi that 'the phenomenon was a miracle', especially
if the second appeared in the same place as the first. Yet he contradicts himself
by saying 'It is in any case highly unlikely that the magi would have regarded a
meteorite fall as a miracle.'[6]

As well as their short-lived existence, this lack of symbolic meaning is a
problem for the meteor theory (despite the year of Julius Caesar's birth [100 BCE]

being marked by a falling meteor.) There is however, one event in which a meteor attained cultic significance.

> At Aphaca in Syria, where there was a famous temple of Astarte [Venus], the signal for the celebration of the rites was apparently given by the flashing of a meteor, which on a certain day fell like a star from the top of Mount Lebanon into the river Adonis. The meteor was thought to be Astarte herself.[7]

* * *

However, a meteor could never have acted as Matthew describes. Not even Moore's appeal to poetic license can salvage the meteor as Matthew's source.

CHAPTER 13:
THE STAR AS VENUS, THE MORNING STAR

Patrick Moore commented that, 'If the wise men could be deceived by Venus, they could not be very wise!'[1] Yet the symbolism and mythology surrounding Venus (Anat, Astarte, Asherah, Isis, Inanna, Ishtar, Aphrodite in the ancient world does present a possible link to the birth of the messiah. Indeed, it's the one phenomenon that's specifically described as rising in the east.

Also linked to Venus are Eos (goddess of dawn) and the Titan, Astraeus (dawn wind) who were the parents of Phosphorus (Φωσφόρος) the *light-bringer* (*Lucifer*). As a personification of Venus, Phosphorus is the only planet mentioned in Greek literature prior to the fourth century BCE. In mythical language, the emergence of dawn in the east caused the stars to merge with the light and Astaeus, the fertilising wind, acts on Eos who becomes the mother of the morning star, Venus. This event also occurs for Venus as the evening star.

The morning star is thus Eos' son Φωσφόρος and the evening star is her other son Ἔσπερος. Indeed, knowledge of these as two aspects of the same planet was identified as far back as 540 BCE.

Apart from the references to Asherah, Venus is a planet specifically mentioned in the Old Testament.

Isaiah 14.4b–21 is a poem (c. 734–705 BCE), which presents joy at the fall of an unknown Babylonian tyrant (14.12–15):

How you are fallen from heaven,
O Day Star [הֵילֵל] son of the Dawn!
How you are cut down to the ground,
you who laid the nations low!
You said in your heart,
'I will ascend to heaven;
I will raise my throne
above the stars of God;
... I will make myself like the
Most High.'

But you are brought down to Sheol,
to the depths of the Pit

This day star or light of the morning has been seen as representing Venus, the morning star. The LXX reads, Πῶς ἐξέπεσεν ἐκ τοῦ οὐρανοῦ ὁ ἑωσφόρος ὁ πρωὶ ἀνατέλλων (*Look how you have fallen from the sky, O shining one, son of the dawn!*) and Jesus makes a reference to this passage in Luke 10.18, when he says that, Ἐθεώρουν τὸν Σατανᾶν ὡς ἀστραπὴν ἐκ τοῦ οὐρανοῦ πεσόντα (*I watched Satan fall from heaven like a flash of lightening*).

The Hebrew הֵילֵל means 'the shining one' or 'light-bearer', which Jerome's (383–405 CE) Latin Vulgate translated as 'Lucifer' (*Quomodo cecidisti de caelo, Lucifer, qui mane oriebaris? Corruisti in terram, qui vulnerabas gentes* [Isaiah 14.12]). In the *Aeneid*, Venus and the Morning Star are also called *Lucifer*.

According to George Grey, this association of the king with Venus is the result of phraseology connected with an astral hero myth plus Venus as a natural phenomenon (as Venus can contrast between brilliant visibility and total disappearance). Edward Kissane likewise sees an unknown myth behind this poem, an allusion to a minor god who tried to overthrow the Chief of the Gods, and was cast out of heaven. To this end, Kissane notes that הֵילֵל is mentioned as the son of (Canaanite/Babylonian) Shahar (son of El) in one of the *Ras Shamra* documents. Isaiah 14.12 could refer to 'Helel, son of Shahar' that is, 'Morning, son of the Dawn.'

'Morning star' in the New Testament

The morning star is specifically mentioned twice in the New Testament. In Revelation 22.16 when Jesus says, ἐγώ εἰμι ἡ ρίζα καὶ τὸ γένος Δαυίδ, ὁ ἀστὴρ ὁ λαμπρὸς ὁ πρωϊνός (*I am the root and descendant of David, the bright morning star*) and in 2 Peter 1.19 (c. 100–150 CE) where the author writes:

Καὶ ἔχομεν βεβαιότερον τὸν προφητικὸν λόγον, ᾧ καλῶς ποιεῖτε προσέχοντες ὡς λύχνῳ φαίνοντι ἐν αὐχμηρῷ τόπῳ, ἕως οὗ ἡμέρα διαυγάσῃ καὶ φωσφόρος ἀνατεί λη ἐν ταῖς καρδίαις ὑμῶν,

So we have the prophetic message more fully confirmed. You will do well to be attentive to this as to a lamp shining in the dark, until the day dawns and the morning star rises in your hearts

Note that Revelation refers to 'a bright morning star', while Peter uses the specific word φωσφόρος (cf. ἑωσφόρος, i.e. Eosphoros—another name for Venus rising in the east.) In 1.19, 2 Peter tells us that Jesus is the morning star, Venus, who will return to illuminate the world. As Venus heralded the dawn, so will Jesus bring light to the darkness.

Luke 1.78 refers to ἀνατολῇ ἐξ ὕψους (lit. *rising sun from heaven*). E.M. Sidebottom interprets Luke 1.78 as referring to the day (the sun) and interprets 2 Peter 1:19 in the same manner. Ray Summers also sees the φωσφόρος of 2 Peter 1.19 as being the sun, but J.N.D. Kelly disagrees with such interpretations and sees the morning star imagery being derived directly from Numbers 24.17 and the 'star out of Jacob'. Indeed, Revelation 22.16 is associated most with Numbers 24.17 and Isaiah 11.10.

As Venus was a special celestial body, associating Jesus with this planet wouldn't have been a random occurrence. It's possible, given the status of Venus in the ancient world, that the author of Revelation was making Jesus palatable to the pagan world beyond Judaism by portraying him as equal to or greater than the many Venus deities of the times.

Outside the New Testament, Tertullian associated Venus with Jesus' birth via a messianic interpretation of Psalm 110:

> Now they say that this Psalm was a chant in honour of Hezekiah, because 'he went up to the house of the Lord,' and God turned back and removed his enemies. Therefore, (as they further hold,) those other words, '*Before the morning star* [προ Εωσφόρου] *did I beget thee from the womb*,' are applicable to Hezekiah, and to the birth of Hezekiah.

Psalm 110 may be described as a royal psalm, an enthronement or public address, perhaps part of a royal liturgy or the annual liturgy of the autumn festival. It was interpreted messianically by Christians but doesn't feature in pre-Christian Jewish literature.

Though Tertullian believed Psalm 110 referred to King Hezekiah, it's much more likely it was addressed to David or some other Davidic king. Justin Martyr applies the Psalm to Jesus and refutes Trypho's claim that Hezekiah was the one referred to in the Psalm. Modern interpretation dates the psalm to the early monarchy period, though M. Treves derives a Hasmonean date from what he perceives to be an acrostic in the psalm: שמען אים = '*Simon* [Maccabee] *is terrible*'.

Tertullian's reference to Jesus' birth being at night and before the morning star indicates, through his interpretation of Psalm 110, what he thought the Star was. The Hebrew of Psalm 110.3 says מרחם משחר (*mērehem mišḥār*)—'from the womb of the morning'—and the word משחר (*morning*) can be translated as 'dawn'. The morning star of Venus, rising before the dawn, is the interpretation given in the Vulgate translation of *ex utero ante luciferum geniu te*.

Psalm 110.3b suffers from textual corruption that's made translation difficult, although William Brown translates 110.3 as, 'In holy splendour, out of the womb towards the dawn go forth! Like (the) dew. I have begotten you'.[2]

Gary Rensburg comments that Brown's version, 'bears only slight resemblance to what has been transmitted by the ancient Jewish tradents' and interprets מרהם to mean 'rain' and not 'womb' translating the passage as, 'In the manifestation of holiness, with the rain of the dawn, yours is the dew of your youth.'[3] This presents a much different meaning to v3 than the usual 'womb' translation would give.

The connection between מֹשָׁחַר and the dawn morning star of Venus is highly probable, so we can conclude that Tertullian's interpretation of Psalm 110, plus 2 Peter 1.19 and Revelation 22.14 all associate the morning star (Venus) with Jesus. Indeed, if the 'association is presupposed', 'it would have been easy to read the psalm's words as prophesying the events Matthew narrates.'[4]

G. Mackinlay

Mackinlay argues that Venus had guided the magi to Jesus in 8 BCE; specifically, the 8 April to 10 December 'morning star' period. He gives 20 September for the date of Jesus' birth. The year 8 BCE is based on his belief that this was the date of an enrolment decree of Augustus, which he equates to Luke 2.1–3, Acts 11.28. The day and month aren't based on any specific chronology, but due to Mackinlay's desire to have as much time as possible between the first rising of the morning star and the magi's visit.

J.G. Frazer

Frazer's theory is more mythological. He noted that when the Emperor Julian first approached the city of Antioch in Syria, he was praised as a god and people cried out that the star of salvation had dawned on them from the east. The Emperor may have arrived in the city during the celebrations of Adonis when the rising star, Venus, was emerging on the eastern horizon.

Venus was associated with Astarte, Adonis' mistress and the festival of Adonis was timed (according to Frazer) to coincide with the rising of Venus as the Morning star:

> We may surmise that it was the morning star which guided the wise men
> of the east to Bethlehem, the hallowed spot which heard, in the language
> of Jerome, the weeping of the infant Christ and the lament for Adonis.[5]

Jerome (*Epistle* 58.3) and Origen refer to Bethlehem as a centre for the cults of Adonis and Tammuz. According to Frazer, this gives an Adonis/Venus morning star rite in Antioch, home of Matthew's community.

Myrrh (σμύρνα or ζμύρνα in the alternative spelling, Latin *murra*), one of the magi's three gifts, was also used as incense in the festivals of Adonis (who was born from a myrrh tree or had a virgin mother called Myrrh). It's more likely that the arrival and gifts of the magi is part influenced by Isaiah 60, Psalm 72 as well as Psalm 110. Here a Solomon/Jesus typology emerges as gold and frankincense is associated with Solomon and the Temple.

Joseph Campbell

The folklorist and anthropologist Joseph Campbell (1904–1987), who fused Frazer's ideas with the archetypal psychology of Jung, also notes the rising star of Sirius and points out that the traditional date of the visit of the magi, 6 January, was also the date of the birth of Aion (Osiris, Horus, Mithras, Tammuz, etc) from the Greek goddess Kore (Isis), 'the maiden', as celebrated in Alexandria. Epiphanius (315–403 CE) describes this festival of Kore (*Penarion* 51):

> On the eve of that day it was the custom to spend the night in singing and attending to the images of the gods. At dawn a descent was made to a crypt, and a wooden image was brought up, which had the sign of a cross and a star marked on hands, knees and head. This was carried round in procession, and then taken back to the crypt; and it was said that this was done because 'the maiden' had given birth to 'the Aion'.[6]

Isis, as another Venus-deity, was associated with Sirius (the Dog Star), a bright star at the feet of Orion, which represented Osiris. The first heliacal appearance of Sirius announced the rising of the Nile floodwaters (great inundation) and was the start of the Egyptian Sothic year. It was also seen as the restoring power of Osiris with the star foretelling his coming.

J. Noiville

Noiville also draws a connection between the birth of Jesus and Kore. He saw Venus as the representation of a Nabataean Sun-God known as Dushara whose mother was Chaamu (Kore). This God, in the form of a black stone, had its cult centre at Petra. However, Noiville appears to be wrong when he refers to Kore as Dushara's mother for this was in fact Kaaba. It was Dushara's consort Allat who was later Hellenised to be equated with Venus in her aspect of Caelestis ('celestial').

＊

Was Venus the Star? As one of the best known and symbolic planets in the ancient world with a mythology dating back millennia before Matthew was composed, Venus couldn't have been the Star. Venus removes any of the uniqueness that's essential to Jesus' star and, apart from being visible in the east, meets none of the required criteria.

CHAPTER 14:
PORTENTS AND SIGNS

Matthew's Gospel is distinctive in having a larger number of oracles, portents, dreams and miracles, all designed to disclose God's divine purpose in Jesus. Here we shall also focus on Jesus' death, whose portents greatly surpassed those of his birth, and why this has an impact upon our interpretation of his birth.

Matthew not only records the darkness (σκότος) from 'noon till three in the afternoon' and the splitting of the Temple veil but further phenomena special to his Gospel; an earthquake that splits rocks, the raising of *saints* who (after Jesus' own resurrection) left their tombs and wandered into Jerusalem *for all to see*, and a second earthquake (σεισμὸς) when the angel descended to roll back the stone. The purpose of such eschatological and apocalyptic miracles and motifs in Matthew are to intensify and signify both the coming of a new age and the confirmation of Jesus' divinity and righteousness.

All have parallels in Greco-Roman literature. For example, *of earthquakes and splitting rocks* see Judges 5.4; Isaiah 5.25; 24.18; Ezekiel 37.7; 38.19 and Jeremiah 4.23–24 and *of opening tombs and rising of the 'holy ones'* see Ezekiel 37.12–13, 24–25 and LXX Isaiah.

If such miraculous events, witnessed by Jerusalem, High Priests, and Roman troops (and no doubt Pilate himself) are absent from Josephus, contemporary literature or eyewitness oral tradition, the events of Matthew 2 are in good company. Indeed, 'not a few interpreters balk at the thought of many known risen dead being seen in Jerusalem—that large-scale a phenomenon should have left some traces in Jewish and/or secular history!'[1] Both can be classed as examples of Matthew's idiosyncratic style, 'playing up of Jesus' majestic deity.'[2]

This thesis is in agreement with Raymond Brown's interpretation that Matthew has 'reshaped and rewritten' *popular* material, perhaps, 'the same circles that supplied some material in the infancy narrative (especially the story of the magi, the star, and the wicked king.'[3] Also:

> The star that came to rest over the place where the child Jesus could be found belongs in the same context as the dead rising from the tombs

and coming into the holy city to be seen by many on the occasion of Jesus' resurrection.[4]

Thus, Brown calls Matthew the more 'folkloric' of the two Infancy accounts. Of further significance is how much Matthew 2 and 27-28 parallel each other structurally.

This doesn't preclude the possibility that a real historical event lies behind the Star, but it does make it easier to present the Star as an idiosyncratic portent, a poetic product of Matthew's theology.

The danger we face in zooming into such a detailed analysis of the Star is that of missing the wider picture. 'Unless the details are seen against the background of the larger whole, we are liable to be seriously misled.'[5] Although the astrological background to Matthew 2 is well represented (as are detailed astronomical calculations), what's missing is a clear socio-political background. *If* the Star had been as Matthew described, it should have caused an effect significant enough to have generated ripples throughout Roman administered Judea *and* the wider Empire.

Roman political background: Eastern frontier

After the surprise defeat at Carrhae of the Roman Triumvir M. Licinius Crassus in 53 BCE, the Parthians of Iran quickly became Rome's single prime threat to her eastern frontier. Being the only threat comparable in size and power to the Roman Empire itself, over the succeeding centuries campaigns against Parthia were waged by such figures as Mark Anthony, Octavian, Tiberius, Nero, Trajan and Septimus Severus.

As the front line, Syria was always under threat and Rome's entire Syrian defensive system was diverted towards Parthia. The threat became real in 40 BCE when the Parthians invaded and, turning towards Judea, interfered with Hasmonean rule by removing Hyrcanus II and installing Antigonus onto the Judean throne.

It was on 'the East' that subjects of the first century placed hopes of liberation. For the eastern direction having connotations of paradise and righteousness see Isaiah 41.2; Baruch 4.36–7; 5.5; and LXX Psalm 97.11. It also has a link to 'mighty deeds'.

Apart from being a military buffer zone between Rome and Parthia, Israel was also a vital source of corn and helped to safeguard the Empire's largest corn supplier, Egypt. Thus, any social destabilising of the region would have had serious military and economic consequences for Rome. At all costs, it had to remain under tight control.

Herod the Great

Herod (a Roman supporter, whose father, Herod Antipater, had been appointed governor of Judea in 47 BCE by Julius Caesar) was forced by these invading Parthians to flee to Rome (via Alexandria where he was met by Cleopatra). In Rome, he was greeted by both Mark Anthony and Octavian and there the Senate proclaimed him king of Judea. His reputation in the Empire was great enough for the Neronian satirist Persius (34–62 CE) to cite his name in connection with Jewish festivities.

With help from Mark Anthony and two Roman legions, Herod re-conquered Jerusalem in 37 BCE, disposing of Antigonus and installing himself as king. However, Anthony's later disastrous campaign against Parthia caused Herod to fear a second Syrian invasion, especially as the Hasmonean Hyrcanus II resided in Parthia and was favoured by the Babylonian Jews.

Fortunately for Herod, no further invasion took place and he would spend the rest of his reign (until his death in 4 BCE) fortifying his military and social position (with palace-fortresses) and executing those who threatened his rule (family, friends and subjects alike). Herod was also aware that, being an Idumean, he was regarded as a foreign ruler and not entitled to rule. Hence his early marriage to Mariamne, the granddaughter of Hyrcanus II. His effective removal of Jewish self-rule, ending of Sanhedrin power and his interference in the appointment of High Priests increased his unpopularity.

Given that Herod had even killed his sons in a dispute over succession, if, into this social and political context, a magian embassy ($\pi\rho\acute{\epsilon}\sigma\beta\hat{a}$) arrived by caravan on the difficult and dangerous roads from the Parthian east, stating that another *non-Roman appointed* royal claimant to the throne had come, particularly a messianic one, it would have generated serious political and religious fallout. (The popular Christmas image of three lone wise men travelling on camels through the desert would probably have led them to certain death long before they reached Bethlehem. A combination of bad roads and the ever-present danger of bandits meant that travel by protected caravan was the only way to arrive safely.)

Augustus would soon be entering into a formal diplomatic treaty with Parthia (c. 1 CE), one that defined their spheres of influence and gave Rome the power to proclaim the kings of Armenia, an independent kingdom which acted as a kind of buffer zone. Again, we would have expected a noticeable political reaction if an eastern group, influenced by astrology (Augustus had made astral divination relating to a ruler illegal and punishable by death) wandered into Jerusalem proclaiming the arrival of a king.

Augustus relied on Herod, his client-king, to keep the province under tight control and free from social unrest. Herod, as part of the patron-client relationship with Augustus, offered allegiance/loyalty through political and financial support to Rome. Hence, the magi's news wouldn't have pleased the already paranoid and increasingly ailing Herod, by now a nearly seventy-year-old ruler, still fearful of potential Parthian invasion and continued Hasmonean popularity in addition to social unrest from a population resistant to high taxes, foreign rule and his 'Hellenistic' approach to Jewish religion and architecture.

Herod may even have harboured messianic aspirations himself. The connections between the Davidic Messiah and Temple imagery could also shed light on his motives for rebuilding the Temple—to proclaim himself as the legitimate βασιλεὺς τῶν Ἰουδαίων (Matthew 2.2) in the eyes of Israel.

Messianic hope and expectation

Messianism during the intertestamental period saw the post-exilic hope of a restored Davidic dynasty shifting to the expectation of a divinely *anointed* (not a messianic figure who was himself divine) eschatological figure. Though there's little literary evidence for messianism between 500–200 BCE, evidence suggests that the idea of royal kingship began to revive during the Hasmonean period.

Messianic doctrines were complex, varied and diverse, and Oegema's study of messianic texts from c. 300 BCE to 135 CE reveals the many and varied forms of messianic expectation. It's clear is that no single form of Jewish 'messianic expectation' existed in the first century BCE. However, enough evidence survives to be certain that at least some form of Davidic Messiah expectation did exist.

When discussing messianism in the framework of the New Testament it's important to be aware of the difference between the expected Jewish messianic king and the later Christian Christ. The danger is in viewing Jewish messianic literature through the lens of later Christian messianic thought.

N.T. Wright, looking for a pattern in Jewish messianism, states that it's wrong to assert that Jewish messianic ideas was quickly abandoned by the early Church and suggests that early Christians retained a modified Jewish form of messianism as applied to Jesus.

The *Psalms of Solomon* and the Dead Sea Scrolls present a concentration of extra-biblical writings devoted to Davidic hope in the first century BCE.

Psalms of Solomon

These *Psalms*, written not long after Pompey's entry in Jerusalem in 63 BCE or perhaps later during Herod's reign (c. 37 BCE), have been called the, 'earliest explicit intertestamental expectation of a Davidic messiah' and the first Jewish text, 'to express unmitigated hostility to Rome.'⁶ ⁷

The Psalms looks forward to the day when God will bring forth a new king, *one descended from David*, to rid Jerusalem of the Gentiles. For example (17.21–22):

Behold, O Lord, and raise up unto them their king, the son of David

[αὐτοῖς τὸν βασιλέα αὐτῶν υἱὸν Δαυιδ]

At the time in the which Thou seest, O God, that he may reign over Israel Thy servant.
And gird him with strength, that he may shatter unrighteous rulers,
And that he may purge Jerusalem from nations that trample (her) down to destruction.

This righteous Davidic saviour, who is referred to in 17.32 as χριστὸς κύριος (*Christ the Lord*), will wage 'Holy War' against Israel's enemies—the Gentiles, though more through speech and wisdom than actual physical combat. At the least these psalms tell us that the title 'son of David' was in messianic use during the first century CE.

Messianism in the Dead Sea Scrolls

Though more prominent in later first-century CE literature, the Davidic kingly messiah was also a key figure in the eschatological sectarian writings of the Essenes. However, differing messianic concepts appear in the Dead Sea Scrolls revolving around two figures: an anointed priest and royal messiah.

We've already examined the existence of astrological texts in the scrolls, but what's also clear is the Essenes' eschatological ('militant') Davidic messianism and apocalyptic expectation of the 'End of Days'. Of special consideration is their messianic use of Numbers 24.17.

For example, in 4Q174, an eschatological Midrash from around the early first century BCE, appears:

> The Lord declares to you that He will build you a House [2 Sam. 7.11c]. I will raise up your seed after you [2 Sam. 7.12]. I will establish the throne of his kingdom [for ever] [2 Sam. 7.13]. [I will be] his father and he shall be my son [2 Sam. 7:14]. He is the Branch of David who shall arise with the Interpreter of the Law [to rule] in Zion [at the end] of time. As it's written, I will raise up the tent of David that is fallen

[Amos 9.11]. That is to say, the fallen *tent of David* is he who shall arise to save Israel. . .

[Why] do the nations [rage] and the peoples meditate [vanity? Why do the kings of the earth] rise up, [and the] princes take counsel together against the Lord and against [His Messiah]? [Psalm 2.1]. Interpreted, this saying concerns [the kings of the nations] who shall [rage against] the elect of Israel in the last days.[8]

This Davidic 'Branch' or scion was expected to kill the leader of the *Kittim* (the Romans).

We could infer that the authors of the scrolls (who, according to Josephus were favoured by Herod) would also have had an interest in what the magi had to say, especially as there's evidence to suggest that they were resident in Jerusalem as well as Khirbet Qumran.

Essenes, Jubilees and Daniel 9.24–27

Of further significance is Roger Beckwith's argument that the Essenes believed their two messiahs would arrive around 4 BCE. Beckwith suggests that Menahem the Essene's prediction, given after Herod's accession in 37 BCE, that Herod would rule as βασιλέα Ἰουδαίων for *just over 30 years* is based on the Essene belief that these messiahs would arrive in the final seventh week of the tenth Jubilee of the seventy weeks of Daniel's prophecy (9.24–27) that is, between 10–6 BCE and 3 BCE–2 CE.

Noting Matthew 2, Beckwith comments that Herod's actions could be explained by the, 'fact that his predicted thirty years had elapsed, and the Essenes were expecting the Messiahs any year now' suggesting that Herod would more likely take the advice of the Essenes than the Sadducees and Pharisees. By taking this view, Beckwith is presupposes Matthew 2.1–12 to be a historical event:

Essene expectation must have reached fever-pitch towards the end of the first century B.C., with the eschatological war already overdue, and the Messiahs of Levi and Israel expected in the last of *Daniel's* 70 weeks . . . The revolts which followed Herod's death, and the rise of the Zealot movement at the same period, were no doubt encouraged by this atmosphere.[9]

If this understanding of Essene chronology is correct, the silence in Josephus is evidence of there being no unrest relating to the birth of a Messiah.

Absence of recorded messianic unrest

Given the tense social conditions and messianic expectation around the time of Jesus' birth, to announce that Jesus was the messiah and Davidic king of the Jews could have led to a major destabilisation of the region; forming the basis of (peasant) uprising against Herod and the Roman Empire.

> Living thus under an oppressive and illegitimate king [Herod] installed by an alien power, the people were ready for an 'anointed' charismatic leader from among the peasantry, like David of old. It should not be surprising that as soon as Herod died, the pent-up frustrations of the people burst forth precisely in the form of messianic movements.[10]

Marcus Borg likewise notes the 'active resistance to Rome and her client kings' from 37 BCE to 66 CE. Hence, Craig Evans, in his brief study of messianism during the New Testament period concludes that the idea of a saviour figure had, 'disturbing implications for existing political and social structures.'[11]

This appears in the response to such pseudo-messianic prophets and kingly aspirants as Theudas, Judas of Sepphoris, Judas of Gamala, Simon of Perea, Athronges and the unnamed Egyptian Jew. Josephus records many such messianic and prophetic figures *but nothing about the birth of one.*

The closest records we have of social unrest during the period of Jesus' birth are the rebellious peasant uprisings of Judas, Simon and Athronges that occurred in 4 BCE. These led to inevitable conflict with the Roman army and inevitable defeat. Indeed, the lower Galilean town of Sepphoris was, in retaliation for Judas' uprising, burnt to the ground and its inhabitants sent into slavery by Varus, legate of Syria.

A passage echoing this fear of Roman military intervention is in John 11.47–48 (not attested in the Synoptics but cf. Mark 13.2; Luke 21.20). Though a theologically charged after the event passage, it nevertheless retains an element of historicity for it relates the Sanhedrin's fear of a Roman assault as a direct result of public support of Jesus, that is, *the political fallout of a national messianic 'King of Israel'*:

> συνήγαγον οὖν οἱ ἀρχιερεῖς καὶ οἱ φαρισαῖοι συνέδριον καὶ ἔλεγον, Τί ποιοῦμεν ὅτι οὗτος ὁ ἄνθρωπος πολλὰ ποιεῖ σημεῖα; ἐὰν ἀφῶμεν αὐτὸν οὕτως, πάντες πιστεύσουσιν εἰς αὐτόν, καὶ ἐλεύσονται οἱ Ῥωμαῖοι καὶ ἀροῦσιν ἡμῶν καὶ τὸν τόπον καὶ τὸ ἔθνος.

*So the chief priests and the Pharisees called a meeting of the council,
and said, 'What are we to do? This man is performing many signs.
If we let him go on like this, everyone will believe in him, and the
Romans will come and destroy both our holy place and our nation.*

Although 'the story in Matthew 1-2 reflects exactly the situation towards the
end of Herod's reign' it's ironically *this very situation* that makes the events of
Matthew 2 extremely unlikely to have been factual.[12]

One event in particular is relevant. Late in Herod's rule, Josephus records
(*Ant.* 17.42–45) how *social discontent had produced hopes for a future king.*
In return for the kindness of Pheroras' wife paying a fine on their behalf, the
Pharisees:

> Foretold—for they were believed to have foreknowledge through
> God's appearances to them—that by God's decree Herod's throne
> would be taken from him, both from himself and his descendants, and
> the royal power would fall to her and Pheroras and to any children
> that they might have.

The parallel with Matthew 2 is obvious, yet despite the historical verisimilitude
this brings to Matthew, no attestation for Matthew 1-2 is currently known in
Josephus or any other contemporary Jewish, Greco-Roman or Near Eastern
source.

Absence of the Star from historical records

If the appearance of the Star was such a ground-shaking event (*messianically*
and *astrologically*) why wasn't it recorded or, in the plot of Matthew's Gospel
(the only indirect witness), so completely forgotten so soon after the vague
'those who sought' Jesus had died, either in his hometown or by the time he
entered Jerusalem?

Even Jesus' family appear to have no memory of these unique and unusual
events. At the least, the chief priests (οἱ ἀρχιερεῖς) and the Sanhedrin (τό συνέδριον)
the ultimate authorities on religious and legal matters in post-exilic Judaism,
along with those seeking salvation from Roman occupation, shouldn't have
forgotten. As with Matthew's account of the mass resurrection of holy ones,
there's likewise no New Testament memory of the momentous events of
Matthew 1–2.

Silence in Josephus

Josephus' references to Jesus and John the Baptist (though the subject of much unresolved debate with regard to authenticity) is likely to be genuine in its un-redacted pre-Christian form.

If Josephus could mention such minor characters as Ἰωάννου τοῦ ἐπικαλουμένου βαπτιστοῦ (*John, surnamed the Baptist*), James τὸν ἀδελφὸν Ἰησοῦ τοῦ λεγομένου Χριστοῦ (*the brother of Jesus who was called the Christ*) as well as Jesus himself (Ἰησοῦς σοφὸς ἀνήρ) (*Jesus, a wise man*) how could he leave out the Star, his birth and all the events in Herod's court and Jerusalem that the birth brought about? Without the birth, there would have been no James or Jesus to discuss.

Silence in the Greco-Roman and Near Eastern world

When we compare Matthew 2.3 to the fear of comets, fear that comets and conjunctions regularly brought on the royal courts and populations of Europe right up to the eighteenth century, this collective amnesia in the recollective, autographical memory of those Jerusalem eyewitnesses (which had a population of between 25-70,000, swelling to 180,000 during festival periods), along with the rest of the Greco-Roman and Near Eastern world (whose citizens and traders travelled to and from Jerusalem) doesn't sit well with the assumed historical accuracy of Matthew 2.

Does Matthew 2 and Matthean Christology fit the context of late first century BCE?

The astrological theory, though superficially correct, is in fact profoundly wrong. As an independent hypothesis, the conjunction theory might work, but when Matthew 2 is placed in the socio-political religious context of Roman administered Judea and the reign of Herod, it fails as a solid account of historical events.

Two problems for the historicity of Matthew 2 emerge from such a context:

(1) The evidence from the messianic literature (such as we have it) and Josephus suggests that one should perhaps expect to have seen a longer lasting response, and some wider external records, to the magi's visit.

(2) Messianically, Matthew 2 is too simplistic with its reference to one single Davidic Messiah, this being the product of late first-century CE Christianity. It makes no sense in the pluralistic context of first-century BCE Judaism: why did the scribes *automatically assume* a single Davidic Messiah as opposed to any other messianic-type figure?

The meaning behind the Infancy Narrative becomes clearer through an understanding of post-Easter theology. To the Jews, only one who had removed the pagans from Israel and restored the Temple would have been the true Messiah and Jesus, having been crucified at the hands of the Romans, did neither. However, Jesus' followers, through their belief that Jesus had in fact been raised from the dead, believed that he must be the (Jewish) Messiah.

Christ's ἀνάστασις (*resurrection*) marks the significant break between Judaism and Jewish Christianity with Matthew's infancy narrative (and the conflict in the Gospel as a whole) being the result of this development from Jewish to Christian Messianism. The Jewish notion of the 'messiah' was fluid and flexible. There was no single model that had to be followed.

> We are increasingly aware that at the time of Jesus there were almost certainly no standard or widely acknowledged 'Jewish expectation about the Messiah' such as birth in Bethlehem, about which Matthew or other followers of Jesus of Nazareth would supposedly have been embarrassed.[13]

Hence, Matthew 1–2 is just an example (Luke 1–2 is another) of one community's messianic origin for Jesus.

The work of Warren Carter, in his socio-political reading of Matthew, lends support to the two problems. Though Carter notes that the magi and Star presented a 'challenge to the political stability' of Herod and that the magi lacked 'political astuteness' by asking him for advice (he explains this through reference to the tradition of conflict between magi and kings), he is applying his socio-political methodology from the *later perspective* of a marginal Matthean community c. 85–90 CE, one in conflict with the urban elite. Richard Horsley and Warren Carter provide support for my conclusions (even if they wouldn't agree with them) by emphasising Matthew's political portrayal of Herodian Judea from a point in time *nearly ninety years after the event*.

> Our knowledge of the history of Judea in this period is very partial, and the events recorded in Matt 2 are not of such a character as to demand the attention of Josephus, our only significant source.[14]

What Matthew describes in 2.1–23 is *too powerful politically and messianically* to have been ignored and the absence of their effects on any contemporary or later source is significant. If the Star and events of Matthew 2 were real, they happened *in* history, and would have shaped historical events. Yet there's nothing in surviving contemporary accounts that would lead us back to the events described by Matthew. This suggests why the Star, and the social unrest it should have caused, is absent from any contemporary or later record.

As there's no historical verisimilitude in the picture, the most probable hypothesis is that the magi and the Star are 'creations' serving a theological purpose.

CHAPTER 15:
THE FORM OF THE MATTHEAN INFANCY NARRATIVE

The Jewishness of Matthew's Gospel along with his use of Old Testament Scripture suggests it would be more beneficial to examine the larger Infancy Narrative unit through the methodology of Old Testament form criticism by placing it within the controlling fixed patterns of ancient Near Eastern literature.

Advances in literary criticism in recent decades have created a pluralistic field of study where the definition of 'genre' and genre 'types' (especially with regard to 'Gospel' genre) remains an active area of debate. In current scholarship, the majority view has moved away from the early form critical derivational interpretation of the Gospels and more towards an analogical approach. Hence, a broad movement of study seeks to find genre analogies (to the Gospels as a whole) from both Jewish and Greco-Roman literature. This aims to place the Gospels in the classical genres of biography, encomium (rhetorical pedagogy), and aretalogy (θεῖος ἀνήρ; a form of sacred biography where a deity's attributes are listed, in the form of poem or text, in the first person).

The comparison of the Gospels to Greco-Roman biography has been one of the more fruitful areas of genre study with the most influential work in recent years being Richard Burridge's *What are the Gospels?* This is an analogical approach to Gospel genre for it's the shared *generic features* with Greco-Roman biography that is of importance.

Jack Sasson, in his folkloristic study of Ruth, suggested that definitions of genre lay behind the inability to define the text: was it tale, romance, story, folktale? His view is that textual interpretation is only possible when its literary category is known. Only then is it possible, 'to draw conclusions that are applicable to any literature of the same genre.'[1] In reality, genres can be hard to pigeon-hole into neat classifications.

Ancient biography wasn't clearly defined, with texts covering a range of genres blurring into one another. Such ancient genres had flexible boundaries and βίος overlaps with the subgenres of biographical novel, moral philosophy, teaching, encomium, story, political beliefs, historical monograph and history.

Burridge examined ten Lives in order to identify the patterns of Greco-Roman biography (five pre-dating and five post-dating the Gospels.) In chronological order these are:

1. Isocrates, *Evagoras*

2. Xenophon, *Agesilaus*

3. Satyrus, *Euripides*

4. Nepo, *Atticus*

5. Philo, *Moses*

6. Tacitus, *Agricola*

7. Plutarch, *Cato Minor*

8. Suetonius, *Lives of the Caesars*

9. Lucian, *Demonax*

10. Philostratus, *Apollonius of Tyana*

He then looked at each work via a series of generic features ('opening', 'subject', 'internal' and 'external') to establish commonality before turning taking the same approach to the Gospels. Although genre isn't defined by any one of these features individually, together they build up an identifiable genre. Such a method has also been used to classify ancient novels.

Title and opening preface (opening features): Formal titles are absent in the Gospels and the title ΚΑΤΑ ΜΑΘΘΑΙΟΝ (*according to Matthew*) wasn't originally part of the autograph.

Allocation of space (subject): The allocation of space to the life of Jesus in the Gospels reveals that little is given about his childhood but much is written about his death. Though some have cited this as an argument *against* a biographical genre, it does closely match the content percentage of Greco-Roman biographies.

Burridge follows the narratrive + discourse structure of Matthew as discussed above. Taking this structure, he presents a statistical content analysis of Matthew.

TABLE 9: MATTHEW'S ALLOCATION OF SPACE

Chapters	Verses	Topic	N or D	% of work
1-2	48	Prologue and infancy	Narrative	4.5
3-4	42	Preparation and beginnings	Narrative	3.9
5-7	111	Sermon on the Mount	Discourse	10.4
8-9	72	Ministry	Narrative	6.7
10-11:1	41	Mission of disciples	Discourse	3.8
11:2-12	79	Ministry and conflict	Narrative	7.4
13:1-52	52	Parables of the Kingdom	Discourse	4.9
13:53-17:27	136	Ministry/Peter's confession	Narrative	12.7
18	35	Christian community	Discourse	3.3
19-23	195	Journey to Jerusalem	Narrative	18.2
24-25	97	Eschatology	Discourse	9.1
26-28	161	Last Supper, Passion and Resurrection	Narrative	15.1
	1,069			100

These percentages significantly match the contents of Greco-Roman biography. For example, of Jesus' death, Matthew, Mark and Luke each respectively allocate the following content percentages: 15.1%, 15.6% and 19.1%. Even in Acts, Luke devotes 24.7% to Paul's arrest and detention.

As these closely match the percentages of the deaths presented in Plutarch's *Cato Minor* (17.3%), Nepos' *Atticus* (15%), Tacitus' *Agricola* (10%) and Philostratus' *Apollonius of Tyana* (26.3%), Burridge concludes that 'the evangelists' concentration on the Passion and death of Jesus can no longer be used as an argument against the gospels' as biography.

Mode of representation (external feature): Being continuous prose narratives their 'mode of representation . . . is like historiography or βίοι.'[2]

Size (external feature): A word count of the Synoptics (Matthew 18,305, Mark 11,242 and Luke = 19,428) shows that they fit into the medium-length category and share this feature with Greco-Roman biography. E.P. Sanders and Margaret Davies note of Luke, 'there is a lack of focus on the hero... It is not a biography of Jesus but a story of God bringing salvation to his people.'[3] Against such a view, Burridge conducted a verbal analysis and found that Jesus *is* the main focus and subject of the Synoptics (Mark = 24.4%, Matthew = 17.2%, Luke = 17.9%) with no other single person getting above 1%. Groups of individuals fared only slighter higher. Matching this to the percentage of hero focus in ancient biographies, he concludes that such figures are a 'clear indicator' of the Gospel's *biographical* interest. Of the large level of 'teaching' materials that Matthew contains (42.5% against Luke's 36.8% and Mark's 20.2%), this matches well his scribal background and the didactic purpose of his Gospel.

Structure (external feature): Structure refers to *the overall sequence of events* and not the specific features of each Gospel. There's a clear chronological structure that flows from Jesus' baptism (even earlier in Matthew and Luke) to his Passion and resurrection. In between, there's a geographical progression (especially in Luke) from Galilee to Jerusalem, with inserted teaching materials. Burridge finds this 'not dissimilar from βίοι', particularly those about philosophers and teachers (for example, Moses, Apollonius and Pythagoras). Indeed, travel and teaching were common features of θεῖος ἀνήρ biographies. He concludes that, 'The Gospel's exterior framework of a chronological sequence with topical material inserted is a structure typical of Graeco-Roman βίοι.'[4]

Scale (external feature): The scale of the Synoptics is narrowly focused on Jesus with characters existing only to relate to him and talk about him when he is absent. Hence, Burridge concludes that the gospels, 'all restrict their scale to the person of Jesus in a manner typical of βίος literature.'[5]

Literary units (external feature): Units (forms) such as anecdotes (ἀποφθέγματα, παραδείγματα), sayings (γνῶμαι), legends, remarks (χρεῖαι), stories, discourses, and speeches are interwoven in the narrative, and have been the basic blocks of biography since Aristotle. Various types of literary forms appear in the Gospels. Rudolf Bultmann refers to apophthegms (sayings), miracle stories, historical stories and legends. Martin Dibelius finds paradigms, tales, legends, myths and exhortations. V. Taylor sees pronouncement stories, miracle stories and sayings. In more recent scholarship, R. Tannehill terms such units 'apophthegms', '*chreiai*' and 'pronouncement stories' (defining the latter as, 'a brief narrative in which the climactic [and often final] element is a pronouncement which is presented as a particular person's response to something said or observed').[6] These units that make the building blocks of the Synoptic Gospels can also be observed in Satyrus, *Euripides*, Tacitus' *Agricola* and Plutarch's *Cato Minor*. They also match the pronouncement stories in the central section of Lucian's *Demonax*, while legends and miracles stories are also evident in Philostratus' *Apollonius of Tyana* 1.4–5. Matthew 1–2 as a literary unit fits into the generic genre of biography.

Use of sources (external feature): Burridge follows Markan priority with Q. Through the methodology of redaction criticism, the Gospel authors are now seen as editors selecting their sources in the same manner as Greco-

Roman biographers. For example, he refers to Luke's preface as biographical-historiographical in style.

Methods of characterisation (external feature): The traditional argument against the Gospels as biography (that they don't give a *modern style* account of his physical and mental make-up) is refuted by the ancient style of showing character through *words and deeds*. To this end, Burridge provides six passages that demonstrate the employment of stories and anecdotes (literary units) as an indirect method of characterisation in the Gospels: Mark 1.24; 12.13–34; 15.15; Matthew 8.27; 9.36; Acts 1.1. He concludes that lack of character development can't be used as an argument against their being biography.

Topographical settings (internal feature): Though Jesus moves to various geographical locations, he remains the focus of the narrative: *we only arrive at these locations because Jesus has travelled to them*. Even in didactic settings where he is teaching, he remains the primary focus. This focus, Burridge suggests, is a common feature between the Gospels and βίοι (biography).

Topics (internal feature): Though he doesn't refer to the narrative structure of hero folklore, Burridge notes that *'certain motifs can indicate specific genres'* (my italics). He observes that, 'the motif of the child, usually from a rich family, abandoned at birth but preserved by a kindly yokel' is a standard motif in Greek New Comedy.[7] Although topics are only secondary elements that can't serve as genre determinatives, they can serve as a generic link *if various works make use of similar motifs*. Thus, Burridge lists the recurring topics of *ancestry, birth, boyhood and education, great deeds, virtues, death and consequences*. All these are in the Gospel accounts of Jesus.

τόποι *and encomium (writing that praises someone highly)*

H.I. Marrou, outlining the eulogy system of Theon (114–140 CE), presents 36 basic stages that had to be conformed to when eulogising 'a certain person, living or dead, real or mythical.' Of the initial stages, we have:

1. *Exterior Excellences*
    (a) Noble birth
    (b) Environment
        1. Native city
        2. Fellow citizens
        3. Excellence of the city's political regime
        4. Parents and family

(c) Personal Advantages
    1. Education
    2. Friends
    3. Fame
    4. Public service
    5. Wealth
    6. Children, number and beauty of
    7. Happy death

Style (internal feature): Burridge's conclusion (given the range of Greek styles among the Synoptics and their Semitic influences), is that they are 'not unique to themselves' and 'remain within the range of contemporary Koiné, and probably similar to popular βίοι no longer extant.'[8]

Atmosphere (internal feature): The mood and atmosphere of the Gospels is serious, though it does change according to the situation (for example, joy, sadness, fear, excitement) and it's usually always linked to the central figure of Jesus. Burridge sees the tone of the Gospels more as one of *reverence and invitation* rather than the praise and pleading of the encomiastic genre. This sombre tone, he suggests, is in Tacitus' *Agricola* and Philo's *Moses*.

Quality of characterisation (internal feature): Burridge, examining the ancient concept of Ãqoj (and how it must not be confused with modern notions of psychological development in biographies), notes the tendency for βίοι to combine typical and stereotypical characterisations, with a real feeling being obtained through sayings and anecdotes. His conclusion is that, 'The tension between the real and the stereotype in the synoptic gospels is not dissimilar from characterisation in other βίοι.'[9]

Social setting (internal feature): Burridge concludes from the internal and external evidence that insufficient information is given in the texts to know anything specific, saying 'there appears to be nothing about this generic feature preventing them being βίοι.'[10]

Authorial intention and purpose (internal feature): Different purposes have been suggested for the Synoptic Gospels: encomiastic, exemplary, informative, entertainment, memory preservation, didactic, apologetic and polemic. All these *to some extent* can apply to the Gospels.

✳ ✳ ✳

Genre is the key to Gospel interpretation as its conventions, expectations and rules (the generic features) allow the reader-listener to interpret the evangelist's composition process. Burridge's research provides a literary explanation for why Matthew included a birth narrative and in the form he did. Though such introductory birth narratives (or τόποι), literary units and motifs weren't essential (generic) features of Greco-Roman biography, many possessed them *and they tended to follow a particular pattern or form.*

The Gospel genre is closest to Greco-Roman biography, though influenced by other literary forms (typical of Hellenistic literature of the period). Yet they're also *Jewish* biographies, the story of Jesus modified to reach a Gentile audience. As David Aune concludes, 'the *content* is Jewish and Christian while the *form* and *function* is Hellenistic.'[11] And Roger Beck says, 'The vehicle for publicity [for the 'gospel' message] was to hand in the form of prose narrative that manifests itself equally as aretalogy, sacred biography and novel.'[12]

The life of the historical figure of Jesus has been depicted, first by Mark and then in expanded form by Matthew and Luke, as 'sacred biography'—a mixture of Greco-Roman βίοι, fictional prose biography and Judeo-Christian theology, featuring the themes and motifs of Jewish and Gentile miracle workers. If this description of Gospel genre sounds too much like a mixture, it must be borne in mind that Judaism had been under the influence of Hellenism for nearly three hundred years before Mark was written.

CHAPTER 16:
MATTHEW AND THE NARRATIVE PATTERN OF LEGENDARY BIRTH MOTIFS

The terms 'folktale', 'fairy-tale', 'legend', and 'myth' aren't synonymous and are often confused.

Folklore: Coined in the mid-1800s to replace the term 'popular antiquities', 'folklore' has a wide usage. The Oxford English Dictionary defines 'folklore' as 'the traditional beliefs, legends, and customs, current among the common people.'

Myth: A myth essentially encompasses stories of *origins* (of belief, ritual, natural phenomena, etc.) and is primarily concerned with the ancient, distant past.

Legend: Legends are more *human* orientated (less remote in time). They combine historical fact with mythic elements, and are regarded as true by their speakers/audience. The birth stories of heroes and great rulers are 'legends' as opposed to 'myths' and 'folktales'. The Old Testament form critical label is 'Heroic Saga'. They can be seen as stories from the 'periphery of Gospel tradition' and primarily interested in 'secondary things and persons.'[1] The latter is true of Matthew 1–2, where the focus is on Joseph, the magi, and Herod.

Folktale/fairy-tale (Volksmärchen): The English term 'fairy-tale' derives from the French *conte de fées*. Its modern usage is one of (Oxford English Dictionary) 'an unreal or incredible story' (for example, the tales of the Brother's Grimm). A fairy-tale is:

> A work of oral literature, usually presented in prose and only rarely in verse, in which a man must confront marvelous forces in order to win a royal-marvelous spouse, and in so doing he redeems the latter and his/her marvelous world.[2]

The taxonomy of folktales

Though I use 'legend' as the correct term for what's in Matthew 2, the use of 'folktale' is common in secondary literature.

I'll be employing the use of 'tale-types' and 'motifs' to look at birth legends. Tales and motifs are specific products of the Finnish School of folklore studies and the comparative 'historical-geographical' method of Julius Krohn (1835–1888), Kaarle Krohn (1863–1933), Antti Aarne (1867–1925) and Stith Thompson (1885–1976).

According to this monogenesis model, the variants of a story are merely the transmitted corruptions of an original archetype (*Ur*-form) that has geographically migrated (and suffered local redaction). The school's method was to collect variant tales into groups of types in order to recover these original forms.

Though this method has received criticism due to the difficulty in mapping the migrated life history of variants, the use of motifs and tale types remains the most common forms of classifying folktales.

Motifs

A motif is 'the smallest element in a tale having the power to persist in tradition.'[3] According to the *Concise Oxford Dictionary of Literary Terms*, a motif is a:

> Situation, incident, idea, image, or character-type that is found in many different literary works, folktales or myths; or any element of a work that is elaborated into a more general theme.[4]

The primary source for motifs (and that on which more recent lists are based) is Sith Thompson's *Motif-Index of Folk Literature*. In this, motifs are classified by letters and numbers: letters represent the category of the motifs while the numbers are divided into hundreds (representing the general idea of the division), subdivisions of tens (representing general concepts) and further subdivisions (providing more specific ideas). The motifs in Matthew 1–2 are listed in Table 11. (A list of relevant motifs is in Appendix I.)

The Finnish School's use of motifs is blamed by Will Soll for the lack of weight given to the 'non-Jewish fairy tale' elements in Tobit. He argues that the 'emphasis on motifs prevented scholars from seeing any coherent core around which these motifs might crystallize'.[5] Soll employs instead the functional classification of Vladmir Propp. However, a coherent core *does exist around those motifs that relate to birth*: specifically the pattern of the exposed/persecuted and rescued infant culture hero.

Tale-types

The tale-type consists of a collection of motifs forming a more complete and larger narrative unit. Hasan El-Shamy refers to this coherent core as a 'motif spectrum'. This being:

> The various themes that seem to cohere around that given tale-type in all instances of its occurrence... Naturally, some tale texts may include additional motifs while others may incorporate only a few of the motifs cited.[6]

A 'type' relates to the narrative content of a tale, though each type of tale will contain many variants.

Tale types are classified by Aarne-Thompson (AT; Thompson's expanded and enlarged second 1961 edition of Aarne's original 1910 *Verzeichnis der Märchentypen*, a system of cataloguing tales adapted from the historic-geographic method) or simply 'type', followed by their number, then an italicised title.[7] For example, AT 561 *Aladdin*. Variants can also have a letter suffix, for example, AT 934C *Death Forestalls Evil Fates*. The AT has recently been replaced by the 2004 Aarne-Thompson-Uther (ATU) index.

The hero cycle

Central to this chapter is the hero cycle; the literary pattern of birth, life and death common to mythic, legendary and even historical figures. Table 10 lists the cycle as presented by three major figures in the study of hero pattern (my italics):

TABLE 10: THE HERO PATTERN

Von Hahn (1876)	Rank (1909)	Raglan (1934)
1. Hero of illegitimate birth	*1. Child of distinguished parents*	*1. Mother is a royal virgin*
2. Mother is a princess	*2. Father is a king*	*2. Father is a king*
3. Father is a god	*3. Difficulty in conception*	*3. Father related to mother*
4. Prophecy of ascendance	*4. Prophecy warning against birth*	*4. Unusual conception*
5. Hero abandoned	*5. Hero surrendered to the water in a box*	*5. Hero reputed to be son of god*
6. Suckled by animals	*6. Saved by animals or lowly people*	*6. Attempt to kill hero*

7. *Hero raised by childless shepherd couple*	7. *Suckled by female animal or humble woman*	7. *Hero spirited away*
8. Hero is high-spirited	8. *Hero grows up*	8. *Reared by foster parents in a far country*
9. He seeks service abroad	9. Hero finds distinguished parents	9. *No details of childhood*
10. Triumphant home-coming	10. Hero takes revenge on his father	10. He goes to future kingdom
11. Slays original persecutors and sets mother free	11. Acknowledged by people	11. Is victor over king, giant dragon or wild beast
12. Founds cities	12. Achieves rank and honours	12. Marries a princess
13. Extraordinary death		13. Becomes king
14. Reviled because of incest and dies young		14. For a time he reigns uneventfully
15. Hero dies as an act of revenge by an insulted servant		15. He prescribes laws
16. He murders his younger brother		16. Later, he loses favour with his gods or his subjects
		17. Driven from throne and city
		18. Meets with mysterious death
		19. Often at the top of a hill
		20. His children, if any, do not succeed him
		21. His body isn't buried
		22. But he has one or more sepulchres

The pattern breaks down once adulthood is reached, which suggests the absence of a fixed literary form. Such a pattern is 'fudged' by leaping from one trait to another to create the desired hero pattern.

Birth of the hero

Even if the life of the adult hero fails to conform to a regular pattern, *his birth does not* and is more likely to follow the same narrative sequence of events and contain the same folk motifs. Even critics of Dundes' 1976 comparison of Jesus to the hero pattern conceded this point. More recently, Horsley observed that:

> What is at least impressive, on the basis of Dundes' comparison of von Hahn, Rank, and Raglan, is the close correspondence of the first eight motifs in their respective schemes and the degree to which their respective case studies exemplify all or most of those motifs.[8]

Johann Georg von Hahn (1811–1869)

Though the English anthropologist E.B. Tylor (1832–1917) had, in 1871, made reference to a common mythic pattern (the 'recurring operation of imaginative processes') with regard to the exposure birth stories of Cyrus, and Romulus and Remus, modern hero pattern research effectively begins with von Hahn. In his *Sagwissenschaftliche Studien*, von Hahn presented what he termed the *Arische Aussetzungs- und Rückkehr-Formel* ('Aryan Expulsion and Return Formula').

This consisted of a series of sixteen biographical events divided into four sub-groups *birth* (1–3); *youth* (4–9); *return* (10–13); and *additional events* (14–16). Of the hero's birth and youth, we find:

1. Hero is of illegitimate birth
2. Mother is a princess
3. Father a god or foreigner
4. Signs warning of his ascendance
5. Child is abandoned
6. Suckled by animals
7. Brought up by childless shepherd couple

Otto Rank (1884–1939)

The Freudian psychologist Otto Rank, using fifteen hero biographies, presented the following common pattern:

1. Child of distinguished parents

2. Father is a king

3. Difficulty in conception.

4. Prophecy warning against birth (for example, death of father)

5. Hero put into water in a box

6. Saved by animals or lowly people

7. Suckled by female animal/woman

8. Hero grows up

Uniquely for this early period of study, Rank included Jesus among his list of biographies.

Vladimir Propp (1895–1970)

The Russian Formalist and folklorist Propp is concerned with the 'morphology' of fairytales rather than the specific pattern of heroes, although his morphology does cover the birth of the fairytale's hero and his work has become the most widely used in biblical studies.

In 1928, Propp published *Morfologija skazki* (*Morphology of the Folktale*), an attempt at a new classification (against that of the Finnish School) of Russian fairytales (ATU 300–749), more specifically, the 'heroic wonder-tale'.[9] Through a limited analysis of one hundred tales, Propp looked for component parts of the story that didn't change from tale to tale. These constant elements (of which he saw thirty-one) he termed 'functions', that is, 'an act of a character, defined from the point of view of its significance for the course of the action.'[10] These functions (each of which is represented by a symbol) are spread across seven tale roles. However they only serve as abstract slots and variant actions can and do occur.

Propp's *Morphology* is only a summary of his work, which was brought to a premature halt by the Marxist suppression of Formalism in 1929–30. However, he does provide a fuller list of 151 elements which covers the birth of the hero ('Initial Situation'):

1. Temporal-spatial determination (location)
2. Composition of the family (prosperity)
        a.   according to nomenclature and status
        b.   according to the categories of dramatis personae
3. Childlessness
4-5. Prayer for the birth of a son (family enumeration)
6. Cause of pregnancy
        a.   intentional
        b.   accidental
        c.   forced
7. Form of miraculous birth
        a.   from a fish and from water
        b.   from a hearth
        c.   from an animal
        d.   otherwise
8. Prophecies, forewarnings
9. Well-being, prior to complication
        a.   fantastic
        b.   domestic
        c.   agrarian
        d.   otherwise

Though Propp doesn't see the *Initial Situation* as itself a 'function' (as functions imply action) he still sees it as 'an important morphological element'[11] and assigns it the symbol α.

Propp and Matthew 1–2
Applying Proppean analysis to Matthew 1–2 gives:

α Initial Situation—prosperity (2.11); miraculous birth (1.18–25); prophecy (2.3–6)

   ε^1 Function 4: Reconnaissance by villain to obtain information (2.3–8)

   ζ^1 Function 5: Villain receives information (2.6)

   η^1 Function 6: Deceitful persuasion of villain (2.8)

   $G^2 \uparrow$ Function 15: Transference to a different place—Hero is carried (2.13–15)

   A^{13} Function 8: Order to kill (2.16)

   A^{14} Function 8: Murder (2.17)

   $\downarrow$ Return (2.19–23)

The morphology of Matthew 1–2, as defined by Propp, appears as: $\alpha\varepsilon^1\zeta^1\eta^1G^2\uparrow A^{13}A^{14}\downarrow$. Note that the role of the magi (and Star) is reduced to little more than information for the villain (Herod).

Though Propp's analysis is confined to the plot elements of a specific sub-genre of (Russian) folktale, we again see miraculous births, prophecies, and a villain looking for information about the Hero in order to kill him.

When finally published in English in 1958, Propp's study became linked to the emerging (French) study of structuralism (the relationships between part and whole) as pioneered by the linguistic theories of Ferdinand de Saussure and Claude Lévi-Strauss. However, it's also been applied to biblical studies (specifically the Old Testament) where Propp's analysis of folk tales, as a method of classifying texts, has been widely used.

Lord Raglan (1885–1964)

Raglan (though unaware of the work of von Hahn and Rank) was inspired by the myth of Oedipus and examined the common characteristics attached to the heroes of Greek, Roman, Persian and Celtic myths. He found the following to be true of the births of most mythical heroes:

1. The hero's mother is a royal virgin;

2. His father is a king, and

3. Often a near relative of his mother, but

4. The circumstances of his conception are unusual, and

5. His is also reputed to be the son of a god.

6. At birth an attempt is made, usually by his father or his maternal grandfather, to kill him, but

7. He is spirited away, and

8. Reared by foster-parents in a far country.

9. We're told nothing of his childhood, but

10. On reaching manhood, he returns or goes to his future kingdom.

Raglan didn't see any historicity behind the pattern, arguing that it was derived solely from ritual. On 'myth and the historic hero', Raglan notes that the stories of historical characters can become embellished with folk motifs. Noting Henry

V (1387–1422), of whose youth little is historically known, Raglan argues that Shakespeare's depiction of the prince's association with the drunken buffoon Falstaff derives from the perception that all young heroes behaved in this manner.

There's often a gap between the birth of the hero and his appearance as an adult. Raglan writes that the hero's birth:

> Is the central feature in a series of highly dramatic incidents, incidents which are related in considerable detail, and such incidents seldom, if ever, occur in the lives of real people. The most surprising things happen to our hero at birth; the most surprising things happen to him as he reaches manhood, but in the meanwhile nothing happens to him at all.[12]

To Raglan, this is due to the lack of ritual in a child's life between birth and initiation. Whether ritualistic in origin or not, the pattern is a feature of Matthew 2 and Luke 2. The apocryphal Infancy Narratives are later attempts at filling such gaps in the missing years of Jesus.

Jan de Vries (1890–1964)

In his 1963 study of the hero in ancient Greek, European and Near Eastern legend, saga and song, de Vries laid out 'the pattern of a heroic life' and presents his own pattern based on selected examples of Indo-European myth and legend. Of the birth of the hero, he presents:

1. Hero is begotten
    a. Mother is a virgin.
    b. Father is a God
    c. Father is an animal
    d. Child conceived in incest
2. Hero is born
    a. In an unnatural way.
    b. By caesarean section.
3. His youth is threatened
    a. Child is exposed ('either by father who has been warned in a dream that the child will be a danger to him, or by the mother who thus tries to hide her shame.')
    b. Exposed child is fed by animals.
    c. Child is found by shepherds.
    d. Child raised by mythical figures.

4. He is brought up
   a. Reveals strength and courage from an early age.
   b. Slow in development.

Brian Lewis

In his monograph on the Sargon legend Lewis devotes two chapters to the study 'The Tale of the Hero who was Exposed at Birth'. After examining seventy-two tales (spanning the sixteenth century BCE to the twentieth century), he concludes that seven basic components create the exposed-hero tale:

I. Explanation of abandonment
   a. Fear or shame over circumstances of birth
   b. To save the hero's life
   c. To avert an unfavourable prophecy
   d. Child is unwanted
II. Infant of noble birth
   a. Noble or royal parent
      i. Father is a king
      ii. Mother is a queen
      iii. Mother is a princess
      iv. Mother is priestess
   b. Divine parent
   c. Animal parent
III. Preparations for exposure
   a. Box, basket, chest, receptacle
      i. Receptacle made waterproof
      ii. Comfortable fittings or valuables (placed in receptacle)
   b. Parent's agent observes fate of abandoned infant
IV. Exposure
   a. In or near water
   b. In wilderness, forest, mountain, or desolate area
   c. In a cave
   d. Multiple exposures
   e. Mother and child exposed together
V. Infant protected or nursed in an unusual manner
   a. By an animal
   b. By a human or humanoid
      i. Nursed by a deity
      ii. Nursed by a human who is the natural mother

       iii.   Nursed by another female
VI. Discovery and adoption
      a.   Herder
      b.   Other commoner
      c.   Aristocracy/deity
VII. Accomplishments of hero
      a.   Noteworthy deeds
      b.   Kingship

He adds a final eighth component of miscellaneous events:

VIII. Miscellaneous factors
      a.   Twin heroes involved
      b.   Dream, omen, or prophecy and its fulfilment
      c.   Disclosure of the hero's origin
            i.   Hero is informed of the secret of his birth
            ii.   Hero informs natural parent of his identity
            iii.   Birth tokens lead to disclosure of identify
            iv.   Mother's milk miraculously flows
      d.   Etymology of hero's name given
      e.   Etiological element present
      f.   Miraculous events surrounding birth
            i.   Miraculous conception
            ii.   Miraculous birth or growth of the infant
      g.   Incest
            i.   Incest without consequences
            ii.   Incest with slaying of the father
      h.   Adopted child slays natural child
      i.   Mutilation of limbs
      j.   Jealousy of principle wife over inferior wife
      k.   Death letter
      l.   Adoptive parents childless
      m.   Repetition of components

Ur-form, type and sub-types
Attempting to reconstruct an *Ur*-form of the original tale via the Finnish historic-geographic method, Lewis sees a basic story that consists of two types: Type A (exposure on water, rescued and adopted) and Type B (exposure on land,

nursed by animal before discovery and adoption). He also presents five sub-types (Semitic, Greek, Latin, Indian, and Persian).

According to Lewis, the *Ur*-form consisted of the seven basic components based around Type A. Hence, he looks towards an area where rivers were of importance, probably somewhere in the Near East (Mesopotamia/Western Asia) circa end third millennium BCE.

In his 1967 study of thirty-two such tales, D.B. Redford differentiated between water and land versions. Viewing the water type as the earliest form (due to the early date of the Sargon legend), he looked towards the Tigris-Euphrates region as its literary home and suggested that the land type could have originated in the mountainous regions of Armenia, northern Zagros and eastern Mesopotamia.

Marc Huys

Huys, in his study of the 'tale-pattern' of the hero exposed at birth in nine of the works of Euripides (d. 406 BCE), sees ἔκθεσις (*exposure*) as the 'central motif'. Examining 150 exposure tales, he presents the following 'motif-complex':

1. *Antecedents and causes of* ἔκθεσις

Illegitimate or unusual sexual intercourse, mostly of a god with a mortal princess.

Omen and/or prophecy

2. *The child abandonment proper and its circumstances*

Who? The person exposing the child.

Where? The place where the child is abandoned.

How? The object (basket, chest, vessel) in which the child is exposed and the συνεκτιθέμενα (objects placed with child)

With what intent and expectation? The ἔκθεσις as a compromise between death and rescue.

3. *The survival of the child and its growing up as a hero.*

Rescuing and menacing animals.

Deities or humans (herdsman, priest or priestess, royal couple) rescue and adopt child.

The extraordinary capabilities of the foundling and the conflict with his inferior social position.

Huys finds these motifs in the following plays:

    Ion (1.1; 2.1-4; 3.1-3)

    Alexandros (1.2; 2.1-4; 3.1-3)

Melanippe Desmotis (1.1; 2.1-4; 3.1-3)
Antiope (1.1; 2.1-2, 4; 3.2-3)
Oidipous (1.1-2; 2.1-4; 3.2-3)
Danae (1.1-2; 2.1-4; 3.2-3)
Melanippe Sophe (1.1-2; 2.1-2, 4; 3.1-3)
Alope (1.1; 2.1-4: 3.1-3)
Auge (1.1; 2.1-4; 3.1-2)

Exposed/persecuted child as tale type/literary form

In the ATU there's no specific tale-type that applies to the collection of motifs surrounding the birth of the exposed culture hero. Of those tales that do include such motifs, the following can be listed: ATU 327, 450, 675, 920, and 930. The closest are those stories classed as 'tales of fate'.

An example is ATU 930 *The Prophecy*). Here, a prophecy tells that a poor boy will become the son-in-law of the king, whereupon the king plans to avoid this fate. According to Thompson, the motifs in such tales relate to *prophecy*, *exposure and abandonment* of the child, and his *rescue*. More specific is ATU 931 *Oedipus*.

As the stories of heroes and gods don't end with their birth, it isn't surprising that a specific 'birth tale' has not been classified. Such motifs form only a part of the larger narrative that covers the life of the hero. Nevertheless, a core motif-spectrum has been clustered around the birth accounts of gods, divine heroes, and dynasty founders since the late third/mid-second millennium BCE, generating a *semi-fixed* controlling pattern/literary form.

Such a pattern also echoed reality since the exposure and abandonment of children was an accepted part of life in the ancient world and wasn't just the product of fiction (though 'only in myth are they saved and suckled by animals').[13] This social connection with such stories could explain its long survival in a wide range of literary genres. Alternatively, Morgan, states that the abandoned child story exists in so many genres due to it holding 'obvious attractions as a basis for an exciting plot.'[14]

Lewis, noting the absence of a specific tale-type, opted for '*The Tale of the Hero who was Exposed at Birth*' as a suitable title. I propose instead the wider '*Legend of the Persecuted and Rescued (Royal) Child*' as a literary form, for not all variants concern exposure.

Legend of the persecuted and rescued (royal) child

Greek New Comedy

The motifs of the abandoned child adopted by poor parents was a feature of Greek New Comedy. Though more 'tale' than 'legend', this feature will now be expanded on in a little more detail.

In an article on the various elements in New Comedy, Gilbert Murray suggests five stages, of which the first is, 'the ravished maiden and the exposed or foundling baby.' He begins by listing those plays of Euripides that contain this first stage: *Ion, Alope, Antiope, Auge, Melanippe Sophe, Melanippe Desmotis*, plus three not examined by Huys: *Alchene, Tyro* and (possibly) *Hypsipyle*. Murray doesn't cite *Danae* or *Oidipous*.

In New Comedy, the 'exposed' and rescued child motif appears most clearly in Menander (c. 342–290 BCE), the founding father of European comedy. Here are the motifs of abandonment (with identifying trinkets), adoption and later recognition in his *Epitrepontes* (120–137), *Perikeiromene*, and (to some extent) *Samia*. However, only a small percentage of his 108 plays have survived, with *Dyskolos* being the only complete play. A more complete knowledge of how often such motifs appeared in his remaining corpus relies on future discoveries.

Oscar Wilde's *The Importance of Being Earnest* (1895) exhibits a modern version of this pattern: The hero, Jack Worthing, tells of how he was abandoned in a handbag at Victoria station, with the handbag (the 'identification trinket') acting as the catalyst for his recognition later in the play.

New Comedy had borrowed these motifs from earlier tragic prototypes, particularly Euripides (for example, *Ion*). There were two changes: the first (which also represents the stylistic changes from the more extravagant Old Comedy to the more domestic New Comedy) was that they were treated more realistically in comparison to the mythological and legendary elements in tragedy (religious element removed; no miraculous survival; child of human parents not divine, etc.) and second, *they became technical devices for the plot*.

Zeus

Of the birth of Zeus, Apollodorus records that Gaia and Ouranos had prophesied that Cronos would be removed from power by one of his sons. To avoid this fate, he swallowed his children (by Rhea) as they were born. While carrying Zeus, Rhea fled to Crete and gave birth to him in a cave on Mount Dicte. There he was suckled by the she-goat (or nymph), Amalthaea. To fool Cronos, she gave him a stone wrapped in swaddling clothes to swallow. Hesiod records that it was Gaia who hid the child in a cave and who gave the stone to Cronos.

Motifs

A112, B535, J641, K1847 (in this case, a stone), K515, K515.1, M300, M311, M311.4, M370, M375.1, M376.3, R153.4, S146.2 (in this case, mother takes son to the cave), S330.

Romulus and Remus

The twin sons of the Vestal Virgin Rhea Silvia and the god Mars (by rape, at which heavenly signs occurred) were ordered to be thrown into the Tiber by Amulius, the uncle of Rhea (who had deposed his brother, Numitor). Amulius had made Rhea a Vestal Virgin to avoid any of her children later trying to depose him. The box drifted on the flooded Tiber to the shore whereby the twins were suckled by a wolf until they were discovered and raised by Faustulus, a herdsman, and his wife, Acca Larentia.

Motifs

A511.0.1§, A511.1, A511.2.1, A511.3.1, A511.10.2.1, A512.3, A515.1.1, F960.1, M375.1 (in this case, their grand-uncle, Amulius), R131, S330, S331, S350, S350.2, S351.2.

Oedipus

The birth of Oedipus, the son of Laius, king of Thebes, and Iocasta (or Epicaste) is as follows: Laius is warned by Apollo that if he had a son, that son would kill him. Ignoring the warning, Laius had a son whom he had exposed (spiking his feet for good measure) to avoid this fate. Later found by a shepherd of Corinth, the baby was adopted by King Polybus, who named him Οἰδίπους (*swollen-foot*). Hyginus' later Latin variant leaves out the shepherd and almost suggests an 'exposed on water' element.

Variants of the Oedipus story span centuries of literature. Though the earliest references appear in Homer and Pindar, the definitive account derives from Sophocles' *Oedipus Tyrannus* (fifth century BCE). How much the Old Testament is based on earlier lost literature or oral tales is unknowable.

The Oedipus story is recorded as tale type ATU 931 *Oedipus* in which are listed these motifs:

M343	'Parricide Prophecy'
M344	'Mother-incest prophecy'
M371.2	'Exposure of child to prevent fulfilment of parricide prophecy'.
[K512	'Compassionate executioner' (This motif is listed in the AT but

not in the ATU)

R131   'Exposed or abandoned child rescued'
S354   'Exposed infant reared at strange king's court'
N323   'Parricide prophecy unwittingly fulfilled'
T412   'Mother-son incest'

El-Shamy provides a larger list of 42 motifs that include L111.2, M342.2, R131 and S354.

Telephus

The son of Heracles and Auge (daughter of King Aleos). In Arcadian tradition, after his birth (by rape), Auge hid him in an Athenian temple whereupon the land became plagued/infertile. Aleos had him exposed on Mount Parthenion where he was suckled by a hind/doe until being rescued by shepherds. Hence his name 'Τήλεφος', which derives from θηλᾶν (*to suckle*) and ἔλαφος (*deer* or *hind*). In other versions, Auge and Telephus are set adrift in a chest.

> Here are the stock incidents of romance—a hero's child, exposed, nursed by a wild animal, rescued and brought up by a shepherd. It might be the beginning of another *Daphnis and Chloe*![15]

In this late second, early third-century CE romance/pastoral novel by Longus, a goatherd finds a boy (Daphnis) being suckled by a she-goat whom he adopts. Two years later, a shepherd finds a girl (Chloe) being suckled by a sheep in a cave.

Motifs
A511.2.1, K515, S141, S147, S312, S322.1, S350.2, S351.2.

Sargon

Of the Sargon legend, four texts (three Neo-Assyrian and one Neo-Babylonian) recount the story of his birth. This translation is taken from Column i of the neo-Assyrian text K3401+Sm 2118:

1. Sargon, strong king, king of Agade, am I.

2. My mother was a high priestess, my father I do not know.

3. My paternal kin inhabit the mountain region.

4. My city (of birth) is Azupiranu, which lies on the bank of the Euphrates.

5.   My mother, a high priestess, conceived me, in secret she bore me.

6.   She placed me in a reed basket, with bitumen she caulked my hatch.

7.   She abandoned me to the river from which I could not escape.

8.   The river carried me along; to Aqqi, the water drawer, it brought me.

9.   Aqqi, the water drawer, when immersing his bucket lifted me up.

10. Aqqi, the water drawer, raised me as his adopted son.

Discovered during the 1848–50 excavations of Assurbanipal's library at Nineveh, the legend's parallel with Moses' birth was quickly observed in the earliest translations of the 1870s.

Motifs

A511.0.1§, A511.1, A511.2.1, A511.3.1, R131, S312, S331, S350, S350.2, R131.4? (fisher = water-drawer?).

Cyrus

Cyrus II, King of Babylon, is presented as a saviour figure in the Old Testament for releasing the Jews from captivity and ordering the rebuilding of the Temple. Indeed, Isaiah 45.1 specifically calls him 'anointed' (MT, מָשִׁיחַ; LXX, Χριστῷ) and sent by God to redeem Israel and deliver the exiles from captivity.

Herodotus' fifth-century BCE account can be summarised as follows:

> [Astyages]... had a daughter called Mandane and he dreamt that she urinated so much that she not only filled his city, but even flooded the whole of Asia. He described this dream to some of the Magi, who interpret dreams, and the details of what they told him frightened him... his fear of the dream made him refuse to marry her to any [Mede]; instead, he gave her to a Persian called Cambyses... [A few months later] Astyages had another dream in which a vine grew from Mandane's genitals and overshadowed the whole of Asia. He told the dream-interpreters what he had seen and then had his daughter, who was pregnant, sent from Persia. When she came, he kept a close watch on her, because he wanted to kill the child... for the Magi had interpreted his dream to mean that his daughter's offspring would rule in his place... when Cyrus was born, Astyages summoned... Harpagus... 'I want you to get the baby Mandane bore, take him to your own home, and kill him. How you bury the body

is up to you.' Harpagus gave the Cyrus to a herdsman to expose but
the herdsman substituted him for his own recently still-born son. So the
dead child was exposed upon the mountain and Cyrus was adopted and
raised by the herdsman and his wife.[16]

Motifs

This long account allows us to apply a far wider range of motifs:
A511, A511.2.1, A511.2.3, A511.3.1, D1810.3, D1810.8.2, D1810.3,
D1810.8.3.3, D1812.3.3, P481?, K1847.1.1, K512, M302.7, M370, M371,
M371.1, S147, S310, S350, S350.2, S351.2, T581

In Herodotus' version, Cyrus is never himself exposed and abandoned. Only
the dead replacement child is 'exposed' on the mountain.

Herodotus' stories have raised the issue of mythological patterns in historical
narratives, and his use of mythic elements, as in Cyrus' birth, have been seen as
problematic for his standing as a historian. In her view (in complete opposite to
studies of Matthew 1–2):

> Perhaps because the legendary elements in the birth stories of Cyrus
> or Demaratus are so transparent, there has been little temptation for
> scholars to try to separate factual kernels from mythological chaff in
> those tales.[17]

For example, I.M. Diakonoff sees the birth story of Cyrus as a folklore motif
common to stories about, 'famous kings, conquerors and founders of dynasties'
while T. Cuyler Young states that 'the stories of his childhood as related in
Herodotus can be dismissed as charming legend.'[18]

Jan de Vries, writing of the historicity of heroic legends, notes how Herodotus
would have heard such legends during his Persian travels of c. 450 BCE.

> We may at least suppose, then, that about 480 B.C.E. this legend about
> Cyrus was in circulation. Now this Persian king died in 529, so that in
> about half a century his history had grown into a true legend.[19]

Herodotus has preserved for us an early example of a historical figure that has
been given a legendary birth. Similarly, Campbell writes, 'If the deeds of an actual
historical figure proclaim him to have been a hero, the builders of his legend will
invent for him appropriate adventures in depth.' These suggest a parallel to how
such a heroic birth pattern might have attached itself so soon to stories about
Jesus: *being a response to questions regarding his origins.*

Augustus

In his account of the birth of Augustus, Suetonius records a bolt of lightening hitting the wall of Velitrae (Augustus' birthplace) that was later interpreted as an omen foretelling his rule of the world. He then records another more significant portent, this time seen in Rome:

> Auctor est Iulius Marathus, ante paucos quam nasceretur menses prodigium Romae factum naturam parturire; senatum exterritum censuisse, ne quis illo anno gentius educaretur; eos qui gravidas uxores haberent, quod ad se quisque spem traheret, curasse ne senatus consultum ad aerarium deferretur.

> *According to Julius Marathus, a few months before Augustus was born a portent was generally observed in Rome, which gave warning that nature was pregnant with a king for the Roman people; thereupon the Senate in consternation decreed that no male child born that year should be reared; but those whose wives were with child saw to it that the decree was not filed in the treasury, since each one appropriated the prediction to his own family. (Aug. 2.94.1-6)* [20]

Suetonius also relates a tale that Augustus was the son of Apollo ('Apollonis filium') and that his mother, Atia, had also, 'somniavit intestina sua ferri ad sidera explicarique per omnem terrarium et caeli ambitum.'

Motifs
A512.3, F960.1, D180.8.2, M311 (M311.4, M311.5) M370, M375, K512.

The usual events are somewhat reversed in parts, for there are those who *want* the prophecy to be fulfilled in their own children, and there's no exposure/ abandonment and return. However, Suetonius provides Augustus with an illustrious birth via a standard collection of motifs: portents, prophecies of greatness and future rule, and divine genealogy.

Apollonius of Tyana

The close attention received by Philostratus' *Apollonius* is due to his record of Apollonius' miraculous birth as the son of Zeus and his life as a wise teacher and healer who imprisoned, executed then raised from the dead, a pattern often contrasted to the life of Jesus. Indeed, to Roger Beck, its close parallel to the Synoptics is due to Philostratus, whether intentionally or not, 'setting up a philosophical counterpart to the Christian saviour/hero.' [21]

1. The Greek sea-god Proteus, in the guise of an Egyptian demon appears before Apollonius' mother and tells her that she will give birth to himself.

2. His mother is warned in a dream to pick flowers in a meadow where she falls asleep, surrounded by dancing swans.

3. Apollonius is born in the meadow.

4. At his birth, a thunderbolt falls to earth but then rises back up into the sky.

5. Apollonius is regarded by some as a son of Zeus.

Motifs
A511, A512.3, F960.1

CHAPTER 17:
BIRTH NARRATIVES IN BIBLICAL LITERATURE

In the Old Testament, birth stories typically follow a particular literary form (connected with barrenness and fertility), the 'Biblical Annunciation of Birth.'

1. The *appearance* of an angel of the Lord (or of the Lord)

2. *Fear* or prostration of the visionary confronted by a supernatural presence

3. The divine *message*:

    a. The visionary is addressed by name
    b. A qualifying phrase describes the visionary
    c. The visionary is urged not to be afraid
    d. A woman is with child or is about to be with child
    e. She will give birth to a (male) child
    f. The name by which the child is to be called is revealed
    g. An etymology interprets the name
    h. The future accomplishments of the child are indicated

4. An *objection* by the visionary as to how this can be, or a request for a sign

5. The *giving of a sign* to reassure the visionary.

Alternatively, Robert Neff presents the simpler fixed form ABND:

    AB: Announcement of birth (introduced by the particle *hinnēh*)
    N: Designation of the name
    D: Specification of the child's destiny

Such annunciations can be seen with regard to Ishmael, Isaac, Samson, Josiah, 'Immanuel', and Solomon. It can also be seen in the birth stories of John the Baptist (Luke 1) and Jesus, though Samson's birth:

Contains all the elements common to the legends about the birth
of mythological heroes: the barren mother, the intervention of a
supernatural (usually divine) being, and the resulting miraculous birth.[1]

This doesn't readily parallel the exposed-persecuted child pattern. Though
abandonment of children does occur in the Old Testament, the birth legend is
clearest in the birth story of Moses and apocryphal stories of Abraham.

Abraham

Abraham (a converted Gentile), the first descendant of Jesus listed in the
genealogy is, for Matthew, the beginning of salvation history being linked
chiasticically with David in the first artificial set of fourteen generations.

The birth of Abraham in Gen 11.27 is mentioned only briefly. After a
toledot-formula introduces the story of Terah, we learn in a genealogy only
that (LXX): '*Terah was the father of Abram*' Josephus' account (*Ant.* 1.149) is
likewise short: '*For Therrus begat Abraham at the age of 70*'. Later apocryphal
narratives follow the form of the persecuted and exposed child.

The Hebrew *Sefer ha-Yashar* (*Book of Jashar*) claims to be the book referred
to in Joshuah 10.13 and 2 Samuel 1.18. It's a midrashic history of the biblical
world from Creation to the Israelite invasion of Canaan.

Dated to between the ninth and sixteenth century CE, it at first appears too
late to be of any use as a source for Matthew 2. However, Geza Vermes argues
that, though indeed late (no earlier than the eleventh century in his opinion),
it exhibits continuity with Second Temple tradition; further reflecting the
haggadaic influence of the Rabbinic Tannaim (20–200 CE) and later Amoraim
(200–500 CE). His conclusion is that it preserves 'a valuable amount of pre-
Tannaitic exegetical traditions'.[2] *Sefer ha-Yashar* 8.1–36 relates a variant on the
birth of Abraham where the story tells of Nimrod's 'wise men' and 'conjurers'
who observe an astronomical portent at the time of Terah's birth of Abraham:

> 8:11 And thy servants were astonished at the sight which we saw,
> and were greatly terrified, and we made our judgment upon the sight,
> and knew by our wisdom the proper interpretation thereof, that this
> thing applies to the child that is born to Terah, who will grow up and
> multiply greatly, and become powerful, and kill all the kings of the
> earth, and inherit all their lands, he and his seed forever.[3]

Nimrod then demands Terah's son and offers to pay for him:

> 33 And Terah hastened, (as the thing was urgent from the king), and
> he took a child from one of his servants, which his handmaid had born
> to him that day, and Terah brought the child to the king and received
> value for him.

Abraham is saved and spends the early years of his life safely concealed in a cave.

Motifs
A511.0.1§, A511.1, A511.2.3, D1812.5.1.6, F960.1, K512, K515, K1847,
M302.4?, M370, P481, R153, S310, T581, Z159§

A variant account (with a closer parallel to Matthew 2) appears in the
Ma'ase Abraham from the *Bet Ha Midrash*:

> King Nimrod, a king well versed in astrology, learns from the stars that
> a child will be born who would overthrow the gods. Fearing this he
> called together all his chief priests and councillors to ask them 'What
> can I do against this child of destiny?' The priests and councillors advise
> him to slaughter every male child as soon as he is born, but to spare the
> females. Upon observing this the Angels cry out to God 'Have you not
> seen how Nimrod [sic] the blasphemer murders innocents?'. Escaping
> the slaughter Amitlai, Abraham's mother, gives birth to him in a cave
> by the river Euphrates. Left alone for twenty days, in which he grows
> into a boy with great speed, he is watched over by the Angel Gabriel.[4]

Additional motifs
J641, M311, M311.4, M375, R153.4, S146.2, S302.1, V230, V235, T580, T585

Of the *Sefer ha-Yashar* account, Vermes (arguing that such Infancy
Narratives belong to 'a well-defined class of midrashic literature') observes four
(now familiar) themes:

1. Miraculous birth.

2. Interpretation of miracle.

3. Newborn child condemned to death.

4. Escape and deliverance of child. Themes that Vermes traces
   primarily to Moses haggadah.

However, P. Nepper-Christensen examining the Abraham-Nimrod tale in the *Sefer ha-Yashar*, suggests that such traditions should cause pause in any claims as specific Moses typology with Matthew as such legendary birth motifs occur across many hero stories. Dale Allison, on the other hand, doubts this view due to the age of the legend (being later than the Moses story of Philo and Josephus; the late development of the Nimrod birth account to Abraham could explain Josephus' silence with regard to the legend in his own account) and the assimilation of later Abraham traditions with those of Moses.

Moses

Moses, the most important figure in Israelite salvation history (Moses is referred to more times in the New Testament than any other biblical figure) provides an example of the heroic pattern. According to Raglan (following his outline given above):

> His parents (1 and 2) were of the principal family of the Levites, and (3) near relatives; he is (5) also reputed to be the son of Pharaoh's daughter. Pharaoh (6) attempts to kill him at birth, but (7) he is wafted away, and (8) reared secretly. We are told (9) nothing of his childhood.

James Frazer also notes folkloric features and suggests that Moses' birth narrative is an 'embellished invention of the narrator'.[5]

In the short scriptural account in Exodus, the Pharaoh commands that all the newborn male children be killed by being thrown into the Nile in order to control the fast growing slave population. Dead Sea Scroll, 2Q2 2.14 adds, 'Egypt was in dread because of the children of Israel.'

The tale of Moses birth and survival is told in 2.1–10; an unnamed man and woman marry and have a boy. After three months he is hidden in a papyrus basket along the banks of the river where he is found and raised by the Pharaoh's daughter.

The general consensus on the literary composition of Exodus 1–2 is that 1.13–14 is P (seventh to fifth century BCE), while 1.15–22 and 2.1–10 is the work of E (c. 850 BCE). Martin Noth, however, suggests that 1.15–21 is E, with 1.22 (joining onto vv8–12) and 2.1–10 being J (c. 850–1000 BCE). The division isn't definite, as, 'Both J and E seem to follow the same major lines of the tradition and therefore show few characteristic peculiarities.'[6] Though debate continues over the designation and dating of Pentateuchal sources (and whether such nineteenth-century scholarship is even valid), we can assume an early date for the Moses birth story.

Exodus contains a number of literary forms, but into which does Moses' birth fit? The most commonly cited source is that of Sargon who, as seen above, was likewise set adrift in a basket. From this legend, H. Gressman, examining similar birth parallels, concluded that the Moses birth story was based on this common *Märchenmotif*, that of the rescued promised child. Brevard Childs, however, argues that Gressman has made an error: noting (in line 2 of the Sargon text) that *enitum* (or *ēntu*) means 'priestess', to Childs, the Sargon legend isn't the story of a child rescued from danger but the story of the concealment of an illegitimate child.

It's been argued that the threat from Pharaoh *wasn't an original part of the birth story*, but added to provide the motivation for the author's use of the exposure motif.

As evidence of Exodus 1's literary purpose as prologue to Exodus 2, Childs has pointed to the illogical actions of a nation trying to wipe out its work force, and by killing males, instead of females. He also notes the lack of further references to this event later in Exodus or the Old Testament. This parallels our conclusions with regard to Matthew 1–2.

The legend of the child exposed on water (whether Sargon or some other early 'Type A' source) remains the primary influence. Whether the original Sargon tale is one of illegitimacy or danger is irrelevant, because the narrative structure remains the same. Later first-century CE commentators would have known the *final redacted form* and these versions of the story closest in time to Matthew would have had the most influence.

Philo relates the birth of Moses in *Moses* 1.2–6. He presents the same basic Exodus story though he extenuates the Pharaoh's cruelty, with the motivation for his decree being a fear that the Israelites would take control of Egypt, fear (in connection with avoiding fate) being a common motive for exposure and persecution in birth legends.

In Philo's account, Moses parents are named as Jochebed and Amran and he relates the post-biblical detail that Jochebed didn't require a midwife at the birth. Due to the omnipresence of Pharaoh's spies, both parents (not just his mother as in Exodus 2:3) decide to expose him in the Nile to perish and he relates their grief and guilt. God's providence brings Moses to the childless Egyptian princess, whereby he is raised in the royal household, with Pharaoh as his adopted grandfather.

Though the fear of losing power is the cause of Pharaoh's decree to kill all newborn male infants, Philo does have those in authority put *further* fear into Pharaoh by suggesting that Moses, after killing the slave master, wished to usurp his sovereignty. At this point Moses flees the wrath of his adopted grandfather and travels to Arabia for safety, only returning to Egypt after his encounter with God. God informs Moses that it's safe to return as his grandfather is dead and the new ruler doesn't know him.

Josephus amends the story in his *Antiquities* (written perhaps not long after Matthew, in c. 93–94 CE) where another example of his *rewritten Bible* appears. Here, the significant addition is his embellishment of the Exodus account.

In *Antiquities* 2.205–209, a 'sacred scribe' (ἱερογραμματέων), one who could *predict the future*, warned the king that a child would be born to the Israelites, a saviour who would surpass all in virtue and renown. The scribe then advises the alarmed (δείας) king to have all newborn male infants killed. Thackeray (perhaps with Matthew in mind) translates Josephus' φθειρομένων... τῶν τικτομένων (literally, 'the destruction of that brought into the world') as 'the massacre of the infants.'

In *Antiquities* 2.209, Moses escapes from the clutches of the king's decree by the will of God:

> For this child, whose birth the sacred scribe had foretold, was reared eluding the king's vigilance, and the prophet's words concerning all that was to be wrought through him proved true.

The story of this escape is related in *Antiquities* 2.210–223. Moses' father, Amram, asks God for deliverance from Egyptian oppression. God appears *in a dream* to Amram and assures him that his son, 'whose birth has filled the Egyptian with dread' will be born safe and escape death.

Of Moses' actual birth, Josephus only records that it was an unusually gentle and painless birth (*Antiquities* 2.218).

The Psalm–Jonathan *Targum* on Exodus 1.15 records that Pharaoh had a dream in which he saw a set of scales. On one side was a lamb (טליא) and on the other all of Egypt, but the lamb was heavier. Pharaoh's 'chief magicians', Jannes and Jambres (who are seen in later tradition as the sons of Balaam) interpret this to mean that, 'a son is about to be born in the congregation of Israel, by whose hand the whole land of Egypt will be ruined.'

Astrologers/magicians warn Pharoah of the birth of a saviour in *Midrash Shemoth Rabbah* 1.18, 24, *Sanh.* 101b, *Sotah* 12a, 12b, and *Pirqe R. El.* 2. In these passages, water is seen by the astrologers as the means of averting this fate.

In *Exodus Rabbah* 1.22 a heavenly sign appears in the form of light flooding the room. Allison suggests that the Star of Matthew 2 *could* parallel the light 'phenomena' associated with Moses' birth, but concludes that this isn't a 'confident' parallel *for folklore reasons*—it was common enough not to have, 'reminded ancient readers of Moses in particular.'[7]

Motifs

Exodus: A511.1, A511.2.1 (in this case, after 3 months), J641, M375.1 (in this case, overcome Egypt), R131, S302.1, S310, S330, S331, S350, S350.2, S354 (in this case, Pharaoh's own court), T581.

Philo: story includes T584.0.3.

Josephus: As Exodus but also D1810.8.2, M310.1, M311, M311.4, M311.5, M370, M391.

Rabbinic: Includes P481.

Jesus and the legend of the persecuted and rescued (royal) child

> If we accept the validity of the general outlines of the European hero pattern, it would appear reasonable to consider that the biography of Jesus does in fact conform fairly well to this pattern.[8]

The general issue is the methodological problem with the definition of the 'hero pattern'. Yet there remains more agreement with regard to the Infancy Narrative's parallel with the legendary birth pattern.

It's traditional to divide Matthew 2 into two acts: the first dealing with the Star and the arrival of the magi (often divided into five sub-sections), and the second dealing with the massacre, flight into Egypt and final settling in Nazareth. This second section has also been sub-divided. Thus, Gerd Lüdemann presents Matthew 2 as follows:

A.   The Magicians
   a.   Arrival of the Magicians in Jerusalem
   b.   Privy Council in Jerusalem
   c.   Interrogation of the Magicians
   d.   Magicians travel to Bethlehem
   e.   Adoration of the Magicians
   f.   Return of the Magicians

B.   Flight to Egypt

C.   Herod's infanticide

D.   Return of the family from Egypt

W.D. Davis and Dale Allison structure Matthew 1–2 as follows (also with six stages to the Magian visit):

I. Early history (1:18–4:22)
    1. Conception and infancy of Jesus (1:18–2:23)
        A. The virginal conception (1:18–25)
        B. Visit of the Magi (2:1–12)
            b1. Magi arrive looking for king of the Jews (2:1–2)
            b2. Herod asks chief priests and scribes for location (2:3–6)
            b3. Herod asks magi for help (2:7–8)
            b4. Magi follow Star (2:9–10)
            b5. Magi pay homage with gifts (2:11)
            b6. Magi warned not to return to Herod and leave (2:12)
        C. Infants and Herod (2:13–23)
            c1. Joseph warned to flee to Egypt (2:13–15)
            c2. Massacre of the Innocents (2:16–18)
            c3. Return from Egypt to Nazareth after Herod's death (2:19–23)

A shorter pattern is presented by Leon Morris:

C. Infant Jesus (2:1–23)
    1. Visit of the magi (2:1–12)
    2. Flight into Egypt (2:13–15)
    3. Killing of the children (2:16–18)
    4. Return from Egypt (2:19–23)

Craig Keener divides Matthew 2 into three sections:

Pagans worship Jesus (2:1–12)
Persecuted child (2:13–18)
Settling in Nazareth (2:19–23)

R. E. Brown outlines two structures:

Introduction:	1:1–17	Genealogy
Scene One:	1:18–25 (Isaiah7:14)	First dream of Joseph
Scene Two:	2:1–12 (Micah 5:1)	Herod, magi, Bethlehem
Scene Three:	2:13–15 (Hosea 11:1)	Second dream of Joseph

| Scene Four: | 2:16–18 (Jer 31:15) | Herod, children, Bethlehem |
| Scene Five: | 2:19–23 (Isaiah4:3?) | Third dream of Joseph |

1:1–17	Genealogy
1:18–25	Conception
2:1–12	Arrival of the magi
2:13–23	Escape and return to Nazareth

These are artificial divisions as 'chapters' and 'verses' didn't exist in ancient New Testament texts, having only existed in Greek New Testaments since the mid-sixteenth century. This doesn't rule out the possibility that Matthew had such a structure in mind—his Gospel is full of structural patterns and devices.

Matthew 1–2 appears to be constructed as a *single narrative unit*:

1. Joseph learns that Mary is pregnant via the Holy Spirit (Matthew 1.18–19)

2. The angel of the Lord reminds (*in a dream*) Joseph of Isaiah's virgin birth prophecy (Matthew 1.20–23; Isaiah 7.14)

    1. [*Event occurring outside of narrative—Past event—Star appears to Magi*].

    2. Magi arrive in Jerusalem (Matthew 2.1–2)

    3. Past event revealed; Herod and Jerusalem worried (Matthew 2.3)

    4. Herod calls council for advice (Matthew 2.4)

    5. It's learnt that Bethlehem would be the birthplace (Matthew 2.5–6; Micah 5.1 and 2 Samuel 5.2).

    6. Herod asks magi to report to him (Matthew 2.7–8)

    7. Magi follow Star and find Jesus, worshipping him with gifts (Matthew 2.9–11)

    8. Magi warned (*in dream*) and do not return to Herod (Matthew 2.12)

    9. Joseph warned by angel (*in a dream*) and flees to Egypt with Mary and Jesus (Matthew 2.13–15; Hos. 11.1).

10. Herod kills newborn children in Bethlehem (Matthew 2.16–18; Jeremiah 31.15).

11. Joseph told to return from Egypt (*in a dream*) and settlement in Nazareth (Matthew 2.19–3; Isaiah 11.1–2?; Judges 13.1–5, 16.17?).

TABLE 11: MATTHEW 1–2 AND HEROIC BIRTH PATTERNS

Pattern of:	Motifs Evident
Von Hahn	3. Father is a god; 4. Signs warning his ascendance.
Rank	4. Prophecy warning (Herod) against birth.
Propp	$\alpha\ \varepsilon^1\ \zeta^1\ \eta^1\ {}^1G^2{\uparrow}A^{13}A^{14}{\downarrow}$
Raglan	1. Virgin mother; 4. Unusual conception; 5. Hero reputed to be son of god; 6. Attempt to kill hero, 7; Hero spirited away, 8; Reared by foster parents (Joseph); 9. No details of childhood.
de Vries	1a. Mother is a virgin; 1b. Father is a god; 3. Youth is threatened.
Lewis	II.b. Divine parent; VIII.b. Prophecy and its fulfilment; VIII.f. Miraculous events surrounding birth

At first it seems that (apart from Raglan and Propp) the number of matching points is limited. Indeed, the absence of a more complete birth pattern is due to the obvious lack of any *exposure and adoption* element in Matthew 2. However, the order of events indicates that the *general pattern and form* of the 'persecuted child' tale is present:

1. Unusual conception—miraculous (virgin) birth of new 'king'

2. 'Old' king warned by portent (Star), told of meaning by magi (interpreters) and location (prophecy) by chiefs priests/scribes

3. Attempt by fearful king to kill newborn threat/avert fate

4. Child escapes persecution (death) via safety in foreign land

5. [Eventual return to homeland]

These events cover nearly every verse of Matthew 1–2 with the exception of the genealogy (which serves its own semi-independent purpose) and the magian homage. Thus, individual folk-motifs applied to Matthew 1–2 reveals a literary unit consisting of the 'motif-spectrum' of generic features.

TABLE 12: BIRTH MOTIFS IN MATTHEW 1–2

Matthew 1-2	Motif
1:18	A511, A511.0.1§, A511.1, T510, T540
1:18, 25	A511.1.3, T547
1:20–25	D1810.8.2, D1812.3.3
1:22–23	M300, M369.7, V230, V235, V235.0.1
2:1	P481, T581
2:1–2	E741.1.1.2, F960.1, F961.2.1, P481, Z159§, Z159.4.4§
2:4–6	M300, M310.1, M311, M311.0.2, M311.4, M311.5, M369.7
2:7–8	M370, P481
2:9–10	D1314.13
2:12, 16	D1810.8.2, D1810.3, M370, M375, M375.1, S330
2:13–15	D1810.8.2, D1810.3, D1810.8.3.3, V235.0.1, J641, K515, K515.1
2:17–18	M300
2:19–20	D1810.8.2, D1810.3, V235.0.1
2:23	M300

Early form critics were aware of such parallels with folk motifs. Rudolf Bultmann writes that 'it seems more likely that use has been make [by Matthew] of a folk-saga or a fairy-tale motif' and observes the use of such motifs in classical literature, 'whether in the form of the old ruler who sets traps for his newborn future rival and dethroner or in conjunction with the motif of child slaying.'[9] Martin Dibelius is more cautious though still willing to accept the use by Matthew of a 'general pattern'.[10]

Charles Potter writes that the wise men and Star, 'all bear the authentic marks of folklore, paralleling the Infancy Narratives of the founders of other faiths' where the persecution of the prophesied child was 'stock first-act situation in the dramatic folk histories of many others.'[11] Likewise, Thomas Fawcett, though stating that the Old Testament remains the prime influence, notes the persecuted child theme and states that, 'Matthew has written a Jewish variant of a story with wide currency.'[12] Alan Dundes also refers to the life of Jesus as 'a variant of the standard biography of the hero of tradition.'[13]

As Jesus isn't abandoned, Brian Lewis sees Matthew 1–2 as a 'defective or incomplete version of our tale type', though D.B. Redford argues that 'the abandonment of the child in a deserted spot is replaced by a flight *through* the desert to Egypt'.[14] However, abandonment isn't a essential motif and the reason it's missing from Matthew 2 might be the simple historical reason that Jesus' mother and family were so closely connected with his life.

Horsley has also observed the close parallels between Matthew 1–2 and the hero pattern, and sees the use of the birth pattern as socio-political, as most hero tales concern the founders of new social and political orders.

Whether Matthew was consciously aware of the 'founding culture hero' origin or using a familiar biographical folk form in his presentation of Jesus as the promised saviour is impossible to establish. What *is* easier to establish is the similarity between the birth of Jesus and of haggadic accounts (legend, folktale, fairytale) of Moses' birth.

Matthew 1–2 and the birth of Moses

All comparisons between the births of Moses and Jesus highlight the same general points. For example, R.E. Brown and A.D.A. Moses present the following parallels from Exodus.

TABLE 13:
A COMPARISON OF BIRTH NARRATIVES
OF JESUS AND MOSES: BIBLICAL

Matthew 1–2	Exodus 1–4
2.1,3. Herod is called king ($\beta\alpha\sigma\iota\lambda\acute{\epsilon}\omega\varsigma$).	1.8, 15, 17, 18. Pharaoh is called 'the king of Egypt.'
2.3. Herod and Jerusalem afraid.	1.8–10 (cf. 2Q2 2.14). Egypt afraid of Israel.
2.13–14. Herod was going to search for the child to destroy him, so Joseph took the child and his mother and went away.	2.15. The Pharaoh sought to kill male infants, so Moses went away.
2.16. Herod sent troops to Bethlehem and massacred boys aged two years and under.	1.22. The Pharaoh commanded that every male born to the Hebrews be cast into the Nile.
2.19. Herod died.	2.23. Pharoah died.

2.19–20. The angel of the Lord said to Joseph in Egypt: πορεύου εἰς γῆν Ἰσραήλ· τεθνήκασιν γὰρ οἱ ζητοῦντες τὴν ψυχὴν τοῦ παιδίου (go to the land of Israel, for those who were seeking the child's life are dead).	4.19. The Lord said to Moses in Midian: Εἶπε δὲ Κύριος πρὸς Μωυσῆν ἐν Μαδιάμ, βάδιζε, ἄπελθε εἰς Αἴγυπτον, τεθνήκασι γὰρ πάντες οἱ ζητοῦντες σου τὴν ψυχήν (...go back to Egypt; for all those who were seeing your life are dead).
2.13–15, 22–23. Jesus protected.	2.1–10. Moses saved.
2.14. Joseph ἀνεχώρησεν εἰς Αἴγυπτον (departed for Egypt).	2.15. Moses fled (ἀνεχώρησεν) from the face of Pharaoh.
2:21. Joseph took the child and his mother and went back to the land of Israel.	4:20. Moses took along his wife and children and returned to Egypt.

Of Matthew 2.19–20 and Exodus 4.19–20, Allison refers to this as evidence of 'implicit citation' and the parallelism of exile and return, especially given the similar use of language between Matthew and the LXX. However, more specific parallels and allusions exist in post-biblical literature (particularly Josephus).

TABLE 14:
A COMPARISON OF BIRTH NARRATIVES
OF JESUS AND MOSES: POSTBIBLICAL

Jesus	Moses
1.18–21. Jesus will save. Angel appears to Joseph (who is worried) in a dream.	Jos. *Ant.* 2.210–216, 228. God appears to Amram in a dream and tells him that Moses is Israel's saviour. Name associated with Egyptian vb. 'save'.
2.2. Star of Bethlehem.	*Exodus Rab.* 1.22; cf. *Sotah* 13a; *Meg.* 14a; *Cant. Rab.* 1:20. Bright light at Moses' birth.

2.2–18. Herod learning of the birth of a Jewish saviour from chief priests and magi results in 'Massacre of Innocents.' 2.4–6. ἀρχιερεῖς καὶ γραμματεῖς *(chief priests and scribes)*	Jos. *Ant.* 2.205–209, 234; *Tg. Psalm On Exod* 1:15; *Midrash Shemoth Rabbah* 1.18, 24; *b. Sanh.* 101a-b, *Sotah* 12b. Pharaoh learns of saviour via dream/scribes/astrologers/chief magicians. ἱερογραμματέων *(sacred scribe)*
2.3. Herod and Jerusalem gripped by fear.	Jos. *Ant.* 2.206; Philo *Mos.* 1.2.8. Pharaoh seized by fear.

Order and structure of Moses' birth

In Exodus 1.15–2.15, 4.20, the order of events runs as follows:

1. Order from king of Egypt for midwives to kill newborn males

2. Midwives do not obey

3. New command for every newborn boy to be thrown in the Nile

4. Parents of Moses hide child in basket by side of river

5. Moses found and adopted by king's daughter

6. Adult Moses kills an Egyptian and flees to Midian

7. Lord tells Moses to return to Egypt as those seeking him are dead

Of Josephus' postbiblical account, Allison observes a three act structure:

2.205–209: Pharaoh's dream and its interpretation
2.210–216: The dream of Amram
2.217–223: Moses' birth and providential deliverance

Or:

1. Prophecy to deliverer's foes and decree of death

2. Prophecy (in a dream) to Moses' family

3. The deliverance of Moses from danger

What is evident is that Matthew 2, the Exodus account and especially Josephus' postbiblical account agree significantly in order and structure.

We can step back further and conclude that the structure wasn't even the invention of Jewish tradition, but the result of widespread Near Eastern birth traditions extending far back into the second millennium BCE. Therefore, it's no surprise to observe such similarities in order between the two narratives.

CHAPTER 18:
PRE-MATTHEAN NARRATIVE AND MATTHEAN REDACTION

Some critics have argued for the existence of pre-Matthean narratives/sources.

> Given the rampant attraction to astrology in their culture and official Jewish polemic against it, *Matthew and his Jewish church would probably not have made up the story* about Magi believing in Jesus, *though they might put a pre-existing story to good use.*[1] [my italics]

Did Matthew use earlier sources (independent magi and Herod traditions), redacting them into the form now seen in Matthew 2? If so, how does such a redaction of such sources affect the argument that Matthew 2 is a single narrative based on a Moses haggadic 'persecuted child' motif?

Pre-Matthean narrative in recent scholarship

W.D. Davies and Dale C. Allison

Davies and Allison argue that these two chapters are the result of earlier pre-Matthean traditions combined with later redactional work by Matthew. Dismissing free creation by Matthew or the stringing together of two or more separate pericopae (due, they say, *to evidence of unity in the whole infancy structure*), they present five observations that reveal three stages of development.

1. The redactional nature of the formula citations

2. The redactional nature of Matthew 2.22–23

3. That the 'Matthean style' of the remaining material could be the result of 'fluid sources' and 'thorough editing'

4. Jewish haggadic traditions about Moses

5. The existence of certain historical elements such as names (Jesus, Mary, Joseph), Herod and Nazareth.

After subtracting the redactional and historical elements plus the Moses Haggadah, we're left with elements of Davidic Christology—the virgin birth, the magi and the Star, and the birth in Bethlehem. From the remaining text, Davis and Allison extract three stages of development:

1. A birth narrative influenced by Moses traditions, with long dream annunciation to Joseph. The group behind this stage could also have been behind the Moses traditions found in Acts 3 and 7.

2. The development of Davidic Christology. The annunciation is conflated with the virgin conception, legend of the magi and Star, merged with the Herod story and with Bethlehem added. No specific community can be deduced for this stage of development.

3. Matthean redaction. Formula citations added along with 2.22–23. Whole narrative re-written in Matthew's style and vocabularly.

R.E. Brown

In his *Birth of the Messiah*, Brown devotes a great deal of space to the question of pre-Matthean narratives. His method of extracting what is Matthean from what isn't is through detecting Matthean vocabularly, structure and style, internal tensions and parallels with other narratives.

Though appreciating the difficulty of such extraction, he points to a number of 'raw materials' which Matthew used to create 1–2:

(1). Lists of patriarchs and kings

(2). Old Testament patterns of annunciation

(3). The patriarch Joseph and the birth of Moses

(4). Numbers 22–24, and (5) scriptural citations

Thus, Brown finds three pre-Matthean blocks:

(1). Angelic dream sequences based on Joseph

(2). A magi story based on Balaam and Balak

(3). An Herodian story based on the Moses narrative

Added to these three narratives are the five formula citations 1.22–23; 2.5b–6, 15b, 17–18, 23b.

George M. Soares Prabhu

Soares Prabhu likewise sees three sources behind Matthew 1–2, though he provides different blocks of passages:

(A). Dream narrative source

(B). Magian source

(C). Herodian source

Soares Prabhu sees in vv1–2 primarily redactional material containing elements from both the magi and Herod narratives. He argues that though the six units of 1.1–17, 18–25; 2.1–12, 13–15, 16–18 and 19–23 form a unified whole, Matthean vocabulary and style, the absence of chronological links, the juxtaposition of scenes and the recurring dream sequences point towards an Infancy Narrative built on skilfully edited pre-Matthean sources into which the formula citations have been inserted.

For example, Soares Prabhu argues that in 2.1–12 we have two independent traditions that have been redacted together by Matthew. He sees the appearance of Mary as a 'particularly strong indication of a pre-Matthean tradition' as in Matthew 1–2 she makes few appearances (as opposed to Luke).[2]

Soares Prabhu refers to the magi story as 'long', 'lacking in unity of time and place', and 'confused in its action', pointing to the illogical nature of the Star first appearing as a portent, disappearing then reappearing again to act as a guide.

> The Magi, instead of being led directly to Bethlehem (as would have been expected in a story of divine guidance), appear unexpectedly in Jerusalem. No reason is given for their sudden appearance there, though everything else in the story is clearly explained. They are then led to Bethlehem by two different indications: the directions of Herod, based on a passage of scripture (2,5f), and the guidance of the star (2,9b). All this suggests that two separate stories have been joined together here.[3]

These two narratives are joined together by v9b, which continues 2:2b.

C.T. Davis

Davis provides one of the most detailed studies of pre-Matthean Infancy sources. He argues that Matthean style helps to reveal four narrative units of pre-Matthean material in Matthew 1–2 (1.18–21; 24–25; 2.1–2 (in part), 9b, 11; 2.13–15a and 2.19–21) with the remainder being redactional in nature (1.23; 2.1–2 (in part), 3–9a; 10, 12, 15b, 16–18 and 22–23b—essentially the formula citations and narrative linking sections).

The redactional parts of 2.1–2 are verses 1b and 2a (which look towards the redactional 2.3–9a). What remains is linked to the pre-Matthean 9b and 11. Parallels between 2.3–6 and 2.22–33; 4.12–16 and 21.14–16 reveal a redactor at work. Matthew 2.7–9a is presumed by 2.12. Matthew 2.10 is redactional as this passage has the magi viewing the Star again and ought to follow 2.9a. This leaves verses 9b and 11 as pre-Matthean: the magi are led directly to Bethlehem, as they had only to follow the guiding star and no help from Jerusalem should be required. Matthew 2.12 is redactional as it's linked to 2.16–18 and interrupts the flow from 2.15a to 2.19a.

To Davis, the reasons behind the threat from Herod aren't needed as Herod's hostility is all that is needed to motivate the flight. This matches the 'economy of narration' that explains the return from Egypt.

Finally, 2.15b and 2.22–23b are redactional due to the citation of Hosiah 1.11 and Jeremiah 31.15. Davis comes to the conclusion that an earlier tradition has been, 'enlarged on the basis of scriptural interpretation.'

John Nolland

Nolland attempts to present credible independent 'Herod' and 'magi' narrative sources that can survive certain difficulties presented by Ulrich Luz who suggests that a *single narrative* lies behind Matthew 2. Stating that the idea of two pre-Matthean sources has 'little cogency', he notes that:

> A Herod narrative without the Magi would be incomplete; one would not know from where Herod received his information about the royal child. Conversely, the Magi narrative is designed with a view towards the Herod episode: The Magi are Gentiles; that required some form of confrontation with Israel.[4]

Countering the idea of a single redacted source, Nolland highlights a 'considerable number of narrative tensions and unevenness' in the current text (not all of which, he states, can be explained away as 'Mosaic Haggadah') which point to a multiple pre-Matthean source.[5] He lists the following tensions:

(1). The focus on Herod and the magi can more naturally be explained as the joining of two independent sources.

(2). In the current text, once the magi have reached Jerusalem the Star isn't needed to lead them onto Bethlehem: its purpose now is to locate Jesus *in* Bethlehem—despite taking up a guiding role only *after* the magi leave Jerusalem. This suggests a separate magi narrative in which they didn't visit Herod in Jerusalem and in which the Star (not the priests and scribes) identified Bethlehem.

(3). Herod's need for the magi to provide him information on Jesus is evidence of a merger of separate Herod and magi narratives due to Herod being 'so well provided with informers.' Why use the magi instead of his own spies?

(4). Matthew 2.11 points to separate origins for the magi and Herod narratives given the focus on Joseph in 1.18–25 and 2.13–21.

Magian Source
Nolland presents the following reconstruction of the magian narrative:

(1) [Τοῦ δὲ Ἰησοῦ γεννηθέντος] ἰδοὺ μάγοι ἀπὸ ἀνατολῶν παρεγένοντο εἰς Ἱεροσόλυμα (2) λέγοντες, Ποῦ ἐστιν ὁ τεχθεὶς βασιλεὺς τῶν Ἰουδαίων; εἴδομεν γὰρ αὐτοῦ τὸν ἀστέρα ἐν τῇ ἀνατολῇ καὶ ἤλθομεν προσκυνῆσαι αὐτῷ. (3) καὶ [πᾶσα Ἱεροσόλυμα] ???

(9-11) ἰδοὺ ὁ ἀστήρ, ὃν εἶδον ἐν τῇ ἀνατολῇ, προῆγεν αὐτούς, . . . καὶ σμύρναν.

(12) καὶ ἀνεχώρησαν εἰς τὴν χώραν αὐτῶν.

(1) [Now having been born], behold, magi from the East arrived in Jerusalem

(2) asking, 'Where is the child who has been born king of the Jews? For we observed his start at its rising, and have come to pay him homage. (3) and [all Jerusalem] ???

(9-11) there, ahead of them, went the star that they had seen at its rising, ... and myrrh.

(12) they left for their own country.

In this narrative, the Star leads the magi to Jerusalem, where they receive no assistance. It's the Star and not the Jews of Jerusalem (whose precise attitude, in this reconstruction, remains unknown) that leads them onto Bethlehem where they offer worship (the gifts being a later Matthean expansion). With the absence of Herod, there's no need for the warning dream (2.12) and the episode ends with the departure of the magi. Nolland is satisfied that this pre-Matthean reconstruction suggests:

> That a coherent narrative has emerged which is not at all vulnerable to Luz's criticisms of sources with the Magi and which allows easy development from source to final Matthean form.[6]

Herodian source

As a starting point, Nolland follows R.E. Brown's construction but with 'refinements'. The reference to 'the days of King Herod' is absent, being only necessary for the later redacted version whereupon the magi and Herod actually meet. No reference to Jesus' birth in Bethlehem is given in the introduction (nor in 1.18–25) so the reader must infer that the knowledge of the scribes and priests is assumed to be correct.

Herod hears about the birth through rumour, and his instructions to the magi are (in this original source), instructions to his own servants who are given the task of killing all male children two years and under (just to be sure). In Matthew 2, this time period of two years is the result of Matthew merging the two narratives: the magi become both the servants/spies and the source of the rumour (the Star).

Nolland suggests that the failure of the servant's quest to find Jesus in Bethlehem could be due to the population of Bethlehem refusing to help them. This is pure conjecture. The account ends with the family's return to Israel.

What were the reasons for Matthew's merger of these two sources?

> If, as is likely, Matthew was aware of the function of the haggadic material on Moses in the narrative about Herod, a final reason for Matthew's deciding to merge the two accounts may have been the closer echoing of the Mosaic haggadah which he could achieve in this manner.[7]

Matthew, then, merged the two sources to make his account more closely match that of Moses' birth.

Problems with reconstructed pre-Matthean sources

There appears to be a 'four-pronged' approach at work with regard to pre-Matthean and Matthean material:

1. Vertical analysis of vocabulary, style and structure

2. Horizontal analysis of looking at parallels from similar Near Eastern Infancy Narrative literature

3. The existence of tensions and inconsistencies

4. The redactional 'addition' of the formula citations, presupposing that there was an earlier narrative to add them 'to'

Using such an approach, most commentators agree that two or three sources (the *Deus ex machina* style dream sequences, magian and Herodian stories) have been heavily redacted by Matthew.

It's common to argue that the tension between the Star leading the magi to Jerusalem and its diminished second role after they're sent out by Herod suggests the presence of two sources (one magian and one Herodian). This is to *misunderstand* the role of Star and to apply narrative logic to a christological text. In fact, the Star has *four* roles.

Its first role is to be a *sign* of the Messiah's birth (*it isn't followed by the magi*).

Its second and third roles (and second appearance (*it seems to shun appearing to Jerusalem*) a sign of Jewish denial and disbelief in Jesus as the Messiah) are that of *confirmation* of the accuracy of the scribes (God working through a supernatural event, hence the joy of the magi) and revealing the *exact* location of Jesus, not just the general direction of Bethlehem (which is unnecessary), and to *specifically* mark him out as the one born King of the Jews—the objective of the magi's journey (as worshipping Gentiles) and the ultimate objective of the Star (hence it no longer plays a part in the events that follow).

The fourth role of the Star (perhaps actually an extension of the first) is to alert Herod, through the magi, to the Messiah's existence, and act as prime mover for the entire story: it allows Matthew 2 to follow the motif of the persecuted child. Jesus can't flee to Egypt and return to Nazareth and can't parallel the Pharaoh-Moses story *unless there is a threat*. Hence, the magi and Herod story *is more likely to have been from one source from the beginning*.

It can be argued that the source of the threat was rumour or a dream, not requiring any visiting magi, but we'd then be guilty of dividing the text based on a few perceived tensions. By creating hypothetical Herod and magi stories, we're is in danger of having to invent (for example) dreams, Herodian spies, and uncooperative citizens of Jerusalem, to plug the gaps and make them work as separate stories. The tensions that have led to such modern creativity don't exist.

Redaktionsgeschichte

George Soares Prabhu has provided considerable detail in his redactional study of Matthew 1–2 to the point where he appeals to individual words and grammatical constructions, if they appear 'clumsy' or 'un-Matthean' in style and vocabulary, as evidence of earlier narratives; being uncorrected pre-Matthean language. For example, he suggests that Matthew 2.9e, ἐπάνω οὗ ἦν τὸ παιδίον (*over the place where the child was*), is 'awkward and imprecise' and 'much too clumsy to be Matthew's formulation.'

This extremely narrow focus of redaction criticism isn't helpful in determining Matthean sources. Given the Greek text we currently possess, we aren't in the position to be able to argue about the level of Matthew's passive and active Greek knowledge. It's dangerous to argue for sources based on 'awkward' constructs or usage of vocabulary, especially when matched to the perception that the narrative is illogically constructed.

Matthew as *author* of the Infancy Narrative

The motif-spectrum clustered around birth legends, and the fact that 2.13–23 wouldn't have taken place if it weren't for the events of 2.1–12 (which creates the threat from Herod), suggests that Matthew 2 must be taken as a *complete narrative unit*. A tale that begins with a prophecy and fearful king, leads to attempts to avoid fate by exposure/murder of the newborn threat and this pattern clearly flows though Matthew 2.

So the Infancy Narrative *is* 'pre-Matthaean', though by this I don't mean a selection of known early 'Christian' traditions redacted together by Matthew with some formula citations, but the *creative* use by Matthew of genealogy; the 'annunciation' pattern; Moses haggadah (the 'persecuted-exposed child'); dream sequences and scriptural citations (fulfilment formulas) drawn from Old Testament and ancient Near Eastern forms and patterns to produce a theological prologue that provided both a familiar (and expected) biographical birth pattern and christological/didactic message.

In so doing, Matthew created a version of the Moses birth story that bridged the gap between Judaism and developing Christian theology. Hence, though Matthew didn't invent the literary form of the story's pattern, *he was the first to present the birth of Jesus in such a manner*. Before Matthew 'picked up his quill' no one had heard of the visit of the magi, the Star of Bethlehem or the Massacre of the Innocents. This helps explain why no Star tradition appears to exist outside Matthew's community and the single attestation of Matthew 2.

The difference between the presentation of Herod in Matthew and Luke also becomes more understandable. In Luke, Herod is a time reference and shows no interest in (or even knowledge of) Jesus' existence. In Matthew, Herod takes on the classic role of the old king trying to remove a new rival, countering the prophecy (cheating fate) by murderous means. That Herod *was* a tyrant, and protective of his kingship is *only a coincidence* and this fact clouds our understanding of the Infancy Narrative's sources.

The evidence of folk-motifs in Matthew 1–2 also solves the 'problem' of God apparently allowing innocent children to be killed in order to save Jesus (why were the magi not guided directly to Bethlehem?)—it was part of the pattern. It likewise explains the absence of such events from the more 'historical' account in Luke.

Given that the birth motifs of the (divine/royal) culture hero are evident in a wide range of ancient literary genres throughout the ancient Near Eastern world, it's likely that Matthew adapted this same folk pattern/literary form to add a christological birth story to his 'sacred biography' of Jesus. And it's also *unlikely* that the Star is anything other than a literary and theological motif.

CHAPTER 19:
THE MESSIANIC STAR: THE 'STAR OUT OF JACOB'

The Old Testament passage most associated with the Matthew 2.1–12 is Balaam's fourth oracle to Balak found in Numbers 24.15–19. Specifically, the prophetic reference at 24.17 to: *a star shall come/rise out of Jacob*. This 'rising star' (Gk. ἀνατελεῖ ἄστον) and its messianic interpretation during the later intertestamental period is the subject of this chapter.

The Document of Balaam (Numbers 22–24)

The Book of Numbers is so named due to its many census lists. However, the Hebrew title 'In the Wilderness' more accurately portrays the book's contents: the forty-year journey of the Israelites of the Exodus from Matthew Sinai to Canaan. According to the Documentary Hypothesis, Numbers is traditionally attributed to the J and E sources (ninth to eighth century BCE).

The section known as the Document of Balaam (Numbers 22–24) is set towards the end of their journey when the Israelites are camped near the eastern shore of the Dead Sea. King Balak of Moab (a small kingdom east of the Dead Sea), fearful of Israelite military successes against the Amorites, hires Balaam the son of Beor to curse the people of Israel before they cross into Canaan. Numbers 22-24 describes how Balaam travels on an donkey with two servants *from the east* to visit Balak. After three encounters with God (one in the form of a sword wielding angel), and, much to Balak's increasing anger, Balaam refuses to curse Israel as commanded and (acting as the mouthpiece of God) instead blesses them via a series of seven oracles. After foiling the King's plans, he returns home. His fourth oracle is relevant here:

> [24.15] And he took up his discourse, and said, 'The oracle of Balaam the son of Be'or, the oracle of the man whose eye is opened,
> [24.16] the oracle of him who hears the words of God, and knows the knowledge of the Most High, who sees the vision of the Almighty, falling down, but having his eyes uncovered:
> [24.17] I see him, but not now; I behold him, but not nigh: a star [*kokhab*]

shall come forth [*darakh*] out of Jacob, and a sceptre [*shevet*] shall rise
out of Israel; it shall crush the forehead of Moab, and break down all the
sons of Sheth.

[24.18] Edom shall be dispossessed, Se'ir also, his enemies, shall be
dispossessed, while Israel does valiantly.

[24.19] By Jacob shall dominion be exercised, and the survivors of cities
be destroyed!'

The later Greek LXX (third to first century BCE), perhaps influenced by
Isaiah 11.1 (shoot/branch), refered to 'a man' (ἄνθρωπος) rising from Israel), *not*
a sceptre.

This oracle references a future Israelite king who will smite the lands of
Moab and Edom. The king is interpreted as David (c. 1000 BCE), who had
conquered both nations. The star (*kokhab*) is a symbol of royalty, linked to
the 'morning star' of Isaiah 14.12 and Revelation 22.16. This star has been
associated with the 'star' symbol that appears on the coinage of the Hasmonean
king, Alexander Jannaeus 'to symbolise he was the conquering star that rose
from Jacob. However, *kokhab* could also mean 'host' as the Hebrew *darakh*
('there shall come forth') can also mean 'march/tread/trample'. Alternatively, it
can mean 'tribe' in the military sense. The fourth oracle could be interpreted as
referring to a military force or a royal king marching forth in conquest.

The sceptre (*shevet*) was also linked to royalty and rulers and the staves of
Moses and Aaron and has been translated as 'comet' or 'meteor'.

Numbers 24.17 in post-Biblical interpretation

During the intertestamental period (200 BCE to 100 CE) Numbers 24.17
developed into what Geza Vermes called a 'messianic proof-text.'[1] Amongst the
Dead Sea Scrolls such an interpretation appears in 1Q28b 2.22–5.29; 4Q175
lines 9–13; the 'War Scroll' 1QM 11.4–6; 15.2.

At Qumran, the star and sceptre was interpreted as both a single figure and
two separate figures in the Scrolls. For example, CD 7.18-21 proclaims:

(18) And the star is the Interpreter of the law, (19) who will come to
Damascus, as is written: *Num 24:13* 'A star moves out of Jacob, and a
scepter arises (20) out of Israel'. The scepter is the prince of the whole
congregation and when he rises 'he will destroy (21) all the sons of
Seth'. *Blank* These escaped at the time of the first visitation, while the
renegades were delivered up to the sword.[2]

Here the star is the priestly 'Interpreter of the Law' (Teacher of Righteousness), while the sceptre is the 'Prince of the Congregation', a military messiah-king (and 'branch of David') who will rise against Israel's enemies (Rome). However, in 4Q175 (*Testimonia*) and 1QM, the star and sceptre refer to a single messianic figure.

The *Testaments of the Twelve Patriarchs* likewise contain a messianic interpretation. These *Testaments* (though they contain later second-century CE Christian interpolations) can be dated to around the mid second century BCE. The *Testament of Judah* 24.1–6 states that 'there shall arise for you a star from Jacob' who will 'illuminate the sceptre of my kingdom and from your root will arise the Shoot' while the *Testament of Levi* 18.1–3 states:

> [1] When vengeance will have come upon them from the Lord, the priesthood will lapse.

> [2] And then the Lord will raise up a new priest
> to whom all the words of the Lord will be revealed.
> He shall effect the judgement of truth over the earth for many days.

> [3] And <u>his star shall rise in heaven like a king</u>; [καὶ ἀνατελεῖ ἄστρον αὐτοῦ ἐν οὐρανῷ ὡς βασιλεύς];
> kindling the light of knowledge as day is illuminated by the sun.
> And he shall be extolled by the whole inhabited world.[3]

The passage has also been linked to Josephus' application to his future patron (the Emperor Vespasian) of an unnamed and (unfortunately) unspecified Jewish 'oracle' (χρησμός) circulating during the First Jewish Revolt (66–74 CE), which proclaimed the coming of a 'world ruler' (*War* 6.310–315):

> But what more than all else incited them to the war was an ambiguous oracle, likewise found in their sacred scriptures, to the effect that at that time one from their country would become ruler of the world. This they understood to mean someone of their own race, and many of their wise men went astray in their interpretation of it. The oracle, however, in reality signified the sovereignty of Vespasian, who was proclaimed Emperor on Jewish soil.

That the oracle was Numbers 24.17 remains a speculative conclusion (Daniel 9 is the popular alternative). Josephus does refer to a star and a comet. However, they don't appear related to the oracle reference, nor are they interpreted messianically, being instead part of a longer list of portents.

In Book 5 of the *Sibylline Oracles* (of Egyptian origin between 70-130 CE) four eschatological passages relating to a saviour figure allude to Numbers 24.17 (108–110; 155–161 (Dan 7.13); 256–259 and 414–417). For example:

[108] and then a certain king sent from God against him
[109] will destroy all the great kings and noble men.
[110] Thus there will be judgement on men by the imperishable one.

[155] But then after the fourth year a great star shines
[156] which along will destroy the whole earth, because of
[157] the honour which they first gave to Poseidon of the sea,
[158] a great star will come from heaven to the wondrous sea
[159] and will burn the deep sea and Babylon [Rome] itself
[160] and the land of Italy, because of which many
[161] holy faithful Hebrews and a true people perished.

[256] There will be one exceptional man from the sky
[257] who stretched out his hands on the fruitful wood,

[414] For a blessed man came from the expanses of heaven
[415] with a sceptre in his hands which God gave him, [4]

Finally, in later rabbinic tradition, the Aramaic Targums associated Num 24.17 with a warrior messiah king who would destroy Rome. For example, Targum Onqelos: 'When a king shall arise out of Jacob, and the Messiah will be anointed out of Israel.'; Targum Neofiti: 'A king is to arise from those of the house of Jacob and a redeemer and ruler from those of the house of Israel... 'and Targum Pseudo Jonathan: 'When a mighty king from those of the house of Jacob shall rule, and the Messiah will be anointed, and a mighty sceptre out of Israel...'

Numbers 24.17 in Matthean reception history and early art

Given the messianic status of Numbers 24.17, it isn't suprising to see the association of the prophetic 'star out of Jacob' with Matthew 2 and Christ appearing early in the reception history of the Church Fathers and Apologists. For example, the association (whether 'star', 'man' or 'leader') is in Origen, Justin, Athanasius, Ephraem the Syrian, Chrysostom, Jerome, Hippolytus, Leo the Great and Amphilochius of Iconium. The magi were often described as descendants of Balaam or aware of his oracle.

In Christian art, a figure suggested to portray Balaam occasionally appears in scenes depicting the Adoration of the Magi. Prime examples include the aforementioned fresco from Priscilla, a fourth-century funeral plaque (also from Priscilla) and the 'Dogmatic' sarcophagus from Rome (c. 315 CE), all of which depict a figure standing near Mary that may allude to Balaam. In addition, a 56 x 38 cm wall painting from the fourth-century Vita Latina catacomb in Rome depicts a solitary figure in a white toga or tunic and mantle (interpreted as Balaam) pointing towards an eight-sided star. Over a thousand years later, Balaam might be seen in the Prado Epiphany, an altar triptych by Hieronymus Bosch dated c. 1494. Depicting the Adoration of the Magi, he can be seen in the central panel as a pale white figure standing in the doorway of the stable, holding the crown of the second Magus. In the background, the Star is high in the sky, standing over Bethlehem.

Absent formula citation

Today, it's almost universal for scholarly opinion to associate Matthew 2.1–12 with Balaam's 'star out of Jacob'. The LXX's ἀνατελεῖ ἄστρον (*rising star*; messianic king) and ἄνθρωπος (*man* from Israel) foretold by Balaam (a magus) 'from the east' (Numbers 23.7: ἀπέ ἀνατολῶν), who thwarted a king before returning home (Numbers 24.25), provides natural parallels to the individual pericope of the magi and messianic star. The problem is that Matthew, whose central Gospel theme was 'fulfilment', does *not* cite Numbers 24.17 in connection with the Star or the magi. If there was such a close link between this messianic passage and the Star, why doesn't Matthew use such a citation as one of his formula-citations?

Matthew is a Gospel where much is implied rather than made explicit. It's full of tacit references, invokes tradition through allusion, and requires external texts and implied knowledge to interpret fully. In other words, it's a 'closed' text—opaque and ambiguous to modern readers but transparent and clear to his intended audience. These conclusions regarding the *implied reader* of Matthew's Gospel coupled with the widespread interpretation of Numbers 24.17 as an allusion to (or image of) the Davidic Messiah could provide an explanation for the absence of an explicit formula citation: it was perhaps *too obvious* to have required one. Just because Matthew makes no reference to Numbers 24.17, that doesn't mean he had no interest in it: 'Since Jesus has already been introduced as David's son, Matthew expects his readers to catch such allusions; or he takes private delight in them.'[5] As a star represented the Messiah, a specific formula citation was unnecessary.

An alternative view is that Numbers 24.17 was absent because the citations in Matthew 2 refer *only to geography*: Bethlehem (Mt 2.5b–6 = Mic 5.1, 3; cf. 2.12–13: hometown of David), Ramah (Mt 2.15b = Jer 31.15: association with

Rachel's tomb), Egypt (Mt 2.17–18 = Hos 11.1: Moses typology) and Nazareth (Mt 2.23b = ??). Martin Pickup suggests that Matthew's citation of Hosiah 11.1 is 'reminiscent' of Balaam. Noting the association of Numbers 24.17 with the messiah and Matthew 2, he observes that Numbers 24.8 states that 'God brings him out of Egypt' and that a 'Jewish-Christian reader like Matthew... could not have helped but read Balaam's words midrashically and seen in the phrase... a striking applicability to Jesus.'[6]

George van Kooten argues against Numbers 24.17 as a source for the Magi/Star. Reviewing Matthew's repeated use of Old Testament scripture and formulaic citation, he concludes that 'Matthew's dependence on Balaam's oracle seems unlikely because he does not refer to it.'[7] The issue of 'symbol-sign' has been another criticism. To John Nolland the star in Numbers *is* the ruler, while the Star in Matthew is merely the *signal or sign* that the ruler has arrived. However, this is too rigid an interpretation given the post-biblical response.

K. J. Woollcombe observes that 'the number of Matthew's references to the Old Testament is not equivalent to the number of his direct quotations.'[8] For example, why were 1 Kings 10.10; Isaiah 60.3, 5–6 or Psalm 72.10–11 not used as fulfilment citations with regard to the magi? (Such passages being responsible for the magi becoming 'kings' in later centuries.) Indeed, the UBS[4] lists fifty-four Old Testament citations and over 250 further allusions/verbal parallels in Matthew. Raymond Brown argues that this shift from 'Star as Messiah' in Numbers to 'sign of the Messiah' in Matthew 'is quite intelligible once the king has been born.'[9] Michael Shepherd also observes that both Targum Onkelos and Targum Pseudo-Jonathan remove the 'star' and refer instead to a king rising/ruling from Jacob. He associates this substitution of 'star' for 'king' (Messiah) as being in agreement with Matthew: the star becomes the king in the Targums, while Matthew goes further and associates the star with Jesus himself as the king/messiah.

If Matthew were making creative use of Old Testament scripture in this manner, the absence of a primary or a secondary interpretation of Numbers 24.17 in support of the Star reinforces the view that it required no formula. Matthew didn't need to make any specific apologetic appeal to Old Testament scripture to convince his audience. Indeed, it's the magi themselves who provide apologetic legitimacy to the Star.

CHAPTER 20:
THE MESSIAH-KING

Possibly the earliest non-literary representation of the messianic star is the star-like ornament struck on silver tetradrachms during the Second Jewish Revolt against Rome (132–136 CE). Despite the evident lateness by some forty years of this numismatic evidence in relation to Matthew, it provides a significant *visual* link between a star and the messiah.

The cause of the revolt remains the subject of debate. The brief account of Cassius Dio states it might have been a combination of Hadrian's plan to rebuild the ruins of Jerusalem (destroyed during the 66–73 CE revolt) into a new colonial pagan city and the construction on the Temple Mount of a temple to Jupiter Capitolinus (god of the Capitoline hill in Rome). According to Dio: 'This brought on a war of no slight importance nor brief duration, for the Jews deemed it intolerable that foreign races should be settled in their city and foreign religious rites planted there.' It's also been suggested that Hadrian's ban on mutilation (including circumcision) was the primary catalyst for the revolt. Hadrian had visited Judaea around 130 CE, and the economic burden surrounding his visit may also have played a part.

Preparation for the revolt (orchestrated by the rebel leader Bar Kokhba) might have begun soon after Hadrian's departure for Egypt (where Hadrian attributed the 130 CE comet/nova to the spirit of the drowned Antonius). The revolt was certainly under way by summer 132 when Hadrian was a suitable distance away). Such preparation (specifically the construction of large numbers of subterranean tunnels and complexes) might explain the initial success of the revolt.

Roman forces were initially commanded by the Judean governor Tineius Rufus, but he may have died early in the campaign as Hadrian assumed control before requesting the transfer of his 'best general' (Cassius Dio 69.13), Julius Severus (governor of Britain), to take command. Initially taken by surprise (the local garrison consisted of two legions), up to eleven legions and auxiliary forces, totalling 27,500 men, were mobilised against the rebels.

The aims of the revolt had been simple: to reclaim Jerusalem, rebuild the temple and create an independent Jewish state free from Roman rule and interference. Such goals can be seen in the dates used during the conflict: 'Year One of the Redemption of Israel', 'Year Two of the Freedom of Israel' and 'For the Freedom of Jerusalem'. Inevitably, following the initial guerrilla war successes, overwhelming Roman forces produced a hard-won victory for Hadrian. The last major battle (late 135, early 136) took place at the mountain fortress of Bethar not far from Jerusalem, where Bar Kokhba was finally defeated. About 50 outposts and 985 villages were destroyed and 580,000 killed.

Did Bar Kokhba claim to be the Messiah? The answer to this is connected to his name. His *real* name, as revealed through the Greek and Hebrew documents discovered in the Cave of Letters and stamped on coins, was *šm'wn bn kwsb' nsy' yśr'l*—'Shim'on ben/bar Kosiva (Simon son of Kosiba, Prince of Israel'). In the Greek letters he's called Χωσιβα (Chosiba). However, in later Christian writings, Justin called him Βαρχωχέβας (*Bar Kokhba*), Jerome 'Barchochabas' while Eusebius, noting the account of Aristo of Pella spelt out its meaning: 'Βαρχωέχβας ὄνομα, ὃ δὴ ἀστέρα δηλοῖ' (*Bar Kokhba, which means 'star'*).

As the sobriquet derives from the Aramaic for 'star' *Kokhba* (Heb. *kokhab*) it's been linked to Numbers 24.17. How and when did 'Kosiba' change to 'Kokhba'? In later rabbinic literature, several legends portray Bar Kokhba in a messianic light, though ultimately as a *failed* messiah, not a saviour. In these sources he's traditionally called 'Bar Koziva'. The first, from the Jerusalem Talmud (c. 350-450 CE) is the proclamation of Rabbi Akiba (*y. Ta'anit* 68d):

> R. Shim'on b. Yohai taught: Akiba my teacher would expound *A star shall step forth from Jacob* thus: Koziva shall step forth from Jacob.

> R. Akiba when he saw Bar Koziba, would say, 'This is the King Messiah.'

> R. Yohanan b. Torta said to him, 'Akiba, grass will grow up from your jaws and the son of David will not yet have come.'[1]

An alternative version of the first line is in the Midrash on Lamentations (*Lamentations Rabbah* 2.5):

> R. Yohanan [late third century] said: Rabbi [R. Judah Ha-Nasi] would expound *A star shall step forth from Jacob* thus: do not read 'Star' (*kokhav*) but 'liar' (*kozav*).

This belief in Bar Kokhba as a messianic *imposter* (son of a lie) appears in the later (c. 500 CE) Babylonian Talmud (*b. Sanhedrin* 93b):

Rava [fourth century CE] said: That he [the Messiah] smells [detect, sense] and judges, as it is written: *And he shall not judge after the sight of his eyes...But with righteousness shall judge the poor, and decide with equity for the meek of the earth'* [Isaiah 11.3–4]. Bar Koziva ruled two-and-a-half years. He said to the rabbis: 'I am the Messiah.' They said to him: 'Regarding the Messiah, it is written that he will small and judge. Let us see whether you can smell and judge.' When they saw that he could not smell and judge, they killed him.[2]

Despite being the products of later centuries, these rabbinic rejections of Bar Kokhba as the true Messiah stems from knowledge of the Revolt's failure. The concept of the false Messiah (deceiver, liar) also appears in the Apocalypse of Peter, a second-century Jewish-Christian apocryphal text, where Bauckham has convincingly argued that the messianic 'deceiver' of the Apocalypse of Peter 2.12 is a specific reference to Bar Kokhba.

The messianic image of Bar Kokhba emerges only from these later rabbinic and Christian texts and not from contemporary literature of the Revolt itself. This is apparent from the absence of messianic references in the documents from the Cave of Letters. For this reason, some scholars reject the claim that Bar Kosiva called himself 'Messiah' or was ever called so by his supporters. However, he does refer to himself as 'Prince (*nasiy*) of Israel', a title found on his coinage. Here, there's a possible messianic link to Ezekiel 37.25 where it states: 'my servant David shall be their prince [*nasiy*; LXX ἄρχων] forever.' It was also used by Ezekiel and the Hasmoneans as a title of authority, and may have been an attempt by Bar Kokhba to draw a parallel between the Hasmonean rulers, who had successfully revolted against the Greek rule of Antiochus IV and restored the temple (the Maccabean Revolt), and his own mission to defeat the Romans and reclaim Jerusalem. Alternatively, it may have been an honorific military title.

It's possible that Bar Kokhba had made the claim *outside* of his letters as later Christian accounts imply. Eusebius (*Historia Ecclesiastica* 4.6.) recorded that Kokhba saw himself as a *luminary/light (star) from heaven* [ἐξ οὐρανοῦ φωστήρ], magically enlightening those who were in misery.' Jerome (*Against Rufinus* 3.31), though writing a century later than Eusebius, specifically cites Bar Kokhba's performance of fake miracles: he would 'hold in his mouth a lighted straw and blow it out so as to appear to be breathing forth flame.' This echoes the miraculous 'destruction by breath' of Isaiah 11.4; 2 Thessalonians 2.8 and the sixth vision of *4 Ezra* (= 2 Esdras) 13.9-11, an apocalyptic text of the first century CE (closer to the time of Bar Kokhba):

I saw only how he ['the man from the sea' of 13.2-3] sent forth from
his mouth as it were a stream of fire, and from his lips a flaming breath,
and from his tongue he shot forth a storm of sparks. All these were
mingled together, the stream of fire and the flaming breath and the
great storm, and fell on the onrushing multitude which was prepared
to fight, and burned them all up, so that suddenly nothing was seen of
the innumerable multitude but only the dust of ashes and the smell of
smoke.

Likewise, the *Apocalypse of Peter* states that the false messiah 'will perform signs
and wonders in order to deceive.' In addition, Justin records that Bar Kokhba
attempted to torture those who followed a *different* 'messiah/star', that is, the
followers of Jesus, already warned against following false messiahs and who
had no need of a rebuilt temple (Mark 14.58). Eusebius, citing Justin, writes
(*Historia Ecclesiastica*. 8.4) that 'it was only Christians whom Bar Kokhba...
commanded to be punished severely, if they did not deny Jesus as the Messiah
(Ἰησοῦν τὸν Χριστὸν) and blaspheme him.' Such later Christian sources are prone
to historical unreliability and are perhaps more influenced by rabbinic traditions
and contemporary Christian attitudes towards Rome. Maybe they shouldn't be
dismissed entirely as a kernel of historical truth may lie behind them. The rabbinic
legends wouldn't have risen in a vacuum; therefore a messianic connection to
Bar Kokhba must have been in existence in order for it to be denied. Justin was
referring to Shim'on bar Kosiba as 'Βαρχωχέβας' (*barkokebas*) a mere twenty or
so short years after the revolt. Therefore, the link between Kosiba and the star
of Numbers 24.17 was evidently early in origin. Certainly, the messianic fervour
and unrest of the First Revolt (with its traumatic destruction of the temple)
would have remained strong amongst the general population of Israel.

> As *institution*, the temple was central to Jewish religious, economic,
> and socio-political life. As *symbol*, it was central to the very existence
> and self-definition of Israel. The temple, in conjunction with the Law,
> defined what it meant to be a Jew.[3]

Indeed, the period between 70 and 132 CE saw the appearance of the three
greatest apocalypses: The Book of Revelation, 4 *Ezra* and 2 *Baruch*. The
messianic expectation in 4 *Ezra* and 2 *Baruch* looked to a messiah who would
liberate Jerusalem and rebuild the temple.

Bar Kokhba's silver tetradrachm

Stars appear rarely on Jewish coinage and only three examples are known. (A fourth could be the star above the goddess Nike on the obverse of later silver coinage minted under Agrippa II, 55-92 CE, the last Herodian ruler of Judea).

One, a large bronze coin from the reign of Herod the Great (minted c. 40-37 CE), which depicts on its obverse a military helmet with a star (or star-like plume) flanked by palm branches/wreaths, remains disputed so it won't be discussed in detail here.

The first star on a Jewish coin appeared on the Hasmonean era bronze prutah/lepton of Alexander Jannaeus (103–76 BCE). This common coin (14mm, 2gms) was the small copper 'widow's mite' ($\lambda\epsilon\pi\tau\acute{o}\varsigma$, $\chi\alpha\lambda\chi\acute{o}\varsigma$) of Mark 12:41–44 and Luke 21.1–4, which depicts an anchor on the obverse and a star with eight points/rays surrounded by a diadem (with a ribbon or knot) on the reverse.

Eight (or variant) pointed stars are on ancient Greek coinage. The inscription 'Yehonatan the King' is written in paleo-Hebrew script between the star's rays. The diadem, a Hellenistic symbol of royalty, is similar to that on the Greek portrait coins of Ptolemy I (first Hellenistic ruler of Judea, 305 BCE). Though the second commandment would have forbidden the image of a star to be struck, the majority view is that this is a star. As the Hasmoneans continued to imitate and utilise the designs of the bronze Seleucid coins they inherited following the defeat of Antiochus IV, this star is a rare example of innovation and Baruch Kanael suggests that the star could be a symbol for kingship/monarchy, *its interpretation derived from Num 24.17*, although Ya'akov Meshorer sees the star as Jannaeus' attempt to express his status as king without breaking the laws on graven images. The star and diadem of Jannaeus and later the helmet and star of Herod both served as alternatives to portraits.

The tetradrachm

All of Bar Kokhba's bronze and silver denominations were overstrikes of existing Roman circulations. The coins used had been minted in Antioch and Tyre, primarily during the reigns of Nero (54-68), Vespasian (69-79), Titus (79-81) and Trajan (98-117). The primary reason for this was two-fold: firstly, political and religious propaganda. As all coins in Judea since the end of the First Revolt were of pagan (Roman) origin, over-striking them re-stamped the authority of the new, independent Jewish state. With no established mint of his own, over-striking was the cheapest and quickest method of producing the coinage he needed to administer the new Jewish state. Dating these coins is made harder by the fact that only the first two years are stamped with a specific time tag. Fortunately, Yadin's excavations at the Cave of Letters has helped significantly with such chronological issues for the legends on the coins can be matched to the dates and legends written on the letters of Bar Kokhba and his subordinates.

In addition, as the most valuable coin, the large silver (AR) provincial Roman tetradrachm (four drachma coin; weight approx 12.18–15.19gms) had the greatest value, politically and monetarily. The first *Jewish* silver coins, based on Tyrian currency, had been issued during the First Revolt where they were minted by the rebels as currency for the temple tribute tax and other sacred uses. Tyrian silver 'shekels' or half-shekels were used for the annual temple tribute due to their availability and good silver content.

Year One of the Redemption of Israel: 132/133 CE (Figure 1)

The obverse, used for ruler portraits and regarded as the most important side of a coin, depicts a Greco-Roman tetrastyle (four columned) temple façade with what appears to be a flat Near Eastern style architrave or entablature represented by two lines (one solid, one dotted) supported by four columns on a thin foundation/podium. The column shafts vary in detail and thickness from coin to coin but appear to be primarily Roman Doric with Attic bases.

Represented in the temple (with two columns on either side) is what appears to be a beaded box-like object as seen from the short side with two dots and a rounded lid. The reverse depicts specific cultic objects related to the temple, a bundle of *lulav* (closed frond of the palm tree) with an *etrog* (yellow citron used during Sukkot) to the lef), which parallel those on coinage of the First Revolt.

Like the earlier Hasmonean coins of Alexander Jannaeus and those of the First Revolt, all Bar Kokhba coinage are inscribed (for propaganda purposes) using the paleo-Hebrew script. The legend 'Jerusalem' is stamped around the obverse façade and 'Year One of the redemption of Israel' around the reverse lulav/etrog. On ancient coins, it was common for an inscription identifying the temple depicted to appear on the architrave or outer perimeter. The word 'redemption' had been used on coins minted during the fourth year of the First Revolt (69 CE) when the 67-68 CE legend 'Freedom of Zion' was changed to 'For the redemption of Zion'. This perhaps depicted a change in the mood of the population. The military freedom the rebels were winning had changed to defeat as all but Jerusalem and Masada had been lost. By 69 CE, Israel was looking for divine redemption. Meshorer suggests that by using the same word ('redemption') on his own coins, Bar Kokhba was applying his own messianic propaganda.

The Herodian temple

The cultic objects stamped on the reverse provide clues as to why a temple façade appears on the large coins of Bar Kokhba. The façade symbolised the prime objective of the rebels and the religious and cultural heart of Jewish identity: the temple sanctuary, razed by Romans forces in 70 CE. Begun c. 20/19 BCE as a gesture of piety (and to secure the support of his new subjects), Herod's vast reconstruction and enlargement of Zerubbabel's Second Temple was the crowing centre of his grand and extensive building programme of fortresses, palaces, temples and urban infrastructure.

A note of caution must be exercised when using coin types to determine architectural features, especially of buildings now lost or only partially standing. Limitation of space can result in simplifications, omissions or artistic license by the die engraver. The nature of coins as representatives of ideas and symbolic iconography means they can't be treated as reliable sources of specific architectural details in isolation.

As the temple no longer stands, its appearance must be derived from a combination of archaeological and literary sources. Archaeological data from the Temple Mount itself is limited as the site can no longer be excavated and other sites need to be examined for comparable evidence. Peter Richardson, for example, has noted the following external influences on Herod's temple: indigenous (the First Temple and Zerubbabel's Second), Nabatean (Temple of Dushara), Palmyra, Syria (Temple of Bel), Egypt (large spaces and courtyards, i.e. Karnak, Luxor) and classical Greco-Roman. Numerous examples of temple iconography exist in later Jewish art such as ossuaries, grave wall reliefs, rock carvings, murals, clay lamps, gold-glass and mosaics. Such artistic sources must also be treated with caution due to their greater application of symbolism and iconography.

Our primary literary sources for the layout and description of the temple derive from Josephus, the New Testament, the rabbinic Mishnah and Philo. Neither Josephus nor *Middot* present exact descriptions and disagree over details, so there remains a lack of consensus over the reliability and reconciliation of these sources. Josephus (though prone to exaggeration) was at least present in Jerusalem during its destruction in 70 CE and is regarded as the most historically reliable, with the earlier *War* (c. 75 CE) taking priority over the later *Antiquities* (c. 95 CE), which perhaps relied more heavily on memory. The later *Middot* ('Measurements'), c. 220 CE, though broadly in line with the details of Josephus' account (and perhaps making use of it), exhibits elements of utopian ideal and the influence of Ezekiel's description of the First Temple. Michael Chyutin observes that it's 'more of a composite literary reconstruction than a reliable historical description'.[4] Nonetheless, some do interpret *Middot* as the more reliable source over Josephus, especially regarding dimensions. But despite a general consensus as to how the temple looked, certain details remain open to subjective interpretation.

It may also be possible to derive details from earlier descriptions of Zerubbabel's temple. The only potential literary sources are from the Dead Sea Scrolls where fragmented temple descriptions appear in Hasmonean era texts dated c. 100-150 BCE such as the New Jerusalem Scroll and the *Temple Scroll*. Though these scrolls present an eschatological or utopian ideal of the 'New Jerusalem' temple, one based primarily on the First Temple, certain architectural features may derive from the temple as it stood during the Hasmonean period.

Herod's construction greatly expanded and enlarged the old temple on Mount Moriah. Though the sanctuary was completed by 18/17 BCE, the larger temple complex was still not fully finished by 63 CE. The sanctuary followed the First Temple's tripartite longroom plan of porch (*ulum*), Great Hall (*heikhal*) and Holy of Holies (*Kodesh Ha-Kodashim*). Such temple plans appear in many of the surviving Syrian temples of the second-millennium BCE. Later classical Doric and Ionic temples likewise consisted of a (usually open) columned front porch/portico (πρόναος) and a main inner room (the ναός). Within the ναός was the 'cella', a room that contained the cult statue.

The Herodian temple sat on a foundation of 6 cubits (*Middot* 4.6). It was a feature of Roman architecture to raise their temples on a high podium with steps leading to a single front entrance. Herod's style of architecture was particularly influenced by the use of expensive and high quality Roman Imperial architectural designs and materials. This can be seen in the use of *opus caementicium* (a horizontally laid 'concrete' of mortar and aggregate), vaults, viaducts, arches and *opus reticulatum* (diamond shaped brickwork) in his building of theatres, villas, amphitheatres and temples.

The eastern exterior façade of the temple (front entrance) was a large square of 100 x 100 cubits constructed of three kinds of marble (blue, white and red) or white stones and plated with gold. Herod spoke of restoring the temple to its Solomonic height and a few sources speak of a 'high' temple. Its upper sections were white, painted or perhaps the same white marble used in Herod's temple to Augustus.

In classical Greco-Roman architecture, the columns supported an entablature consisted of architrave, decorated/sculptured frieze blocks and horizontal cornice (ledge). Above the entablature sat the front facing triangular pediment, a shallow isosceles (a gable created by the sloping roof), with its decorated tympanum (vertical wall of the pediment). However, the Year One obverse depicts only a flat roof/architrave, a characteristic of ancient Near Eastern/Egyptian architecture. Unfortunately, the style of roof isn't explicitly mentioned in any of the literary sources, only that it had a row of crenellations (or crowstep merlons) with 1-cubit high golden spikes (bird 'scarecrows') on a three-cubit high parapet. Crowstep merlons (which could used to provide rooftop protection for guards) can still be seen on the ruins of contemporary architecture such as the first-century CE temple of Bel at Palmyra. Under the parapet, *Middot* 4.6 refers to a wall-frieze (1 cubit), 'place of drippings' (2 cubits), roof-beams (1 cubit) and plasterwork (1 cubit), a total of five cubits. As no source describes anything above the parapet, we could conclude that (unlike Herodian temples built to honour the cult of Augustus at Samaria-Sebaste, Caesarea and Panium) the façade of the Jerusalem temple retained the Syro-Phoenician style flat roof of the original temple design. The majority of later temple iconography depict a flat roof. Though we can only speculate about the skill of the die engravers employed by Bar Kokhba, these large tetradrachms (one inch in diameter) could easily have accommodated a full pediment temple design.

In true Roman style, frontal access into the temple was by ascending 6 cubits up a flight of twelve steps to an open portal 70-cubits high and 25 wide. Tractate *Middot* (3.7) states that this portal had a lintel consisting of five oak beams of increasing width (akin to an inverted isosceles trapezium) with a 'course of stones' between every two beams. Such tall, but narrow, single entrances were a feature of Augustan tetrastyle temples and can been seen in the doors of the Senate House and the Pantheon. Vitruvius' rules for the proportions of temple doorways (*On Architecture* 4.6) states that:

> The opening of the doorway is to be so determined that the height of the temple from the pavement to the panels of the ceiling is to be divided into 3½ parts, and of these 2½ in height are to be fixed for the opening… Let this in turn be divided into 12 parts and of these let 5½ be the breadth of the opening at the bottom.

If the temple was 100 cubits in height, Vitruvius' proportions would result in an entrance approximately 71 cubits high and 32 cubits wide, close to Josephus' recorded dimensions.

Through this large portal lay the inner porch, a narrow, enclosed antechamber (the πρόναος) running north-south 20 cubits deep, 50 cubits in length and 90 cubits high, with a square (20 x 20 cubit) room/wing at either end. Cedar beams helped secure the outer porch façade to the inner sanctuary wall. In this porch was a smaller inner gate around 55 cubits high and 16 wide with two sets of large golden double doors (the inner and outer) covered by a multicoloured veil or curtain that depicted the heavens and the zodiac or purple colours and pillar designs. This inner gate, clearly visible from outside the temple through the open portal, led from the eastern front wall of the inner façade through gold covered walls 6 cubits thick) into the ground floor the main sanctuary hall. Both Josephus and *Middot* state that above this inner gate were ornamental golden vines (trained over posts or fixed by nails) from which hung 'man-sized' grape-clusters. Tractate *Middot* 3.8 records that golden chains hung in a porch which (young) priests used to climb to 'see the crowns'. These (four?) golden crowns are associated by *Middot* to Zech 6.14 (Joshua's crown in the temple) and are also cited in the *Temple Scroll* and 1 Maccabees.

The sanctuary hall was much narrower than the porch at only 20 cubits wide (but 60 cubits in length and height). A 40-cubit high upper floor, perhaps built during the Hasmonean period, lay above the main ground floor. This hall contained a golden seven-branched lamp stand, a golden shewbread table, and an incense altar. Situated at the far end of the hall, concealed behind two curtains, was a second chamber of 20 cubits, the empty Holy of Holies. It was here that the presence of God was believed to dwell and which would have housed the Ark of the Covenant on its foundation stone.

The Tetrastyle temple

An obvious feature of the coin's obverse are the four temple columns, representing a Roman tetrastyle porch/portico. The column shaft design of the façade appears to be Roman Doric with an Attic base. Doric Order columns were thick set fluted shafts with twenty vertically cut concave grooves (flutes) with a plain capital (topmost part of the column) consisting of a ring of convex moulding (the *astragal*), a plain section known as the 'necking' grooves and finally the rounded *echinus*. The whole capital sat under the *abacus*, a square stone slab that supported the architrave. It's the capital that most easily determines the architectural Order of a building (Doric, Ionic or Corninthian). Iconic capitals have scroll-like *volutes* while the more ornate Corinthian depicts acanthus leaves. On some of the more detailed Bar Kokhba coins the plainer Doric style can be seen along with their rounded *astragal* and *echinus* moulded capitals. The bases are interesting as the thicker, more heavily built Greek Doric columns usually sat directly onto the pavement (the *stylobate*). The smaller Roman Doric style *did* sit on a rounded plain or Attic base (a base primarily used to support the taller 24 grooved Ionic columns). This would make more sense given Herod's use of Roman as opposed to Greek architectural design in his building projects, but, again, caution must be exercised when using coins to establish real architectural details.

As with the roof, no outer façade columns are directly recorded in any of the known literary sources. Yet two pairs of engaged columns (or two corner pilasters and two engaged/free-standing columns) are usually depicted or cited by modern scholars as flanking the outer porch entrance. An 'engaged' column wasn't free standing and formed part of the wall where their shallow parallax generated shadows that helped divide the wall. Their presence on temple reconstructions is based primarily on the interpretation of non-literary sources such as the tetradrachm obverse, contemporary temples and the similar designs of the later Jewish iconography. For example, Michael Avi-Yonah notes the short (south) side of temple of Bel, whose corner pilasters and two engaged central columns closely resemble the obverse (minus portal). True free-standing columns rarely reached higher than 62 feet whereas the height of the temple was over 164 feet high. Hence, the use of engaged columns on Avi-Yonah's model of the temple. A close visual resemblance, that parallels the image on the obverse, can also be found in the mid third-century CE Dura-Europos synagogue (located in Syria). Here, painted on the central west wall above a Torah shrine niche, is a detailed tetrastyle temple.

This mural panel, with its moulded row of semi-circular antefixes (representing the crow-step pediment), matches more closely the undated Year Three and Four coins with their 'wavy line' addition. Unlike the coin obverse, the central feature of this temple are *closed* double doors (with two knobs) under a semi-circular conch design: the golden inner gateway into the sanctuary hall. Evidence of columns could be derived from design of the Torah shrine: an architectural focal feature of the Synagogue that contained the Ark of the Scrolls, the chest in which the Torah scrolls were stored. Taking the form of an aedicula, niche or apse, these shrines were common to synagogues from the second century CE though did not appear in Jewish art until the third and fourth-centuries CE. Rachel Hachlili's description of a typical artistic representation presents a now familiar set of features:

> A façade of two, four, or six columns on pedestals or on a base which carry an arcuated lintel (straight or Syrian gable) with a conch that decorates the upper gable; a base on which the Torah shrine is built and a flight of stairs leading up. Inside the façade the Ark of the Scrolls is shown in the shape of a pair of decorated closed doors.[5]

Such a description parallels in part the façade image of the tetradrachm and such Torah shrines depicted on numerous frescoes, mosaic floors and even gilded gold-glass plates. A symbolic depiction of the temple can also be seen carved on the 'Magdala stone', unearthed in 2009 at the Migdal synagogue in Galilee. Dated pre-70 CE, this depiction may have been crafted by an eye-witness to the original Temple. The front facade of the stone consists of a seven-branched menorah and two amphorae, set between two columns (with bases and capitals) under a covering arch. The upper face depicts a large twelve-petalled rosette. We could speculate that such architectural features represent a cultural memory of the Herodian temple. From such sources, it remains the most commonly accepted consensus that the obverse image depicts a four-columned *outer* façade.

Alternatively, it's been suggested that the obverse image is a depiction, not of the larger *outer* façade of the Sanctuary, but of the smaller, *inner* gate of the Great Hall, with the 'wavy line' of the Year Three and Four coins representing the hanging golden vine. In this interpretation of the temple there may be columns on the plain outer façade and the four columns instead flank the double doors of the inner sanctuary façade. Numismatic evidence may derive from a rare Year Three silver didrachm, which depicts a *two* columned (distyle) variation of the façade with a taller *three* bar architrave and three steps. Depicted in the sanctuary is a different object from the tetradrachm, perhaps the golden shewbread table. Side-by-side, the two coins seem to depict different architectural features. Though this image could be a simplified rendition of the larger tetradrachm design on a smaller coin, it's been suggested that this *smaller* coin represents the *larger* outer temple façade portal with its trapezoid beam lintel and twelve steps, while the *larger* tetradrachm represents the *smaller* inner sanctuary gateway.

A possible solution to the façade problem has been suggested by Chyutin. His interpretation of the tetradrachm is that this façade does *not* represent Herod's expanded temple but illustrates the earlier temple as it appeared during the previous Hasmonean period—specifically, the entrance hall as described in the damaged *Temple Scroll*. Chyutin reconstructs 12.15–16 as follows:

> (15) The Entrance Hall <u>and you shall make four columns</u> for the face of the Entrance Hall, the height (16) <u>sixty cubits and the ceiling</u> ten cubits [...][6]

Although Michael Wise notes that 'four columns' may be referenced at 13.1–7 the text is far too fragmentary. Chyutin suggests that Herod hadn't demolished but had expanded the Hasmonean era temple by building around it, enclosing the original four columned façade entrance inside the new, much wider and higher porch/portico. As Josephus records the panic that arose on first hearing Herod's sudden proclamation to rebuild the temple (fear that the current temple would be razed and left a building site for decades to come), this retention and re-use of the original building could explain the quick construction of the new sanctuary. The existence of such columns in the porch/portico can be inferred from Josephus and *Middot*:

The number of crowns in the description of the Entrance Hall in the Tractate *Middot* hints at the number of columns at the façade of the Entrance Hall, one crown per column, i.e., four columns... The columns that remained inside the Entrance Hall in Herod's Temple were the posts described in the Tractate *Middot* and in Josephus, upon which the 'golden vine' was hung. The dimensions of these columns were big enough to bear the weight of the heavy vine.[7]

This conclusion with regard to the obverse façade is based on his view that, as the aim of the Second Revolt echoed the aims of the Maccabean Revolt, the façade is instead an illustration of the earlier Hasmonean era temple (with its four columns), which the devout rebels hoped to rebuild, and not the ruined Herodian temple with its pagan Greco-Roman features. Chyutin also interprets the smaller distyle didrachm as a representation of the First Temple, with its two pillars of Jachin and Boaz.

The central object (chest/door)
The 'beaded box-like object with rounded lid' represented between the two pairs of columns is generally considered to be the Ark as depicted from the side. The object has alternatively been interpreted as the side of the shewbread table, the closed inner double doors into the sanctuary (as depicted in the Dura mural) or even a Torah shrine. The Ark interpretation is strengthened by its symbolic representation for the presence of God, coupled with the Tabernacle/temple as a 'dwelling' place (house) of God. Gregory Stevenson, who favours the Ark interpretation, observes that the 'god in the doorway' motif of ancient coins symbolically represents the open access to the divine presence in the sanctuary. The cult-statue would have a direct line-of-sight (through the open doors) to the altar outside. Thus, with the real temple destroyed, the obverse could be interpreted as a symbol of divine access, with the lost Ark ('cult-statue'), as seen through the 'open' doors of the sanctuary gateway, representing the Holy of Holies and access to God.

Year Two of the Freedom of Israel: 133/134 CE
For the Year Two coins the word 'redemption' was removed and the revised legend now read 'Year Two of the freedom of Israel'. This could be a reverse of the reason for its usage on the First Revolt coinage. Divine redemption was replaced by the real possibility of military victory as Bar Kokhba's campaign against Roman military forces grew ever more successful. The legend 'Jerusalem' was also replaced by Shimon's name on some later Year Two dies. Baruch Kanael conjectures that the change from 'redemption of Israel' to 'freedom of Israel' was

the result of an assembly in Jerusalem in which Bar Kokhba agreed to relinquish the title and remove the messianic connotations of 'redemption' and that changes to the Second and Third Year coins were 'in order to preserve national unity.'[8] It's now accepted that Jerusalem was never occupied by rebel forces and remained under Roman control.

Addition #1: Fence/Balustrade/Steps/Podium
The thin foundation/podium has now gone and two parallel lines with rows of twelve vertical lines now appear below the temple. What these lines represent inconclusive. Martin Price and Bluma Trell interpret these lines as the 3-cubit high front barrier/fence of stone (the soreg) that existed to stop gentiles from entering the inner temple court, while Carol Meyers refers to it as a podium (even though the temple is already standing on one). The twelve lines could also represent the twelve stePsalm leading up into the temple porch. Whatever its purpose, Leo Mildenberg speculates that this line was added to make the façade more accurate to those 'old-timers' who remembered the original temple. It's plausible (though highly speculative) that people remained alive who remembered the original temple.

Addition #2: The 'Star' Ornament
A star or rosette ornament now appears above the temple architrave/entablature. Four main variations are evident. Mildenberg tracks the evolution of this ornament (from succeeding obverse dies) as follows:

O2.   Five, thick dots between the two letters above the temple

O3.   Small cross, formed by two lines

O4.   Longer and thinner lines

O5.   More compact, representing a rosette

O6-15.   Large, detailed star/rosette design

According to Meshorer, the star ornament was initially a plus (+) sign that *evolved* into a geometric stellate flower/star decoration. Mildenberg refers to a 'cross-rosette'. An early form of the ornament (O3-4) is indeed a simple cruciform sign. He suggests that this sign was inserted between the letters W and R of the obverse legend YR-WŠ-LM ('Jerusalem') but was left behind after the legend was shifted to the sides during Year Two, with three letters on each side (YRW-ŠLM), later developing into a star or flower. We could alternatively suggest that the engraver who added the 'star' over-strike on the Year Two obverse may have been a different person or persons to the façade designer of Year One. Indeed, Meshorer notes that the lack of any central mint meant that changes to personal and the use of unskilled labour in coin production was an inevitable part of Bar Kokhba's unstable administration. Hence, the simpler + ornament of O2 to O4 could have been a rough guide that was more fully developed on later dies or produced by a more inexperienced engraver. Yet cross-shaped star ornaments appear on silver and gold coins of Domitian. Minted c. 81-84 CE, their reverse depicts the deified infant son of Domitian seated on a globe surrounded by seven cross-shaped stars.

What is clear is that the majority of obverse die strikes (O5-O15) depict the more detailed star/rosette ornament, which suggest that this was the intended design.

Temple Variation #1: The sides of the architrave are now joined and linked by connecting lines to make an inverted isosceles trapezium-like shape. This parallels *Middot's* description of the outer porch gateway's wooden lintel.

Temple Variation #2: One type of tetradrachm now depicts an architrave with *three* bars (one straight, two beaded) instead of the usual two. This 'beading' brings to mind the 'course of stones' set between every two beams of the outer porch gateway.

Years Three & Four (Undated)—'For the Freedom of Jerusalem': 134/135 CE

The most numerous of the Bar Kokhba coinage, these undated coins (now inscribed 'For the freedom of Jerusalem') were produced for about eighteen months during the third and fourth years of the revolt. Their dating has been ascertained by Mildenberg's invaluable study of die sequences and die cracks. Meshorer suggests that the lack of dates for year three and four coinage is a deliberate omission, due to the belief that counting was a bad omen (Exodus 40.17):

> In Israel, the population maintained the belief that their fate was decided on the first day of each year. Therefore, the cessation of recording the year on the coinage may be connected with the belief that the fate of the army would be decided in a negative manner.[9]

Against this view, a recently discovered letter, dated to c. 140 CE, contains the never before seen date 'Year 4 of the Destruction of the House of Israel' (136 + 4 = 140).

Temple Variation #3 The 'Wavy Line': Though the star is retained on some coins; a replacement wavy line, running along the top of the temple façade, appears on obverse dies O16-17. Die O16 depicts a clear line of four half-circle

(open at the bottom) joined by three lines, while the later O17 die is much
poorer being just a thin wavy line. Such lines, for example, can also be seen on
a Torah shrine mosaic in the synagogue of Beth-shean, gold-glass plates and a
tetrastyle temple depicted on a clay lamp from Jerusalem, c. 300 CE.

This wavy line has been interpreted in a number of ways: as representing the
scarlet that was pinned to the outer façade of temple on the Day of Atonement;
'the cloud hovering over the holy place'[10] or the golden grapevine that adorned
the inner sanctuary. However, Price and Trell interpret the line as 'a row
of Oriental crenellations' as on a coin (c. 375 BCE) that depicts the flat roofed
shrine of Anu 'decorated with palmette antefixes'.[11] The interpretation of this
wavy line is dependent on whether the obverse represents the full outer temple
façade (crow-step parapet on flat roof) or inner sanctuary gateway (golden
vine). It may also be an illustrative composite of both: full outer façade with
representation of golden vine.

***

By combining the independent (albeit contradictory) testimonies of Josephus,
Middot and later Jewish iconography with what is known about the goals and
aims of the rebels, it's highly probable that some form of temple design is being
illustrated. But which temple? Though the consensus is that of the Herodian
temple, the Hasmonean temple hypothesis of Chyutin (though speculative)
provides a working alternative explanation. There isn't enough evidence to
conclude with any certainty what temple or even which part is being represented.
The argument also becomes circular, with models and depictions of the temple
depending on later iconographic and numismatic data, which is then used in turn
to support the obverse. Nevertheless, though there remains an element of risk in
accepting the consensus view, this study will accept from the evidence examined
above that what is being represented on the obverse is the *outer* temple façade
(in whatever form) with its flat roof.

The Messianic claim of Bar Kokhba: Numismatic evidence

Erwin Goodenough refers to the star ornament as a solar-rosette (καλχη) and
the most elaborate of the ornament designs does indeed look more like a rosette
than a star. The rosette was a common funerary symbol on Jewish sarcophagi
and ossuaries. A star or rosette can also be clearly seen depicted on the gable
of two variant peristyle Corinthian temple representations on the west wall of
the Dura-Europos synagogue. Both temples display a star/rosette ornament on

the pediment's tympanum. I. Renov has suggested that the Dura-Europa temple of Aaron, with its gabled roof, is a representation of Herod's temple with the rosette design being the golden lamp donated by Queen Helena of Adiabene during her visit to Jerusalem. A twelve-petalled rosette design appears on the pediment/gable above a Torah shrine on a 1.3m x 0.58m aedicula stone fragment (c. 250–306 CE) discovered at the synagogue of Nabratein in Galilee. A six-petalled rosette surrounded by two concentric circles appears on a rectangular lead weight found in the underground Second Revolt hiding complex at Horvat ʿAlim. Finally, a large twelve-petalled rosette is depicted on the Magdala stone.

Mildenberg interprets the star ornament as a rosette, rejecting the star interpretation as 'a fatal misrepresentation' that 'should never have arisen' by pointing to the clear design of die O6 as well as the Nabratein Fragment.[12] He observes that the fact the 'star' does not appear on the Year One dies, that they're cruciform in shape on early Year Two dies, and are replaced by the wavy line of the final Year Three dies O16-17 and suggests that they're architectural in origin and not 'symbols' linked to Bar Kokhba as the 'Son of the Star'. he states that:

> The deductive procedure employed to identify the rosette as a star is methodologically invalid since the elements interpreted as symbols are observed in isolation and not within the entire development of the ornament over the temple, as they should be. What might the 'Son of the Star' have to do with the cross-rosette and the architectural element, not to mention the wavy line?... it is torn out of its numismatic context and then quoted as the crowning argument for an otherwise unsubstantiated [third/fourth century] literary tradition.[13]

There are several arguments against the architectural feature interpretation. First, the Mishnah and Josephus describe only a *horizontal* sharp edged parapet roof, which supports the flat architrave design of the Bar Kokhba façade. Therefore, there was no tympanum pediment to decorate. Second, the temple murals in Dura-Europos can't be used as source material for Herod's temple as they're of a much later date. Indeed, the gabled temple design didn't appear in Jewish art until the third century CE. Thirdly, no source describes such a specific rosette-type architectural feature on the temple. Though a single rabbinic source does refer to a golden lamp or candlestick, donated by Helena, this lamp only hung *within* the entrance to the sanctuary (reflecting the bright light of the rising sun over the Mount of Olives) and *not* on the outer facade.

Messianic symbol/kingship (star)

The 'star out of Jacob' was a widely employed messianic motif and the link between Bar Kokhba, Numbers 24.17 and his messianic claim was an early attribution. Within the context of messianism and the nature of the revolt, the star, as a symbol of divine kingship provides the most credible solution. Whether the star specifically referred to Kosiba's sobriquet (as messianic warrior king) or was just a generic messianic symbol can't be determined but it must have been of great significance for the rebels. Mildenberg is also incorrect in stating that the changing nature of the ornaments precludes any reference to Bar Kokhba and can only lead to an architectural solution. The rough cross-shape of the first strikes has been discussed above but the change from star to wavy line doesn't imply that the preceding strikes must be architectural. We could also speculate (based on the known history of the revolt and that of the First) that the symbolic appearance of the ornament on the Year Two coins was the result of initial successes against the Romans and its removal in the last two dies of the final year of minting was due to the evident failure of the revolt. Such a hypothesis is plausible (if impossible to confirm). However, the majority of coins struck and in circulation depicted the star ornament, so this solution seems unlikely.

A countermark in the form of a six-pointed star appears on some of the bronze coins of Herod's son, Philip (dated between 8-15 CE), the first Jewish coins to bear such official marking. These marks were used to revalidate worn coins, change their value or introduce them into new circulation (though Meshorer suggests that none of these reasons were applicable in Philip's case). Was the star/rosette symbol of the Bar Kokhba tetradrachm also a countermark? Again, this is unlikely as countermarks were pressed into the coin and were also restricted to bronze coins. A few of the Bar Kokhba medium bronzes do exhibit countermarks but these are features of the original, un-struck Roman coin.

Hillel Newman suggests that the ornament may represent a comet that appeared 129/130 CE during Hadrian's tour of Egypt. He argues that this comet was interpreted as a sign of coming redemption, citing the earlier comets of 163 BCE and 66 CE. Newman also draws a parallel with rosette shaped star ornaments on the coins of Antonius Pius (138-161 CE) minted in honour of Hadrian's 'Divine Antinous'. A. Strobel drew attention to the fact that during the second year of the revolt (133-134 CE) there was a triple conjunction of Saturn and Jupiter.

The interpretation of the star ornament is more difficult to resolve than that of the façade itself, which at least depicts a building. However, the same methodology applies. Under the guerrilla conditions in which the rebels were operating and the materials available to them, the engravers would only have taken the time to produce a die that provided the maximum symbolic impact (hence their employment of First Revolt symbolism and paleo-Hebrew script). The evidence can take us in several different directions but the strongest hypothesis is that the ornament represents a star and it was used to symbolise the messianic nature and expectations of the revolt.

CONCLUSION

The purpose of Matthew 1–2 was to address and respond to specific community concerns and present an argument for the legitimacy of Jesus (a prologue missing from Mark) as the expected Davidic Messiah, a 'new' Moses as foretold by Scripture. This was in direct response to tensions with post 70 CE formative Judaism for (to the Jews of the local synagogue) Jesus' death would have precluded him from being the messiah. In authoring this Infancy Narrative (approximately 85-95 years after the events it describes), Matthew primarily drew on familiar literary elements from both the Old Testament and popular Near Eastern folk motifs relating to the birth of heroic figures. In this traditional birth narrative, Matthew included a guiding Star, a motif derived from the contemporary interpretation of Numbers 24.17, as a supporting sign of the Davidic Messiah, a sign that was given apologetic legitimacy by the observing magi.

The Infancy Narratives are largely unhistorical. Though elements are verifiable (for example, the reign of Herod and the geographical locations), no historical credence can be given to the events of Matthew 2. Having no historical basis, and being the creation of Matthew himself, it's not surprising to find no external record of the dramatic events Matthew 2 narrates. The Star shouldn't be viewed in isolation through the lens of modern astronomy (as a celestial mystery to be solved) but must be viewed against its early first-century socio-political background and Judeo-Christian messianic context.

Matthew 2 isn't a poetic non-technical work of astronomy or astrology but a work of Christology in response to concerns regarding the Christian Messiah. Those who seek an astronomical or astrological solution have misread Matthew's (unintentionally) ambiguous choice of Greek by failing to fully appreciate the wider context behind it (for example, the introduction of observing magi as a narrative plot device). This misreading has led to numerous hypotheses consisting of unnecessarily complex celestial events and imaginative reconstructions. Most astronomers (or those who wish for a real, historical event) don't apply a thorough application of historical and biblical criticism to Matthew 2. They not only treat the infancy narratives as historical records, they also apply modern astronomical thought to a culture that (for example) thought the stars were alive and the sun the breadth of a foot. They are prone to uncontrolled historical reconstruction and over-complication by trying to force astronomical phenomena to fit the narrative.

The evidence is that no *visiting magi and Star* tradition existed outside Matthew's community. Though the Star tradition may have been subject to 'astrological underplay' prior to the Gospel's composition and could (perhaps) provide an answer to its absence from Matthew and later Christian exegesis, if any tradition of the Star as an astrological or astronomical event existed in Matthew's community *it must have been extremely localised and quickly forgotten.*

We can only speculate about Matthew's implied knowledge or intentions. As few details exist with any certainty to establish what the Star was, we can only weigh the probabilities. The most we can conclude is that some unknown celestial event *may* have served as catalyst for the Star. Until new evidence emerges, whether a real historical event lies behind Matthew's use of a Star can't be determined.

APPENDIX I:
TABLE OF FOLK MOTIFS PERTAINING TO BIRTH

The following table lists those relevant motifs from both Thompson' *Motif-Index* and El-Shamy's works on Arabic tales that relate to the birth of the 'exposed-persecuted child/culture hero' as examined in Chapter 7. Non-related birth motifs have not been included. For completeness (in italics) are A512.3.1 §, D1314.13.1 and some of V, all of which have Matthew 1–2 as their original source.[1]

Motif	Description
A110	Origin of gods
A112	Birth of gods
A164.1.1.1 §	‡Deity reborn as his own son via intercourse with own mother
A511	Supernatural birth of culture hero
A511.0.1 §	Infancy and childhood of culture-hero (arch-saint)
A511.1	birth of culture hero
A511.1.3	Culture hero incarnated through the birth from virgin
A511.1.3.3	Immaculate conception of culture hero
A511.2.1	Abandonment of culture hero at birth
A511.2.3	Culture hero is hidden in order to escape enemies
A511.3.1	Culture hero is reared in seclusion
A511.10.2.1	Culture hero suckled by wolf
A512.3	Culture hero as son of god
A512.3.1 §	*Christ as son of God*
A515.1.1	Twin culture-heroes
B535	Animal Nurse
B535.0.9	She-wolf as nurse for child
B535.0.11	She-wolf cares for baby exposed in forest

D1314.13	[star] indicates location of newborn hero
D1810.8.2	Information received through dream
D1810.3	Warning in dreams
D1810.8.3.3	Dream warns of danger which will happen in near future
D1812.3.3	Future revealed in dream
D1812.5	Future learned through omens
D1812.5.1.6	Stars furnish omens
D1314.13.1	Star of Bethlehem
E741.1.1.1	New star for each birth
E741.1.1.2	[star] signifies hero's birth
F960.1	Extraordinary nature phenomena at birth of holy person
F961.2.1	Bright star indicates birth of holy person
J641	escaping before enemy can strike
K1847	Deception by substitution of children
K1847.1.1	Deceptive report of birth of heir
K512	Compassionate executioner
K515	Escape by hiding
K515.1	Children hidden to avoid their execution (death)
L111.2	‡Foundling hero
L111.2.1	Future hero found in boat
M300	Prophecies
M302.4	Horoscope by means of stars
M302.7	Prophecy through dreams
M310.1	Prophecy: future greatness and fame
M311	Prophecy: future greatness of unborn child
M311.0.2	Prophecy—hero's birth at certain time, place
M311.4	Prophecy: child to become king
M311.5	Unborn child will become nation's deliverer
M312.0.4	Mother's symbolic dream (vision) about the greatness of her unborn child
M312.0.4.1	*The dream about a tree which sprouts enormously*, indicates the birth of a hero
M312.2.1	Prophecy: son to be more powerful than father
M369.7	Prophecies about birth
M370	Vain attempts to escape fulfilment of prophecy

M371	'Exposure of infant to escape fulfilment of prophecy
M371.1	Exposure (murder) of child to avoid fulfilment of prophecy of future greatness
M371.2	Exposure of child to prevent fulfilment of parricide prophecy
M375	Slaughter of innocents to avoid fulfilment of prophecy
M375.1	All male children killed for fear that they will overcome parent
M375.3	Child mutilated to avoid fulfilment of prophecy
M376.3	Children swallowed one after the other as they are born for fear one of them will overcome father
M391	Fulfilment of prophecy
P481	Astrologers
R131	Exposed or abandoned child rescued
R131.1	Hunter rescues abandoned child
R131.4	Fisher rescues abandoned child
R150	Rescuers
R153	Parents rescue child
R153.2	Father rescues children
R153.3	Father rescues son(s)
R153.4	Mother rescues son
S141	Exposure in boat
S142	Person thrown into water and abandoned
S143	‡Abandonment in a forest
S146.2	Abandonment in cave
S147	Abandonment on mountain
S147.2 §	Abandonment in sunken valley
S302.1	All newborn male children slaughtered
S310	Reasons for abandonment of children
S312	Illegitimate child exposed
S313	Child of supernatural birth exposed
S322.1	Father casts daughter forth
S330	Circumstances of murder or exposure of children
S331	Exposure of child in boat (floating chest)
S350	Fate of abandoned child

S350.2	Child driven out (exposed) brought up in secret
S351.2	Abandoned child reared by herdsman
S353	Abandoned child raised by supernatural beings
S354	Exposed infant reared at strange king's court
T510	miraculous conception
T540	miraculous birth
T547	Birth from virgin
T547.1 §	virginity supernaturally preserved
T548.1	Child born in answer to prayer
T580	Childbirth
T581	Place and conditions of childbirth
T584.0.3	Birth of holy person painless
T585	Precocious infant
T594 §	Birth of boy (son) is good news
T611	Suckling of children
V211	*Christ*
V211.1	*Nativity of Christ*
V211.1.2.1	*Hairy star appears before nativity*
V211.1.8	*Infant Jesus*
V211.2.3.0.1	*[angel] warns of Christ's danger*
V230	Angels
V235	Visit of angel to mortal
V235.0.1	Mortals visited by angel in vision
Z159 §	‡Celestial (astronomical) symbolism
Z159.4.4 §	‡Guiding star

APPENDIX II:
MAGI: 'PROCESS OF IMPROVEMENT'

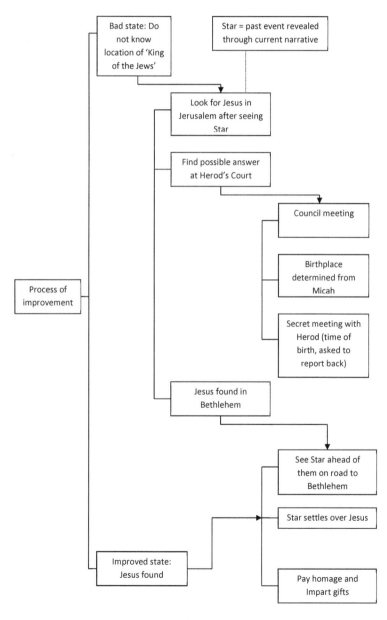

APPENDIX III:
VISUAL CHRONOLOGY OF MATTHEW & LUKE 1–2

Matthew 1–2

Sea of Galilee

Nazareth

5   2   Magi*

'The East'

Jerusalem *(?)   2

2   4

Bethlehem   1, 2*
(Home Town)

The
Dea
d

Sea

3

(Egypt)

1.	Mt 1.18–25
2.	Mt 2.1–12
3.	Mt 2.13–15
4.	Mt 2.16–18
5.	Mt 2.19–23
*	The Star

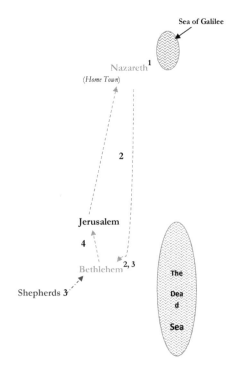

Luke 1–2

Sea of Galilee

Nazareth [1]
(Home Town)

5

2

Jerusalem

4

Bethlehem [2, 3]

Shepherds 3

The Dead Sea

1.	Lk 1.26-80
2.	Lk 2.1-7
3.	Lk 2.8-20
4.	Lk 2.21-38
5.	Lk 2.39-40

NOTES

Notes to Introduction

1   Mark Kidger, *The Star of Bethlehem: An Astronomer's View* (New Jersey: Princeton University Press, 1999), p. ix.

2   N. Denzey, 'A New Star on the Horizon: Astral Christologies and Stellar Debates in Early Christian Discourse', in Scott Noegel, Joel Walker and Brannon Wheeler, (eds.), *Prayer, Magic and the Stars in the Ancient and Late Antique World* (Pennsylvania: Pennsylvania State University Press, 2003), p. 208.

3   David Hughes, *The Star of Bethlehem Mystery* (J.M. Dent, 1979; London: Corgi Books, 1981); Mark Kidger, *Astronomical Enigmas: Life on Mars, the Star of Bethlehem and Other Milky Way Mysteries* (Baltimore: The John Hopkins University Press, 2005).

4   J. Leake, 'Wise Men of the West find the Star of Bethlehem,' *The Times* (24 November 1996), p. 8.

Notes to Chapter 1

1   Richard A. Burridge, *What are the Gospels? A Comparison with Graeco-Roman Biography* (Grand Rapids: Eerdmans, second edition, 2004), p. 205.

2   R.E. Brown and J.P. Meier, *Antioch and Rome: New Testament Cradles of Catholic Christianity* (New York: Paulist Press, 1983), pp. 45-72.

3   David C Sim, *The Gospel of Matthew and Christian Judaism: The History and Social Setting of the Matthean Community*. Edinburgh: T&T Clark, 1998, p. 62.

4   Cited in David Instone-Brewer, 'The Eighteen Benedictions and the *Minim* Before 70CE', *Journal of Theological Studies* 54 (2003), p. 31.

5   N.T. Wright, 'Five Gospels but No Gospel: Jesus and the Jesus Seminar', in Bruce Chilton and Craig A. Evans, (eds.), *Authenticating the Activities of Jesus* (Leiden: Brill, 2002), p. 110.

6   J. A. Overman, *Matthew's Gospel and Formative Judaism: The Social World of the Matthean Community* (Minneapolis: Fortress Press, 1990), p. 4.

7   Craig S. Keener, *A Commentary on the Gospel of Matthew*, (Grand Rapids: Eerdmans, 1999), p. 48.

8   Gerbern S. Oegema, *The Anointed and his People: Messianic Expectations from the Maccabees to Bar Kochba* (Journal for the Study of the Pseudepigrapha: Supplement Series 27; Sheffield: Sheffield Academic Press), p. 161.

9   W.D. Davies and Dale C. Allison, *A Critical and Exegetical Commentary on The Gospel According to Matthew* (ICC; 3 vols; Edinburgh: T&T Clark Ltd, 1988) 3.695.

10   George A. Kennedy, *New Testament Interpretation through Rhetorical Criticism* (Chapel Hill: University of North Carolina Press, 1984), p. 104.

11   M.D. Goulder, *The Evangelist's Calendar: A Lectionary Explanation of the Development of Scripture* (London: SPCK, 1978), p. 212.

Notes to Chapter 2

1   Raymond E. Brown, *The Birth of the Messiah: A Commentary on the Infancy Narratives in the Gospels of Matthew & Luke* (New York: The Anchor Bible Reference Library, Doubleday, 1993; New Updated Edition, New York: Doubleday, 1999), p. 34.

2   Mark Goodacre, 'Beyond the Q Impasse or Down a Blind Alley?', *Journal for the Study of the New Testament* 76 (1999): p. 33.

3   F.G. Downing, 'Redaction Criticism: Josephus' *Antiquities* and the Synoptic Gospels', *Journal for the Study of the New Testament* 8 (1980): 46-65; 9 (1980): 29-48.

4   R.E. Brown, *Birth of the Messiah*, pp. 513-516.

5   G. Theissen and A. Merz, *The Historical Jesus: A Comprehensive Guide* (trans. John Bowden; London: SCM Press, 1998), p. 165.

6   Robert K. MacEwen, *Matthean Posteriority: An Exploration of Matthew's Use of Mark and Luke as a Solution to the Synoptic Problem*. Library of New Testament Studies 501; (London: Bloomsbury T&T Clark, 2015), p. 124.

7   MacEwen, *Matthean Posteriority*, p. 124.

8   Merrill C. Tenney, 'Historical Verities in the Gospel of Luke,' *Biblotheca Sacra* 135 (1978): p. 128.

9   E.P Sanders and Margaret Davies, *Studying the Synoptic Gospels*, (London: SCM Press, 1989), p. 290.

10   N.T. Wright, *New Testament and the People of God*, Christian Origin and the Question of God 1 (London: SPCK, 1992), p. 377.

11   Richard Bauckham, *Jesus and the Eyewitnesses, The Gospels as Eyewitness Testimony* (Grand Rapids, Mich.; Cambridge: William B. Eerdmans, 2006), p. 7.

12   Bauckham, *Jesus and the Eyewitnesses*, pp. 121-122.

13   R.E. Brown, *Birth of the Messiah*, p. 188.

14   R.E. Brown, *Birth of the Messiah*, p. 36.

15   Robert Eisenman, 'Scandals and Rivalries in the Dead Sea Scrolls' *ABC Radio National*, aired 4 December 2005.

16   Gerd Lüdemann, *Jesus after 2000 Years: What He Really Said and Did* (trans. John Bowden; London: SCM Press, 2000), p. 128.

17   C. S. Mann, 'The Historicity of the Birth Narratives,' in *Historicity and Chronology in the New Testament* (London: SPCK, 1965), p. 51.

18   Ben Witherington III, 'Did Jesus Found a Dynasty? James Tabors' New Book' (13 April 2006) at http://benwitherington.blogspot.co.uk/2006/04/did-jesus-found-dynasty-ja_114493136136345584.html (viewed 20 April 2016).

Notes to Chapter 3

1   Stephen Neill and Tom Wright, *The Interpretation of the New Testament* (Oxford: Oxford University Press, 2nd edn, 1988), p. 86.

2   G.J. Toomer, *Ptolemy's Almagest* (London: Duckworth, 1984), p. 21.

3   Johannes P. Louw and Eugene A. Nida, (eds.), *Greek-English Lexicon of the New Testament Based on Semantic Domains. Vol. 1: Introduction and Domains; Vol. 2: Indices* (New York: United Bible Societies, 2nd edn, 1989), 1.30, p. 8.

4   F. H. Colson and G. H. Whitaker, *Philo* (Loeb Classical Library III, 1930), p. 218.

5   Matthew Black, *The Book of Enoch* (Leiden: Brill, 1985), p. 407.

6   J. T. Milik and Matthew Black, *The Books of Enoch. Aramaic Fragments of Qumran Cave 4* (Oxford: Clarendon Press, 1976), p. 289.

7   Aratus, *Phaenomena*, Translated by A.W. Mair and G.R. Mair. Loeb Classical Library 129 (London: Harvard University Press, 2000), p. 202.

8   Ethelbert W. Bullinger, *A Critical Lexicon and Concordance to the English and Greek New Testament* (London: Lampe Press, Ltd, 1957), p. 242.

9   Davies and Allison, *Gospel according to Matthew*, 3.621.

10   Louw and Nida, (eds.), *Greek-English Lexicon of the New Testament.*

11   Davies and Allison, *Gospel according to. Matthew*, 1.244.

12   Robert F. Hock, *The Infancy Gospels of James and Thomas*, (Santa Rose, California: Polebridge Press, 1995), p. 70.

13   Ulrich Luz, *Matthew 1-7:* A Commentary (Edinburgh: T&T Clarke, 1990), p. 137.

14   Michael Molnar, *The Star of Bethlehem:: The Legacy of the Magi* (New Jersey: Rutgers University Press, 2000), p. 92.

15   Molnar, *Star of Bethlehem*, p. 393.

16   Ptolemy, *Tetrabiblos*, trans. F.E. Robins (Cambridge, Massachusetts: Harvard University Press. LOEB Classical Library, 1940; Reprint, London, Harvard University Press, 2001), p. 313, n. 4.

17   Hermann Fränkel, *Apollonii Rhodii Argonautica* (Oxonii: E Typographeo Clarendoniano, 1961), p. 181.

18   Fränkel, *Apollonii Rhodii Argonautica*, p. 260.

19   John Sturdy, *Numbers. The Cambridge Bible Commentary on the New English Bible* (Cambridge: Cambridge University Press, 1976), p. 73.

20   Keener, *Commentary on the Gospel of Matthew*, p. 104.

21   J.P. Migne, *Patrologia graeca* [= Patrologiae cursus completus: Series graeca]. (ed.), 162 vols (Paris, 1857-1886), 57.64.

22   Dale C. Allison, 'What was the Star that Guided the Magi?' *Bible Review* 9 (1993): 24.

23   T. Hegedus, 'Magi and the Star in the Gospel of Matthew, p. 95.

24   Gustav S.J. Teres, *The Bible and Astronomy: The Magi and the Star of Bethlehem* (Oslo: Solum Forlang, 3rd edition, 2002), p. 21.

25   Louw and Nida, (eds.), *Greek-English Lexicon of the New Testament*, pp. 727-728. My emphasis.

26   *Greek-English Lexicon of the New Testament and other Early Christian Literature.* W. Bauer, F.W. Danker, W.F. Arndt, and F.W. Gingrich, Chicago, 3rd edn, 1999, p. 359.

27   Fritz Reinecker, *A Linguistic Key to the Greek New Testament, Testament. Vol. 1; Matthew through Acts* (London: Samuel Bagster and Sons Ltd, 1977), p. 4.

28   O. Neugebauer, *A History of Ancient Mathematical Astronomy, Astronomy* (3 vols; Berlin: Springer-Verlag, 1975), 1.197.

29   Ivor Bulmer-Thomas, 'The Star of Bethlehem—A New Explanation – Stationary Point of a Planet,' *Quarterly Journal of the Royal Astronomical Society* 33 [1992]: 369.

30   Ptolemy, *Tetrabiblos*, p. 45, n. 3.

31   Toomer, *Ptolemy's Almagest*, pp. 15-16.

32   Neugebauer, *History of Ancient Mathematical Astronomy*, 2. pp. 591, n. 16.

33   Neugebauer, *Astronomical Cuneiform Texts.* 3 vols (London: Lund Humphries, 1955), xx. i.

34   Bulmer-Thomas, 'The Star of Bethlehem – A New Explanation', p. 372.

35   Carl J. Wenning, 'The Star of Bethlehem Reconsidered: A Theological Approach,' *Plan* 10 (1981): pp. 2-5.

36   Daniel B. Wallace, *Greek Grammar Beyond the Basics: An Exegetical Syntax of the New Testament* (Grand Rapids: Zondervan, 1996), p. 448.

37   J.C. Fenton, *St Matthew* (London: SCM Press, 1963), p. 47.

38   Meier, John P. Meier, *A Marginal Jew: Rethinking the Historical Jesus. Volume One: The Roots of the Problem and the Person* (NY: Doubleday, 1991), 1.376.

39   R.E. Brown, *Birth of the Messiah*, 165, 170.

40   Davies and Allison, *Gospel according to Matthew*, 1.233.

41   Robert H. Gundry and Jules Lubbock, *Matthew: A Commentary on His Handbook for a Mixed Church Under Persecution* (Grand Rapids: Eerdmans, 1983; 2nd ed, 1994), p. 35.

42   Molnar, *Star of Bethlehem*, p. 96.

43   Carson, *Exegetical Fallacies*, (Grand Rapids: Baker Books, 2002), p. 45.

44   Dale C. Allison Jr., 'Reading Matthew through the Church Fathers' in Allison, Studies in Matthew: Interpretation Past and Present (Grand Rapids: BakerAcademic, 2005), p. 79.

45   John Elwolde, 'Language and the Translation of the Old Testament' in Judith M. Lieu and J. W. Rogerson (eds.), *Oxford Handbook of Biblical Studies* (Oxford: Oxford Handbooks, 2008), p. 155.

Notes to Chapter 4

1   James H. Charlesworth, 'Rylands Syriac Ms.44 and a New Addition to the Pseudepigrapha: The Treatise of Shem Discussed and Translated,' *Bulletin of the John Rylands Library of Manchester* 60 (1978), pp. 382-383.

2   M.R. Lehmann, 'New Light on Astrology in Qumran and the Talmud,' *RevQ* 32 (1975): pp. 599-602.

3   David Pingree, 'Astrology', in Philip P. Wiener, (ed.), *Dictionary of the History of Ideas: Studies of Selected Pivotal Ideas* (5 vols; New York: Scribner, 1973), p. 120.

4   Dorotheus of Sidon, *Carmen Astrologicum*, edited by David Pingree (Leipzig: BSB B. G. Teubner Verlagsgesellschaft, 1976).

5   Geza Vermes, *The Complete Dead Sea Scrolls in English*, Revised Edition (London: Penguin Books, 2004), p. 362.

6   Vermes, *Complete Dead Sea Scrolls in English*, p. 362.

7   Philip R. Davies, George J. Brooke and Philip R. Callaway, *The Complete World of the Dead Sea Scrolls* (London: Thames & Hudson, 2002), p. 134.

8   Martin Hengel, *Judaism and Hellenism: Studies in their Encounter in Palestine during the Early Hellenistic Period* (trans. John Bowden; 2 vols.; London: SCM Press, 1974), 1.237.

9   For English text, see John J. Collins, 'Sibylline Oracles – A New Translation and Introduction' in J.H. Charlesworth, (ed.), *Old Testament Pseudepigrapha*. 2 vols (New York: Doubleday, 1983): 1.317-472.

10   *Old Testament Pseudepigrapha*, 1.367.

11   James H. Charlesworth, 'Jewish Interest in Astrology during the Hellenistic and Roman Period', in: Wolfgang Haase and Hildegard Temporini, (eds.), *Aufstieg und Niedergang der Römischen Welt Geschichte und Kultur Roms im Spiegel der neueren Forschung*. Part II, Principat, 20.2 (Berlin: Walter De Gruyter, 1987): 926-950.

12   Charlesworth, 'Rylands Syriac Ms.44,' pp. 391.

13   Annette Yoshiko Reed, 'Abraham as Chaldean Scientist and Father of the Jews: Josephus, Ant. 1.154-168, and the Greco-Roman Discourse about Astronomy/Astrology', *Journal for the Study of Judaism in the Persian, Hellenistic and Roman Period* 35 (2004): p. 119.

14   Charlesworth, 'Rylands Syriac Ms.44', pp. 389-390.

Notes to Chapter 5

1   Erwin Goodenough, *Jewish Symbols in the Graeco-Roman World* (13 vols; New York: Böllingen, 1950-1959), p.152.

2   Dale C. Allison Jr., 'Reading Matthew through the Church Fathers', p. 117.

3   Hans Lietzmann, *A History of the Early Church,vol.1: The Beginnings of the Christian Church* (trans. Betram Lee Woolf; London: Butterworth Press, 1953), p. 244.

4   Denzey, *A New Star on the Horizon*, p. 213.

5   J.K. Elliot, (ed.), *The Apocryphal New Testament: A Collection of Apocryphal Christian Literature in an English Translation* (Oxford: Clarendon Press, 2006), pp. 84-99.

6   Henry Chadwick, *Saint Augustine: Confessions* (New York: Oxford University Press, 1991), 4.3.4–6; 7.6.8–10.

7   *Corpus Scriptorum Ecclesiasticorum Latinorum,* 32/4, 68.3-4.

8   English translation from Hock, *Infancy Gospels of James and Thomas,* p. 71.

9   Gregory of Nazianus, *Poemata Arcana.* C. Moreschini, D.A. Sykes, Leofranc Holford-Strevens, eds. (Oxford: Clarendon Press, 1997), pp. 23-27, pp. 190-194.

10   Aloys S.J. Grillmeier, *Christ in Christian Tradition*, Vol 1. Trans. J. Bowden (Oxford: Mowbrays, 1965; 2nd Revised edition, Oxford: Mowbrays, 1975), p. 67.

Notes to Chapter 6

1   R.E. Brown and John P. Meier, *Antioch and Rome*, p. 89.

2   David Pingree, '*Kirān*' in Cyril Glasse (ed.), *The Encyclopedia of Islam. New Edition* 5 (Revelation, 2014), p. 130.

3   Dimitri Gutas, *Greek Thought, Arabic Culture, The Graeco-Arabic Translation Movement in Baghdad and Early 'Abbāsid Society (2nd-4th/8th-10th Centuries)* (London: Routledge, 1998), p. 45.

4   *Introductorium in astronomiam albumasaris* (trans. Hermann of Carinthia; Augsburg: Erhardt Ratdolt, 1489).

5   See *Annales prioratus de Wigornia (A.D. 1-1377)* in Henry Richards Luard, (ed.), *Annales Monastici* (5 vols.; London: Longmans, 1864-1869), 4.491.

6   Laura Ackerman Smoller, *History, Prophecy, and the Stars: The Christian Astrology of Pierre d'Ailly, 1350-1420* (New Jersey: Princeton University Press, 1994), p. 64.

7   M. Gaster, 'Abravanel's Literary Work,' in J.B. Trend and H. Loewe, (eds.), *Isaac Abravanel* (Cambridge: At the University Press, 1937), p. 61.

8   *Epistolarum libri XII* (Venice, 1495), book VII. Quoted from P. G. Maxwell-Stuart, (ed.), *The Occult in Early Modern Europe: A Documentary History*, (Basingstoke: Macmillan, 1999), p. 110.

9   Maxwell-Stuart, *The Occult in Modern Europe*, pp. 110-111.

10   Keith Thomas, *Religion and the Decline of Magic: Studies in Popular Beliefs in Sixteenth- and Seventeenth-century England* (London: Penguin Books, repr, 1991), p. 386.

11   Krupp, 'Doctoring the Stars,' *Sky & Telescope* (October, 2004): p. 51.

12   *De stella nova in pede serpentarii, et qui sub ejus exortum de novo iniit, trigono igneo* (Paul Sessi, Prague, 1606) = *Opera Omnia* 2.636 (ed. Christian Frisch, 8 vols, Frankfurt am Main, 1858-1871).

13   Christian Frisch, (ed.), *Joannis Kepleri astronomi opera omnia*, (8 vols.; Frankfurt-Erlangen, 1858-1871; repr, 1971-1995): 4.177.

14   Samuel Herrick, Jr, 'The Jupiter-Saturn Triple Conjunction,' *Leaflets of the Astronomical Society of the Pacific*, 3 (1941), p. 348.

15   Johannnes Bringe, *De vero anno, quo aeternus Dei filius humanum naturam in utero benedictae Virginis Mariae assumsit* (Johannes Bringer, Frankfurt, 1614): 4.347.

16   T.W. Doane, *Bible Myths* (New York: Charles P. Somerby, 1882), p. 140; A. Neander, *The Life of Jesus Christ* (trans. J.M. Clintock and C.E. Blumenthal; New York: Harper & Brothers, 1848), p. 26.

Notes to Chapter 7

1   L. Ideler, *Handbuch der mathematischen und technischen Chronologie* (2 vols.; Berlin: August Rücker, 1825-26), 2.400.

2   Strauss, *The Life of Jesus Critically Examined* (P.C. Hodgson, [ed.]; London: SCM Press, 1973), p. 170.

3   George C. McWhorter, 'Christmas to New Years Eve,' *Harper's New Monthly Magazine* 32.188 (Jan 1866): p. 165.

4   Henry van Dyke, 'The Adoration of the Magi,' *Harper's New Monthly Magazine* 76.452 (Jan 1888): 169.

5   Frederic William Farrar, *The Life of Christ, Illustrated* (NY: Commonwealth Publishing, 1891), p. 26.

6   Farrar, *Life of Christ*, p. 736.

7   Alfred Edersheim, *The Life and Times of Jesus the Messiah* (2 vols.: London: Longmans, 1883; 3rd edn, 1907), 1.211.

8   Edersheim, *Life and Times of Jesus*, 1.211. (Taken from Jellinek, *Beth ha-Midrash* (6 vols., Leipz and Vienna, 1853-1878).

9   J.M. Stockwell, 'Supplement to Recent Contributions to Chronology and Eclipses', *Astronomical Journal* 12 (1892): p. 125.

10   E. Walter Maunder, *The Astronomy of the Bible* (London: T. Sealey Clark & Co, 1908), p. 397.

11   R.S. Richardson, 'Is that the Star of Bethlehem?' *Leaflets of the Astronomical Society of the Pacific* 3 (1937)106: pp. 54-61

12   Werner Keller, *The Bible as History* (New York: William Morrow and Co., 1956), p. 349.

13   John Addey, 'The Astrology of the Birth of Christ,' *The Astrological Journal* 1.3 (1959): pp. 4-12.

14   H. Clark, J.H Parkinson and F.R. Stephenson., 'An Astronomical Re-Appraisal of the Star of Bethlehem – A Nova of 5BC,' *Quarterly Journal of the Royal Astronomical Society 18* (1977): p. 443.

15   Clark et al. 'Astronomical Re-Appraisal, p. 447.

16   Meier, *A Marginal Jew*, 1.410, n. 1.

17   Meier, *A Marginal Jew*, 1, 410, n. 1.

18   Ferrari D'Occhieppo, 'The Star of the Magi and Babylonian Astrology' in *Chronos, Kairos, Christos: Nativity and Chronological Studies Presented to Jack Finegan*. J. Vardaman and E.M. Yamauchi, (eds.), Winona Lake: Eisenbrauns, 1989; p. 47.

19   D'Occhieppo, 'The Star of the Magi and Babylonian Astrology,' *CKC*, p. 48.

20   D'Occhieppo, 'The Star of the Magi and Babylonian Astrology,' *CKC*, pp. 50-53.

21   D'Occhieppo, 'The Star of the Magi and Babylonian Astrology,' *CKC*, p. 44, n. 4.

22   Leake, 'Wise Men of the West find the Star of Bethlehem, p. 8.

23   Stansbury Hagar, 'What was the Star of Bethlehem?' *Popular Astronomy*, 26 (March-July 1918): pp. 253-256.

24   Kocku von Stuckrad, 'Jewish and Christian Astrology in Late Antiquity – A New Approach', *Numen* 47 (2000): p. 31.

25   Kidger, *The Star of Bethlehem*, p. 253.

26   Shelley Jordan, *De Docta Astrologia: Centre Universitaire de Recherche en Astrologie's Book Reviews*, edition 15 (November 2001). Electronic review at http://cura.free.fr/books2.html (viewed 15 December 2013).

27   Kidger, *The Star of Bethlehem*, p. 250.

28   Jacqueline Mitton, *Journal of the British Astronomical Association* 110.1 (2000): p. 39.

29   Angela Tilby, *Son of God* (London: Hodder & Stoughton, 2002), p. 15.

30   Tilby, *Son of God*, p. 102.

31   Allan Chapman, *Gods in the Sky: Astronomy from the Ancients to the Renaissance* (London: Channel Four Books, 2002), p. 119.

Notes to Chapter 8

1   *Times* (22 December 1999).

2   John Mosley, *The Griffith Observer* (Dec, 1980).

3   Ernest L Martin, Ernest L., 'The Celestial Pageantry Dating Christ's Birth', *Christianity Today* 21 (Dec 3, 1976): 2.

4   Mosley, 'The Star of Bethlehem Reconsidered', p. 9.

5   Meier, *A Marginal Jew*, 1. pp. 414-415, n. 18.

6   Michael R. Molnar 'The Coins of Antioch,' 'The Coins of Antioch', Sky & Telescope (Jan 1992): pp. 37-29.

7   Molnar, *Star of Bethlehem*, p. 96.

8   Molnar, *Star of Bethlehem*, p. 5.

9   Michael R. Molnar, 'The Magi's Star from the Perspective of Ancient Astrological Practices,' *Quarterly Journal of the Royal Astronomical Society* 36 (1995): p. 112.

10   Pierre Bayle, *Pensees diversées sur la comète* (1682) in *The Occult in Early Europe*, p. 78.

11   Chown, 'Early Christians Hid Origins of the Bethlehem Star', *New Scientist* (December 2001).

12   Jim Tester, *A History of Western Astrology* (Suffolk: The Boydell Press, 1987), p. 142.

13   Roger Beck, 'The Astronomical Design of Karakush,' *Culture & Cosmos* 3.1 (1999): p. 34, n. 31.

14   Mark Kidger, *Astronomical Enigmas: Life on Mars, the Star of Bethlehem, and Other Milky Way Mysteries* (Baltimore: The John Hopkins University Press, 2005), p. 49.

15   Kidger, *The Star of Bethlehem*, p. 253.

16   Shelley Jordan, *De Docta Astrologia: Centre Universitaire de Recherche en Astrologie's Book Reviews*, edition 15 (Nov, 2001). Electronic review at http://cura.free.fr/books2.html (viewed 28 November 2004).

17   Jacqueline Mitton, *JBAA*.

Notes to Chapter 9

1   Fenton, *Saint Matthew*, p. 46.

2   George M. Soares Prabhu, *The Formula Quotations in the Infancy Narrative of Matthew* (AnBib 63: Rome: Biblical Institute Press, 1976), pp. 277-278, n. 215.

3   Prabhu, p. 299.

4   R.E. Brown, *Birth of the Messiah*, p. 172.

5   R.E. Brown, *Birth of the Messiah*, p. 172.

6   Francis Wright Beare, *The Gospel according to Matthew: A Commentary* (Oxford: Basil Blackwell, 1981), p. 74

7   Davies and Allison, *Gospel according to Matthew*, 1. p. 235.

8   Donald A. Hagner, *Matthew 1-13*. (WBC 33a; Dallas: Word Books, 1993), p. 25, p. 27.

9   Robert W. Funk, Robert Walter and the Jesus Seminar, *The Acts of Jesus: The Search for the Authentic Deeds of Jesus* (San Francisco: Harper San Francisco, 1998), p. 508.

10   Michael Green, *The Message of Matthew* (BST; Leicester: Inter-Varsity Press, 2000), p. 69.

11   J. Neville Birdsall, 'The Star of Bethlehem', *Journal for the History of Astronomy* 33 (2002): pp. 391-394.

12   John Nolland, *The Gospel of Matthew. A Commentary on the Greek Text* (NIGTC; Grand Rapids: Eerdmans, 2005), p. 110.

13   R.T. France, *The Gospel of Matthew* (NICNT; Grand Rapids: Eerdmans, 2007), p. 68.

14   K.L. McKay, 'Aspect in Imperatival Constructions in the New Testament Greek,' *NovT* 27 (1985): p. 214.

15   N.T. Wright and Marcus Borg, *The Meaning of Jesus: Two Visions* (London: SPCK, 1999), p. 174.

16   Soares Prabhu, *Formula Quotations*, p. 277, n. 215.

17   N.T. Wright, 'Christian Origins and the Resurrection of Jesus: The Resurrection of Jesus as a Historical Problem', *Sewanee Theological Review* 41 (1998): pp. 107-123.

18   N.T. Wright, 'Five Gospels but No Gospel: Jesus and the Jesus Seminar', in Bruce Chilton and Craig A. Evans, (eds.), *Authenticating the Activities of Jesus* (Leiden: Brill, 1999), p. 117.

19   David Hackett Fischer, *Historian's Fallacies: Towards a Logic of Historical Thought* (New York: Harper & Row, 1970), p. 47.

20   Ramsay MacMullen, *Enemies of the Roman Order, Treason, Unrest & Alienation in the Empire* (Cambridge, Harvard University Press, 1966), p. 132.

21   N.T. Wright, *New Testament and the People of God*, p. 100.

Notes to Chapter 10

1   W.G. Boswell-Stone, *Shakespeare's Holinshed: The Chronicle and The History Plays Compared* (NY: Benjamin Blom, 1966), p. 137.

2   J.H. Charlesworth, (ed.), *Old Testament Pseudepigrapha*. 2 vols; (New York: Doubleday, 1983), 1. p. 369.

3   Augustine Fitzgerald, *The Essays and Hymns of Synesius the Cyrene* (vol. 2.; London: OUP, 1930), p. 257.

4   *OTP* 1. p. 399.

5   Michael R. Molnar, 'New Nuministic Evidence about the Comets of Mithradates the Great of Pontus (134 and 119 BC)', *Bulletin of the American Astronomical Society* 29 (1997): p. 1262.

6   Christopher Cullen, 'Halley's Comet and the 'Ghost' Event of 10BC', *Quarterly Journal of the Royal Astronomical Society*, 32 (1991), p. 117.

7   Colin J. Humphreys, 'The Star of Bethlehem—A Comet of 5BC—and the Date of the Birth of Christ,' *Quarterly Journal of the Royal Astronomical Society*, 32 (1991): pp. 395-396.

8   Craig S. Keener, *Commentary on the Gospel of Matthew*, p. 101.

9   Jack Finegan, *Handbook of Biblical Chronology* (Peabody, Mass: Hendrickson, rev. edn, 1998), p. 314.

10   Finegan, *Handbook*, p. 314

11   A. Mishcon and A. Cohen, *Hebrew-English Edition of the Babylonian Talmud* (London: The Soncino Press, 1988), p. 10a.

12   Meier, *A Marginal Jew*, 1. p. 420, n. 57.

13   Wayne Horowitz, 'Halley's Comet and the Judean Revolts Revisited,' *Catholic Biblical Quarterly* 58 (1996): p. 459.

Note to Chapter 11

1   C. Sigismondi, D. Hoffleit and R. Coccioli, 'Long-Term Behaviour of Mira Ceti Maxima,' Journal of the American Association of Variable Star Observers 30 (2001): 38.

Notes to Chapter 12

1   R. Campbell Thompson, *The Reports of the Magicians and Astrologers of Nineveh and Babylon* (London: Luzac & Co, 1900), 202 obv. Lines 1-4, rev. lines 1-4).

2   Judith Kingston Bjorkman, 'Meteors and Meteorites in the Ancient Near East,' *Metic* 8 (1973): p. 101.

3   Victoria Combe, 'Star of Bethlehem was Two Brilliant Meteors', *The Daily Telegraph* (30 August 2001).

4   Patrick Moore, *The Star of Bethlehem* (Canopus Publishing Ltd, 2001), p. 99.

5   Moore, *Star of Bethlehem*, p. 97.

6   Hughes, *Star of Bethlehem Mystery*, 195.

7   J.G. Frazer, *Adonis, Attis, Osiris: Studies in the History of Oriental Religion* (London: MacMillian and Co, Ltd, 3rd edn, 1914), p. 259.

Notes to Chapter 13

1   Moore, *Star of Bethlehem*, p. 31.

2   William P. Brown, 'A Royal Performance',: Critical Notes on Psalm 110:3aγ-b,' *Journal of Biblical Literature* 117 (1998): p. 96.

3   Gary A. Rendsberg, 'Psalm CX 3b,' *Vetus Testamentum* 49 (1999): p. 551.

4   Davies and Allison, *Gospel according to Matthew*, 1. p. 251.

5   Frazer, *Adonis, Attis, Osiris*, p. 259.

6   Campbell, *The Masks of God, Occidental Mythology* (New York: The Viking Press, 1964; Reprint, London: Souvenir Press, 2001), p. 338.

Notes to Chapter 14

1   R.E. Brown, *Death of the Messiah*, 2. p. 1131.

2   Gundry, *Matthew*, p. 587.

3   R.E. Brown, *Death of the Messiah*, 2. p. 1138.

4   R.E. Brown, *Death of the Messiah*, 2. p. 1138.

5   Neill and Wright, *Interpretation of the New Testament*, p. 259.

6   Atkinson, 'Herod the Great, Sosius, and the Siege of Jerusalem (37 B.C.E.) in Psalm of Solomon 17', *Novum Testamentum* 38 (1996): p. 313.

7   Emil Schürer, *The History of the Jewish People in the Age of Christ (175BC – AD 135)*. New English Edition by G. Vermes and F. Millar. 4 Vols. (Edinburgh: T&T Clarke, 1973, 1979, 1986), pp. 34-35, 412.

8   Vermes, *Dead Sea Scrolls in English*, p. 493.

9   Roger T. Beckwith, 'Daniel 9 and the Date of the Messiah's Coming in Essene, Hellenistic, Pharisaic, Zealot and Early Christian Computation', *Revue de Qumran* 40 (1981): p. 530.

10   Richard A. Horsley and J.S. Hanson, *Bandits, Prophets, and Messiahs: Popular Movements at the Time of Jesus* New Voices in Biblical Studies (Minneapolis: Winston, 1985), 4: pp. 792-793.

11   Craig A. Evans, 'Messianic Hopes and Messianic Figures in Late Antiquity', *Journal for the Study of Graeco-Roman Christianity and Judaism* 3 (2006): 39.

12   Richard A. Horsley, *The Liberation of Christmas: The Infancy Narratives in Social Context* (New York: Continuum Publishing, 1993), p. 51.

13   Horsley, *The Liberation of Christmas*, p. 7.

14   R.T. France, *Gospel of Matthew*, p. 43.

Notes to Chapter 15

1   Jack M. Sasson, *Ruth: A New Translation with a Philological Commentary and a Formalist-Folklorist Interpretation* (London: John Hopkins University Press, 1979), p. 197.

2   Burridge, *What are the Gospels?, p.* 193.

3   E, P. Sanders and M. Davies, *Studying the Synoptic Gospels*, (London: SCM Press, 1989), p. 288.

4   Burridge, *What are the Gospels?*, p. 196.

5   Burridge, *What are the Gospels?*, p. 196.

6   R. Tannehill, 'Types and Functions of Apophthegms in the Synoptic Gospels', *Aufstieg und Niedergang der römischen Welt: Geschichte und Kultur Roms im Spiegal der nueren Forschung*, 2.25.2: pp. 1792-1824.

7   Burridge, *What are the Gospels?*, p. 118.

8   Burridge, *What are the Gospels?*, p. 204.

9   Burridge, *What are the Gospels?*, p. 205.

10   Burridge, *What are the Gospels?*, p. 205.

11   David. E. Aune (ed.), 'Gospels as Hellenistic Biography,' 9; idem, *Graeco-Roman Literature and the New Testament, Selected Forms and Genres* (Sources for Biblical study 21; Atlanta: Scholars Press, 1988), pp. 107-126.

12   Beck, 'Mystery Religions, Aretalogy and the Ancient Novel', in L.M. Wills, *The Jewish Novel in the Ancient World* (Ithaca, N.Y.; London: Cornell University Press, 1995), p. 142.

Notes to Chapter 16

1   M. Dibelius, M., *From Tradition to Gospel*. Translated from the Revised Second Edition of *Die Formgeschichte des Evangeliums* by Bertam Lee Woolf (London: Ivor Nicholson and Watson Ltd, 1934), p. 132.

2   Heda Jason, 'The Story of David and Goliath: A Folk Epic', *Biblica* 60 (1970): p. 62.

3   Thompson, *The Folktale* (New York: The Dryden Press, 1946), p. 415.

4   Chris Baldick, *The Concise Oxford Dictionary of Literary Terms* (Oxford: Oxford University Press, 2nd ed; 2001), p. 162.

5   Soll, 'Misfortune and Exile in Tobit: The Juncture of a Fairy Tale Source and Deuteronomic Theology', *CBQ* 51 (1989): p. 210.

6   Hasan El-Shamy, *Types of the Folktale in the Arab World, A Demographically Oriented Tale-Type Index.* (Bloomington, Ind.: Indiana University Press; Chesham: Combined Academic, 2004), pp. ix, xviii-xix.

7   A. Aarne, *The Types of the Folktale: A Classification and Bibliography,* trans. S. Thompson (FFC 74; Helsinki: Folklore Fellows Communications, 2nd rev. ed., 1973).

8   Horsley, *Liberation of Christmas,* p.165.

9   Vladmir Y.Propp, 'Structure and History in the Study of the Fairy Tale', *Semeia* 10 (1978): p. 63.

10   Vladmir Y. Propp, *Morphology of the Folktale,* Translated by Laurance Scott. 2nd Revised and Edited Edition. Indiana University Research Centre in Anthropology, Folklore and Linguistics, Publications 10 (Austin: University of Texas Press, 1968), p. 21.

11   Propp, *Morphology of the Folktale,* p. 25.

12   Raglan, *The Hero: A Study in Tradition, Myth, and Drama* (London: Methuen, 1936; New York: Vintage Books, 1956), p. 152.

13   R.L. Hunter, *A Study of Daphnis and Chloe* (Cambridge: Cambridge University Press, 1983), p. 16.

14   Longus, *Daphnis and Chloe,* trans. with an introduction and commentary by J. R. Morgan (Oxford: Aris & Philips, 2004), pp. 151-152.

15   Mary Grant (ed.), *The Myths of Hyginus,* Humanistic Studies 34 (Lawrence: University of Kansas Publications, 1960), p. 88.

16   Part of this summary is taken from Herodotus, *The Histories,* trans. Robin Waterfield (Oxford: Oxford University Press, 1998), pp. 49-52.

17   D. Boedeker, 'Epic Heritage and Mythical Patterns in Herodotus', in *Brill's Companion to Herodotus*: pp. 111-112.

18   I.M. Diakonoff, 'Medea', in Ilya Gershevitch, (ed.), *The Cambridge Ancient History of Iran: Vol.2 The Median and Achaemenian Periods* (Cambridge: Cambridge University Press, 1985), p. 144; T. Cuyler Young, Jr., 'Cyrus', in D.N. Freedman, (ed.), *Anchor Bible Dictionary.* 6 vols (New York: Doubleday, 1992), 1. p. 1231.

19   Jan de Vries, *Heroic Song and Heroic Legend* (trans. B.J. Timmer; London: Oxford University Press, 1963), p. 206.

20   Text from Suetonius, *The Lives of the Caesars* (trans. J.C. Rolfe; 2 vols.; LCL 31, 38 (Cambridge, Mass.: Harvard University Press, 1914).

21   Roger Beck, 'Mystery Religions, Aretalogy and the Ancient Novel', in *The Novel in the Ancient World,* p. 143, n. 53.

Notes to Chapter 17

1   Othniel Margalith, 'More Samson Legends', *Vetus Testamentum* 36 (1986): p. 397.

2   G. Vermes, *Scripture and Tradition in Judaism. Haggadic Studies* (Leiden: Brill, 1961), p. 95.

3   Text is taken from Moses Samuel's 1839-40 translation *Book of Jasher Referred to in Joshua and Second Samuel,* http://www.dubroom.org/download/pdf/ebooks/the_book_of_jasher.pdf (viewed 25 October 2006).

4   Translation by Robert Graves and Raphael Patai, *Hebrew Myths: The Book of Genesis* (London: Cassell, 1964), p. 134.

5   James George Frazer, *Folk-Lore in the Old Testament, Studies in Comparative Religion, Legend and Law.* 3 vols (London: Macmillan and Co., Limited, 1919), pp. 437-455, p. 439.

6   Brevard S. Childs, *Exodus: A Commentary* (London: SCM Press, 1974), p. 7.
7   Dale C. Allison Jr,, *The New Moses: A Matthean Typology* (Edinburgh: T&T Clark, 1993), p. 153.
8   Alan Dundes, *The Hero Pattern and the Life of Jesus: Protocol of the Twenty-Fifth Colloquy, The Centre for Hermeneutical Studies in Hellenistic and Modern Culture, 12 December 1976* (Berkeley: The Centre for Hermeneutical Studies in Hellenistic and Modern Culture, 1977), p.10.
9   Rudolf Bultmann, *History of the Synoptic Tradition, The History of the Synoptic Tradition* (trans. John Marsh; Oxford: Blackwell, 2nd edn, 1968), p. 292.
10   Dibelius, *From Tradition to Gospel*, p. 130.
11   Charles Francis Potter, 'Jesus' in *Standard Dictionary of Folklore*, 2.548.
12   Thomas Fawcett, *Hebrew Myth and Christian Gospel* (London: SCM Press, 1973), p. 149.
13   Dundes, *The Hero Pattern and the Life of Jesus*, p. 12.
14   Brian Lewis, *The Sargon Legend,: A Study of the Akkadian Text and the Tale of the Hero who was Exposed at Birth*. American Schools of Oriental Research Dissertation Series 4; Cambridge, MA: American Schools of Oriental Research, 1980, p. 201, n. 41; R.B. Redford, 'The Literary Motif of the Exposed Child', *Numen* 14 (1967): p. 218.

Notes to Chapter 18

1   Keener, *Commentary on the Gospel of Matthew*, p. 98.
2   Soares Prabhu, *Formula Quotations,* p. 273.
3   Soares Prabhu, *Formula Quotations,* p. 268 (also 270).
4   Luz, *Matthew 1-7*, 130-131.
5   John Nolland, 'The Sources for Matthew 2:1-12', *Catholic Biblical Quarterly* 60 (1998): 285.
6   Nolland, 'Sources for Matthew 2:1-12', p. 293.
7   Nolland, 'Sources for Matthew 2:1-12', p. 296.

Notes to Chapter 19

1   Vermes, *Scripture and Tradition*, p. 165.
2   F. García-Martínez & Eibert J.C. Tigchelaar, *The Dead Sea Scrolls Study Edition* (Leiden: Brill, 2000), p. 561.
3   J.H. Charlesworth, *Old Testament Pseudepigrapha*, 1.794.
4   Collins, 'Sibylline Oracles', *Old Testament Pseudepigrapha,* 1. pp. 395, 397, 399 and 403.
5   Gundry, *Matthew*, p. 27.
6   Martin Pickup, 'New Testament Interpretation of the Old Testament: The Theological Rationale of Midrashic Exegesis', *Journal of the Evangelical Theological Society 51* (2008): p. 375.
7   George van Kooten, 'Matthew, the Parthians, and the Magi: A Contextualization of Matthew's Gospel in Roman-Parthian Relations of the First Centuries BCE and CE', in *The Star of Bethlehem and The Magi*, pp. 602-618 (608).
8   K.J. Woollcombe, 'The Biblical Origins and Patristic Development of Typology', in G.W.H. Lampe and Woollcombe, *Essays on Typology* (Studies in Biblical Theology 22; London: SCM Press, 1957), pp. 39-75.
9   R.E. Brown, *Birth of the Messiah*, p. 196.

Notes to Chapter 20

1   Richard G. Marks, *The Image of Bar Kokhba in Traditional Jewish Literature: False Messiah and National Hero* (University Park, Pa: Pennsylvania State University Press, 1994), p. 14.

2   Adin Steinsaltz, *The Talmud: The Steinsaltz Edition* (New York: Random House, 1999), pp. 20, 126-127.

3   Gregory Stevenson, *Power and Placee: Temple and Identity in the Book of Revelation* (Band 17; Berlin: Walter de Gryter GmBH & Co, 2001), p.167.

4   Michael Chyutin, *Architecture and Utopia in the Temple Era,* (trans. by Richard Flantz; LSTS 58; London: T&T Clarke, 2006), p.145.

5   R. Hachlili, *Ancient Mosaic Pavements: Themes, Issues, and Trends: Selected Studies* (Leiden: Brill, 2009), p. 23.

6   Chyutin, *Architecture and Utopia in the Temple Era,* pp. 126-127 (Figure 4.1), pp. 133-134, 160-167.

7   Michael Chyutin, *Architecture and Utopia in the Temple Era,* (trans. by Richard Flantz; LSTS 58; London: T&T Clarke, 2006), p. 162.

8   Baruch Kanael, 'Notes on the Dates Used During the Bar Kokhba Revolt', *Israel Exploration Journal* 21 (1971): p. 44.

9   Ya'akov Meshorer, *Ancient Jewish Coinage,* 2.154. Meshorer, , Ancient Jewish Coinage. 2 Vols. (New York: Amphora Books, 1982), 2.154.

10   E. Mary Smallwood, *The Jews Under Roman Rule: From Pompey to Diocletian.* Studies in Judaism in Late Antiquity 20 (Leiden: Brill, 1976), p. 445, n. 66.

11   Martin Jessop Price and Bluma L. Trell, *Coins and their Cities: Architecture on the Ancient Coins of Greece, Rome, and Palestine* (London: V.C. Vecchi and Sons, 1977) p. 55, Figure 96, p. 177.

12   Leo Mildenberg, *The Coinage of the Bar Kokhba War,* Monographen zur antiken Numismatik; Bd 6 (Aarau: Sauerländer, 1984), p. 43.

13   Mildenberg, *Coinage of the Bar Kokhba War,* p. 45.

Note to Appendix I

1   E.O. James, 'The Influence of Christianity on Folklore', *Folklore* 58 (1947): 361-376.

BIBLIOGRAPHY

Aarne, A., *The Types of the Folktale: A Classification and Bibliography*, trans. S. Thompson (FFC 74; Helsinki: Folklore Fellows Communications, 2nd rev. ed., 1973).

Allison, Jr., Dale C. and W.D. Davies, *A Critical and Exegetical Commentary on The Gospel According to Saint Matthew*. International Critical Commentary. 3 vols. Edinburgh: T&T Clark, 1988, 1991, 1997.

——, 'What was the Star that Guided the Magi?' *Bible Review* 9 (1993): 20-24, 63.

——, *The New Moses: A Matthean Typology*. Edinburgh: T&T Clark, 1993.

Aratus, *Phaenomena*. Translated by A.W. Mair and G.R. Mair. Loeb Classical Library 129. London: Harvard University Press, 2000.

Atkinson, Kenneth, 'Herod the Great, Sosius, and the Siege of Jerusalem (37 B.C.E.) in Psalm of Solomon 17', *Novum Testamentum* 38 (1996): 313-322.

Aune, David E. (ed.), *Graeco-Roman Literature and the New Testament: Selected Forms and Genres* (Sources for Biblical study 21; Atlanta: Scholars Press, 1988).

Bauckham, Richard, *Jesus and the Eyewitnesses: The Gospels as Eyewitness Testimony*. Grand Rapids, Mich.; Cambridge: William B. Eerdmans, 2006.

Beck, Roger, 'The Astronomical Design of Karakush', *Culture & Cosmos* 3.1 (1999).

Beckwith, Roger T., 'Daniel 9 and the Date of the Messiah's Coming in Essene, Hellenistic, Pharisaic, Zealot and Early Christian Computation', *Revue de Qumran* 40 (1981).

Birdsall, J. Neville, 'The Star of Bethlehem', *Journal for the History of Astronomy* 33 (2002): 391-394.

Bjorkman, Judith Kingston, 'Meteors and Meteorites in the Ancient Near East,' *Metic* 8 (1973):101.

Boedeker, D., 'Epic Heritage and Mythical Patterns in Herodotus', in *Brill's Companion to Herodotus*,.

Bultmann, Rudolf, *The History of the Synoptic Tradition* (trans. John Marsh; Oxford: Blackwell, 2nd edn, 1968).

Boswell-Stone, W.G., *Shakespeare's Holinshed: The Chronicle and History Plays Compared*. New York: Benjamin Blom, 1966.

Bringer, Johannnes, *De vero anno, quo aeternus Dei filius humanum naturam in utero benedictae Virginis Mariae assumsit* (Frankfurt, 1614).

Brown, Raymond E., *The Birth of the Messiah: A Commentary on the Infancy*

Narratives in the Gospels of Matthew & Luke. New York: The Anchor Bible Reference Library, Doubleday, 1993; New Updated Edition, New York: Doubleday, 1999.

Brown, William P., 'A Royal Performance: Critical Notes on Psalm 110:3aγ-b,' *Journal of Biblical Literature* 117 (1998): 93-96.

Bullinger, Ethelbert W., *A Critical Lexicon and Concordance to the English and Greek New Testament* (London: Lampe Press, Ltd, 1957).

Burridge, Richard A., *What are the Gospels? A Comparison with Graeco-Roman Biography.* 2nd Edition. Grand Rapids: Eerdmans, 2004.

Campbell, Joseph, *The Masks of God: Occidental Mythology.* New York: The Viking Press, 1964; Reprint, London: Souvenir Press, 2001.

Chapman, Allan, *Gods in the Sky: Astronomy from the Ancients to the Renaissance.* London: Channel 4 Books, 2002.

Charlesworth, James H., 'Jewish Interest in Astrology during the Hellenistic and Roman Period', in: Wolfgang Haase and Hildegard Temporini, (eds.), *Aufstieg und Niedergang der Römischen Welt Geschichte und Kultur Roms im Spiegel der neueren Forschung.* Part II, *Principat*, 20.2. Berlin: Walter De Gruyter, 1987: 926-950.

——, 'Rylands Syriac Ms.44 and a New Addition to the Pseudepigrapha: The Treatise of Shem Discussed and Translated,' *The Bulletin of the John Rylands Library of Manchester* 60 (1978): 376-403.

——, (ed.), *Old Testament Pseudepigrapha.* 2 vols; (New York: Doubleday, 1983).

Childs, Brevard S., *Exodus: A Commentary.* London: SCM Press, 1974.

Chilton, Bruce and Craig A. Evans, (eds.), *Authenticating the Activities of Jesus.* Leiden: Brill, 2002.

Chown, Marcus, 'O Invisible Star of Bethlehem,' *New Scientist* 23/30 Dec 1995: 34-35.

——, 'Early Christians Hid Origins of the Bethlehem Star,' *New Scientist.Com* (Dec 2001) at www.newscientist.com/news/print.jsp?id=ns99991713 (viewed 11/08/04).

Collins, John J., 'Sibylline Oracles – A New Translation and Introduction' in J.H. Charlesworth, (ed.), *Old Testament Pseudepigrapha.* 2 vols; Doubleday: New York, 1983: 1.317-472.

Chyutin, *Architecture and Utopia in the Temple Era,* (trans. by Richard Flantz; LSTS 58; London: T&T Clarke, 2006).

—— *Architecture and Utopia in the Temple Era,* (trans. by Richard Flantz; LSTS 58; London: T&T Clarke, 2006).

Combe, Victoria, 'Star of Bethlehem was Two Brilliant Meteors', *Daily Telegraph*, Aug 30th 2001.

Cullen, Christopher, 'Halley's Comet and the 'Ghost' Event of 10BC', *Quarterly Journal of the Royal Astronomical Society*, 32 (1991), 117.

Denzey, Nicola, *Cosmology and Fate in Gnosticism and Graeco-Roman Antiquity: Under Pitiless Skies.* Leiden: Brill, 2013.

Dibelius, M., *From Tradition to Gospel.* Translated from the Revised Second Edition of *Die Formgeschichte des Evangeliums* by Bertam Lee Woolf (London: Ivor Nicholson and Watson Ltd, 1934).

Dorotheus of Sidon, *Carmen Astrologicum*, edited by David Pingree (Leipzig: BSB B. G. Teubner Verlagsgesellschaft, 1976).

Downing, F. Gerald, 'Redaction Criticism: Josephus' *Antiquities* and the Synoptic Gospels', *Journal for the Study of the New Testament* 8 (1980): 46-65; 9 (1980): 29-48.

Dundes, Alan, *The Hero Pattern and the Life of Jesus: Protocol of the Twenty-Fifth Colloquy, The Centre for Hermeneutical Studies in Hellenistic and Modern Culture, 12 December 1976*. Berkeley: The Centre for Hermeneutical Studies in Hellenistic and Modern Culture, 1977.

Dyke, Henry van, 'The Adoration of the Magi,' *Harper's New Monthly Magazine* 76.452 (Jan 1888): 167-178.

Edersheim, Alfred, *The Life and Times of Jesus the Messiah* (2 vols.: London: Longmans, 1883; 3rd edn, 1907).

Elliott, J.K. (ed.), *The Apocryphal New Testament: A Collection of Apocryphal Christian Literature in an English Translation*. Oxford: Clarendon Press, 2006.

El-Shamy, Hasan, *Types of the Folktale in the Arab World: A Demographically Oriented Tale-Type Index*. Bloomington, Ind.: Indiana University Press; Chesham: Combined Academic, 2004.

Eisenman, Robert, 'Scandals and Rivalries in the Dead Sea Scrolls' *ABC Radio National*, aired 4 December 2005.

Evans, Craig A. 'Messianic Hopes and Messianic Figures in Late Antiquity', *Journal for the Study of Graeco-Roman Christianity and Judaism* 3 (2006): 9-40.

Farrar, Frederic William, *The Life of Christ (Illustrated)*. New York: Commonwealth Publishing, 1891.

Fawcet, Thomas, *Hebrew Myth and Christian Gospel*. London: SCM Press Ltd, 1973.

Finegan, Jack, *Handbook of Biblical Chronology* (Peabody, Mass: Hendrickson, rev. edn, 1998), p.314.

Fischer, David Hackett, *Historian's Fallacies: Towards a Logic of Historical Thought* (New York: Harper & Row, 1970), p. 47.

France, Robert T., *The Gospel of Matthew*. The New International Commentary on the New Testament. Grand Rapids: Eerdmans, 2007.

Frazer, James George, *Folk-Lore in the Old Testament. Studies in Comparative Religion, Legend and Law*. 3 vols; London: Macmillan and Co., Limited, 1919.

Freedman, D.N. (ed.), *Anchor Bible Dictionary*. 6 vols (New York: Doubleday, 1992).

Frisch, Christian, (ed.), *Joannis Kepleri astronomi opera omnia*, (8 vols.; Frankfurt-Erlangen, 1858-1871; repr, 1971-1995).

Funk, Robert W., Robert Walter and the Jesus Seminar, *The Acts of Jesus: The Search for the Authentic Deeds of Jesus*. San Francisco: HarperSanFrancisco, 1998.

García-Martínez F. and Eibert J.C. Tigchelaar, *The Dead Sea Scrolls Study Edition* (Leiden: Brill, 2000).

Glasse, Cyril (ed.), *The Encyclopedia of Islam. New Edition* 5 (Revelation, 2014).

Goodacre, Mark, '*Beyond the Q Impasse* or Down a Blind Alley?', *Journal for the Study of the New Testament* 76 (1999): 33-52.

Goodenough, Erwin, *Jewish Symbols in the Graeco-Roman World* (13 vols; New York: Böllingen, 1950-1959).

Goulder, Michael D., *The Evangelist's Calendar: A Lectionary Explanation of the Development of Scripture*. London: SPCK, 1978.

Grant, Mary (ed.), *The Myths of Hyginus*. Humanistic Studies 34; Lawrence: University of Kansas Publications, 1960.

Graves, Robert and Raphael Patai, *Hebrew Myths: The Book of Genesis*. Cassell: London, 1964.

Gregory of Nazianus, *Poemata Arcana*. C. Moreschini, D.A. Sykes, Leofranc Holford-Strevens, eds. (Oxford: Clarendon Press, 1997).

Gutas, Dimitri, *Greek Thought, Arabic Culture. The Graeco-Arabic Translation Movement in Baghdad and Early 'Abbāsid Society* (2nd-4th/8th-10th Centuries). London: Routledge, 1998.

Hachlili, R.. *Ancient Mosaic Pavements: Themes, Issues, and Trends: Selected Studies* (Leiden: Brill, 2009), p. 23.

Hagner, Donald A., *Matthew 1-13*. (WBC 33a; Dallas: Word Books, 1993), p. 25.

Hagar, Stansbury, 'What was the Star of Bethlehem?' *Popular Astronomy*, 26.253-256 (March-July 1918).

Herodotus, *The Histories*. Translated by R. Waterfield. Oxford World's Classics Paperback, 1998.

Herrick, Samuel Jr, 'The Jupiter-Saturn Triple Conjunction,' *Leaflets of the Astronomical Society of the Pacific*, 3 (1941).

Hock, Robert F., *The Infancy Gospels of James and Thomas*. Santa Rose, Califronia: Polebridge Press, 1995.

Horsley, Richard A., *The Liberation of Christmas: The Infancy Narratives in Social Context*. New York: Continuum Publishing, 1993.

——, and J.S. Hanson, *Bandits, Prophets, and Messiahs: Popular Movements at the Time of Jesus* New Voices in Biblical Studies; Minneapolis: Winston, 1985.

Horowitz, Wayne, 'Halley's Comet and the Judean Revolts Revisited,' *Catholic Biblical Quarterly* 58 (1996).

Humphreys, Colin J., 'The Star of Bethlehem—A Comet of 5BC—and the Date of the Birth of Christ,' *Quarterly Journal of the Royal Astronomical Society*, 32 (1991): 395-396.

Hunter, Richard, *A Study of Daphnis and Chloe*. Cambridge: Cambridge University Press, 1983.

Instone-Brewer, David, 'The Eighteen Benedictions and the Minim Before 70CE', *Journal of Theological Studies* 54 (2003): 25-44.

Introductorium in astronomiam albumasaris (trans. Hermann of Carinthia; Augsburg: Erhardt Ratdolt, 1489).

Jason, Heda, 'The Story of David and Goliath: A Folk Epic', *Biblica* 60 (1970): 36-70.

Keener, Craig S., *A Commentary on the Gospel of Matthew*. Grand Rapids: Eerdmans, 1999.

——, and David Pingree. *The Astrological History of Māshā'Allāh*. Cambridge, Mass: Harvard University Press, 1971.

Kennedy, George A., *New Testament Interpretation through Rhetorical Criticism*. Chapel Hill: University of North Carolina Press, 1984.

Kidger, Mark, *The Star of Bethlehem: An Astronomer's View*. New Jersey: Princeton University Press, 1999.

Krupp, E. C., 'Doctoring the Stars', *Sky & Telescope* (October, 2004): 50-51.

van Kooten, George, 'Matthew, the Parthians, and the Magi: A Contextualization of Matthew's Gospel in Roman-Parthian Relations of the First Centuries BCE and CE', in *The Star of Bethlehem and The Magi*, 602-618 (608).

Lewis, Brian, *The Sargon Legend: A Study of the Akkadian Text and the Tale of the Hero who was Exposed at Birth*. American Schools of Oriental Research Dissertation Series 4; Cambridge, MA: American Schools of Oriental Research, 1980.

Lietzman, Hans, *The Beginnings of the Christian Church*. Vol 1. Translated by Bertram Lee Woolf. London: Lutterworth Press, 1952.

Lieu, Judith M. and J. W. Rogerson (eds.), *Oxford Handbook of Biblical Studies* (Oxford: Oxford Handbooks, 2008).

Longus, *Daphnis and Chloe*. Translated with an Introduction and Commentary by J.R. Morgan. Oxford: Aris & Philips, 2004.

Louw, Johannes P. and Eugene A. Nida, (eds.), *Greek-English Lexicon of the New Testament Based on Semantic Domains. Vol. 1: Introduction and Domains; Vol. 2: Indices*. New York: United Bible Societies, 2nd edition, 1989.

Luz, Ulrich. *Matthew 1-7: A Commentary*. Edinburgh: T&T Clarke, 1990.

MacEwen, Robert K., *Matthean Posteriority: An Exploration of Matthew's Use of Mark and Luke as a Solution to the Synoptic Problem*. Library of New Testament Studies 501; London: Bloomsbury T&T Clark, 2015.

MacMullen, Ramsay, *Enemies of the Roman Order: Treason, Unrest & Alienation in the Empire*. Cambridge, Harvard University Press, 1966.

Margalith, Othniel, 'More Samson Legends', *Vetus Testamentum* 36 (1986): 397-405.

Marks, Richard G., *The Image of Bar Kokhba in Traditional Jewish Literature: False Messiah and National Hero* (University Park, Pa: Pennsylvania State University Press, 1994).

Maunder, E.W., *The Astronomy of the Bible*. London: T. Sealey Clark & Co, 1908

Maxwell-Stuart, P.G., (ed.), *The Occult in Early Europe: A Documentary History* (Basingstoke: Macmillan Press, 1999.

McWhorter, George C., 'Christmas to New Years Eve', *Harper's New Monthly Magazine* 32.188 (Jan 1866): 164-172.

Meshorer, Ya'akov, *Ancient Jewish Coinage*. 2 Vols. New York: Amphora Books, 1982.

Mildenberg, Leo, *The Coinage of the Bar Kokhba War*. Monographen zur antiken Numismatik; Bd 6; Aarau: Sauerländer, 1984.

Milik, J. T. and Matthew Black, *The Books of Enoch. Aramaic Fragments of Qumran Cave 4*. Oxford at the Clarendon Press, 1976.

Mitton, Jacqueline, *Journal of the British Astronomical Association* 110.1 (2000).

Molnar, Michael R., *The Star of Bethlehem: The Legacy of the Magi*. New Jersey: Rutgers University Press, 2000.

——, 'Firmicus Maternus & The Star of Bethlehem', *Culture & Cosmos: Journal of the History of Astrology & Cultural Astronomy* 3:1 (1999): 3-9.

——, 'Greek Astrology as a Source of the Messianic Portent', *The Ancient World* (1998): 139-150.

——, 'New Numismatic Evidence about the Comets of Mithradates the Great of Pontus (134 and 119 BC)', *Bulletin of the American Astronomical Society* 29 (1997): 1262.

——, 'The Magi's Star from the Perspective of Ancient Astrological Practices', *Quarterly Journal of the Royal Astronomical Society* 36 (1995): 109-126.

——, 'The Coins of Antioch', *Sky & Telescope* (Jan 1992): 37-39.

Neugebauer, O., *Astronomical Cuneiform Texts*. (3 vols.; London: Lund Humphries, 1955), xx. i.

——*A History of Ancient Mathematical Astronomy*, 3 vols (Berlin: Springer-Verlag, 1975).

Nolland, John, *The Gospel of Matthew. A Commentary on the Greek Text*. New International Greek Text Commentary; Grand Rapids: Eerdmans, 2005.

——, 'Review of Matthew and the Margins. A Social-Political and Religious Reading by Warren Carter', *Journal of Theological Studies* 54 (2003): 225-229.

——, 'The Sources for Matthew 2:1-12', *Catholic Biblical Quarterly* 60 (1998): 283-300.

——, 'A Text-Critical Discussion of Matthew 1:16', *Catholic Biblical Quarterly* 58 (1996): 665-673.

——, 'No Son-of-God Christology in Matthew 1.18-25', *Journal for the Study of the New Testament* 62 (1996): 3-12.

D'Occhieppo, Ferrari, 'The Star of the Magi and Babylonian Astrology' in *Chronos, Kairos, Christos: Nativity and Chronological Studies Presented to Jack Finegan*. J. Vardaman and E.M. Yamauchi, (eds.), Winona Lake: Eisenbrauns, 1989.

Oegema, Gerbern S., *The Anointed and his People: Messianic Expectations from the Maccabees to Bar Kochba*. Journal for the Study of the Pseudepigrapha: Supplement Series 27; Sheffield: Sheffield Academic Press, 1998.

Overman, J. A., *Matthew's Gospel and Formative Judaism: The Social World of the Matthean Community* (Minneapolis: Fortress Press, 1990).

Pickup, Martin, 'New Testament Interpretation of the Old Testament: The Theological Rationale of Midrashic Exegesis', *Journal of the Evangelical Theological Society* 51 (2008): 353-381.

Pogson, Norman, 'Magnitudes of Thirty-six of the Minor Planets for the first day of each month of the year 1857'. Monthly Notices of the Royal Astronomical Society. 17: 12–15 (November 1856).

Price, Martin Jessop and Bluma L. Trell, *Coins and their Cities: Architecture on the Ancient Coins of Greece, Rome, and Palestine*. London: V.C. Vecchi and Sons, 1977.

Propp, 'Structure and History in the Study of the Fairy Tale', *Semeia* 10 (1978): 63.

Propp, Vladimir Y., *Morphology of the Folktale*. Translated by Laurance Scott. 2nd Revised and Edited Edition. Indiana University Research Centre in Anthropology, Folklore and Linguistics, Publications 10. Austin: University of Texas Press, 1968.

Ptolemy, *Tetrabiblos*. Translated by F.E. Robins. Cambridge, Massachusetts: Harvard University Press. LOEB Classical Library, 1940; Reprint, London, Harvard University Press, 2001.

Raglan, *The Hero: A Study in Tradition, Myth, and Drama* (London: Methuen, 1936; New York: Vintage Books, 1956).

Redford, D.B., 'The Literary Motif of the Exposed Child', *Numen* 14 (1967): 209-228.

Reed, Annette Yoshiko, 'Abraham as Chaldean Scientist and Father of the Jews: Josephus, Ant. 1.154-168, and the Greco-Roman Discourse about Astronomy/Astrology', *Journal for the Study of Judaism in the Persian, Hellenistic and Roman Period* 35 (2004).

Reinecker, Fritz, *A Linguistic Key to the Greek New Testament. Vol. 1; Matthew through Acts* (London: Samuel Bagster and Sons Ltd, 1977).

Rendsberg, Gary A., 'Psalm CX 3b,' *Vetus Testamentum* 49 (1999): 548-553.

Richardson, R.S., 'Is that Star the 'Star of Bethlehem'?,' *Leaflets of the Astronomical Society of the Pacific* 3 (1937): 54-61.

Sanders E. P. and Margaret Davies, *Studying the Synoptic Gospels*, (London: SCM Press, 1989).

Schürer, Emil, *The History of the Jewish People in the Age of Christ (175 BC – AD 135)*. New English Edition by G. Vermes and F. Millar. 4 Vols. Edinburgh: T&T Clarke, 1973, 1979, 1986.

Sigismondi, C. D. Hoffleit and R. Coccioli, 'Long-Term Behaviour of Mira Ceti Maxima,' Journal of the American Association of Variable Star Observers 30 (2001): 38.

Soll, 'Misfortune and Exile in Tobit: The Juncture of a Fairy Tale Source and Deuteronomic Theology', *CBQ* 51 (1989): 210.

Smallwood, E. Mary, *The Jews under Roman Rule: From Pompey to Diocletian*. Studies in Judaism in Late Antiquity 20. Leiden: Brill, 1976.

Smoller, Laura Ackerman, *History, Prophecy, and the Stars: The Christian Astrology of Pierre d'Ailly, 1350-1420* (New Jersey: Princeton University Press, 1994).

Soares Prabhu, George M., *The Formula Quotations in the Infancy Narrative of Matthew*. Analecta Biblica 63. Rome: Biblical Institute Press, 1976.

Steinsaltz, Adin, *The Talmud – The Steinsaltz Edition*. New York: Random House, 1999.

Stevenson, Gregory, *Power and Placee: Temple and Identity in the Book of Revelation* (Band 17; Berlin: Walter de Gryter GmBH & Co, 2001), p.167.

Stockwell, J.M. 'Supplement to Recent Contributions to Chronology and Eclipses', *Astronomical Journal* 12 (1892)

Strauss, D.F., *The Life of Jesus Critically Examined*. Peter C. Hodgson (ed.). London: SCM Press, 1973.

Stuckrad, Kocku von, 'Jewish and Christian Astrology in Late Antiquity – A New Approach', *Numen* 47 (2000): 1-40.

Sturdy, John, *The Cambridge Bible Commentary on the New English Bible: Numbers*. Cambridge: Cambridge University Press, 1976.

Suetonius, *The Lives of the Caesars* (trans. J.C. Rolfe; 2 vols.; LCL 31, 38 (Cambridge, Mass.: Harvard University Press, 1914).

Tannehill, R., 'Types and Functions of Apophthegms in the Synoptic Gospels', *Aufstieg und Niedergang der römischen Welt: Geschichte und Kultur Roms im Spiegal der nueren Forschung*, 2.25.2: 1792-1824.

Tenney, Merrill C., 'Historical Verities in the Gospel of Luke', *Bibliotheca Sacra* 135 (135): 126-138.

Teres, Gustav, S.J., *The Bible and Astronomy: The Magi and the Star of Bethlehem* .Oslo: Solum Forlang, 3rd edition, 2002.

Tester, Jim, *A History of Western Astronomy*. Suffolk: The Boydell Press, 1987.

Theissen, Gerd and Annette Merz, *The Historical Jesus: A Comprehensive Guide*. Translated by John Bowden. London: SCM, 1998.

Thomas, Keith, *Religion & The Decline of Magic: Studies in Popular Beliefs in Sixteenth and Seventeenth England*. London: Weidenfeld & Nicholson, 1971; Reprint, London: Penguin Books, 1991.

Trend, J.B. and H. Loewe, (eds.), *Isaac Abravanel* (Cambridge: At the University Press, 1937).

Vermes, Geza, *The Complete Dead Sea Scrolls in English*. Revised Edition. London: Penguin Books, 2004.

De Vries, Jan, *Heroic Song and Heroic Legend* (trans. B.J. Timmer; London: Oxford University Press, 1963), esp. 210-226.

Wallace, Daniel B., *Greek Grammar Beyond the Basics: An Exegetical Syntax of the New Testament* (Grand Rapids: Zondervan, 1996).

Wiener, Philip P. (ed.), *Dictionary of the History of Ideas: Studies of Selected Pivotal Ideas* (5 vols; New York: Scribner, 1973).

Wills, L.M., *The Jewish Novel in the Ancient World* (Ithaca, N.Y.; London: Cornell University Press, 1995).

Wright, N.T., 'Christian Origins and the Resurrection of Jesus: The Resurrection of Jesus as a Historical Problem', *Sewanee Theological Review* 41 (1998): 107-123.

——*The New Testament and the People of God*. Christian Origin and the Question of God 1. London: SPCK, 1992.

INDEX